T0208659

The Rapture
2028:
America's Countdown
to Apocalypse!

David Netherton

WESTBOW·
PRESS
A DIVISION OF THOMAS NELSON
& ZONDERVAN

Scriptures marked NASB are taken from the New American Standard Bible®, Copyright © 1960, 1962, 1963, 1968, 1971, 1972, 1973, 1975, 1977, 1995 by The Lockman Foundation. Used by permission.

Scriptures marked NKJV are taken from the New King James Version®. Copyright © 1982 by Thomas Nelson, Inc. Used by permission. All rights reserved.

Scriptures marked NLT are taken from the Holy Bible, New Living Translation, copyright © 1996, 2004, 2007 by Tyndale House Foundation. Used by permission of Tyndale House Publishers, Inc., Carol Stream, Illinois 60188. All rights reserved.

Most scriptures quoted is from the Authorized (King James) Version of the Bible unless otherwise marked, the rights in which are vested in the Crown in the United Kingdom, is reproduced here by permission of the Crown's patentee, Cambridge University Press.

Unless otherwise indicated, Bible quotations are the actual quotes from the Ancient Church fathers or the KJV and not from any modern Bible versions. The verses not marked have been retranslated from the original Greek or Hebrew manuscripts. The author, with three years of Alexandrian Greek, is well qualified to translate any NT verse into English from the original manuscripts.

Verses from the Epistle of Barnabas comes from the J.B. Lightfoot translation.

All links to websites in this book are accurate at the time of this writing but are subject to change with time.

WestBow Press books may be ordered through booksellers or by contacting:

WestBow Press
A Division of Thomas Nelson & Zondervan
1663 Liberty Drive
Bloomington, IN 47403
www.westbowpress.com
1 (866) 928-1240

ISBN: 978-1-4908-5046-7 (sc)
ISBN: 978-1-4908-5044-3 (hc)
ISBN: 978-1-4908-5045-0 (e)

Library of Congress Control Number: 2014915813

Print information available on the last page.

WestBow Press rev. date: 3/11/2015

CONTENTS

ACKNOWLEDGMENTS

I am so thankful to many for the completion of the following body of work. First to Jesus Christ, my Redeemer and Lord, who delivered me from death and set me on this course of writing in the latter years of my life. Thanks for the future things He has revealed to me through His written Word, mostly from the Bible and the Dead Sea Scrolls.

This book would not have been possible if not for L. A. McCown, who relentlessly kept me from butchering the King's English. She protected it with fervor, and I am so thankful for her knowledge of the language. Plus my good friend in Christ Mark Covin helped me work on chapters 6 through 8, keeping my math in line while dealing with the zero year from AD to BC. I at first had figured 2027 as the date rather than 2028, but 2029 or 30 is very possible (no later than 2030).

Last I want to thank my Hebrew and Greek professors, Ron Adema and Al Rosenblum, for their unwavering commitment to the original languages of the Holy Bible and their critical assignment for me to research the Dead Sea Scrolls. Plus thanks to the late Buzzy Sutherland, an evangelist who introduced me to the Koine Greek word Zoë life. Plus I cannot thank John and Shanna enough for our newfound friendship and their efforts to keep me from making grammatical mistakes. They truly unselfishly took me under their wings as I made final revisions to this book. May God richly bless them above all they can ask or think and every one that was a part of my new endeavor of becoming an author.

God has no grandchildren but I have several and I would like to dedicate this book to them, especially Jacob, my oldest grandson. May God richly bless them and keep them from the kingdom of darkness. May God fill them to all the fullness of Jesus as we enter these final days!

PREFACE

For several years I have studied Koine Greek and ancient Hebrew, two of the original languages of the ancient biblical text. I was given a project to research the Dead Sea Scrolls. This project literally changed my understanding of the number of books we have in our English Bibles. We only have sixty-six books and only twelve chapters (Gen. 1-12) that cover this first two thousand-year period of ancient history. Why are certain historical records about this early time period missing from our Bible, and did the Dead Sea Scrolls uncover these ancient writings? Why do the Ethiopian Christians still have these historical books in their Bible? Who gave the Pharisees, who hated Jesus, the authority to remove these early historical books? Should we have seventy instead of sixty-six books in our Bible? These are valid questions to be asking.

Today these historical records are still available to us. They were removed from the Bible during the early church period by the Pharisees and the Council of Laodicea, two very corrupt religious groups. These books that were removed were a part of the Bible during Jesus' time and were abundantly discovered in the Dead Sea Scrolls.

This is what the Lord says—the Lord who made the Earth, who formed and established it, whose name is the Lord: Ask me and I will tell you remarkable secrets you do not know about things to come. (Jer. 33:2-3 NLT)

Howbeit when he, the Spirit of truth, is come, he will guide you into all truth: for he shall not speak of himself; but whatsoever he shall hear, that shall he speak: and he will show you things to come. (John 16:13 KJV)

Now all the world needs is another doomsday book. Thoughts and feelings flooded my heart and mind concerning this book and the last days. I later understood these heartfelt feelings to be the Holy Spirit leading me to write about this ancient history and the end of time. I prayed for God to show me things to come and the ancient history of the past. This book is the result of that prayer, and my studies were not just of the sixty-six books but all seventy books of the Bible. God always reveals the truth. The kingdom of darkness is completely about deception, always. The Devil was a liar from the beginning. He is the father of lies. Why should we be surprised that his children are only following in their father's footsteps?

I discovered that all of time consists in a window of only 7,007 years. I know this sounds strange as we all live in a deceptive Darwinian smokescreen of millions and billions of years. Before the creation there was no time, and after the kingdom there will be no time in the new heaven and the new earth (Rev. 21). We will just eternally exist.

The deeper I researched and prayed, the more God's truth became very clear. Then I realized we only have about twenty-one years until Armageddon, and the urgent need to write this book for true, born-again believers became apparent. *This book will set you free* from the deceptive philosophies of Darwinism and the misunderstood theory of ancient aliens. This book will orient you to God's actual calendar of time, history, and coming events. To God be the glory. His love endures forever. The heavens and earth will pass away but not His Word of truth; it will last forever.

INTRODUCTION

Don't be **left behind** during these coming events. I know we don't know the day and the hour of the rapture or Christ's coming Kingdom. But according to my studies within all seventy biblical books, I estimate the year of the rapture to be around 2028. This book does not go into great detail explaining these actual coming events but more or less establishes my theory of the year they could take place. I selected this title mainly because of the frightening discoveries I found in the Dead Sea Scrolls. These discoveries concern books being removed from the Bible and covered up by religious leaders who could not handle the *truth*. These important ancient writings more accurately help you to see when these expected coming events will occur. These are some of the most anticipated events of the children of God and I truly think I have some answers to help you know when these events could shortly take place. Be sure and prepare your families and your life for these expected events while there is time. Jesus said not to be caught unaware or asleep concerning His return! The Rapture is Jesus metamorphosing all true Christians to heaven without death. In a similar manner God removed ancient believers before Noah's flood. The rapture event will probably be blamed on UFOs and the return of ancient aliens. *Will you be among those* **left behind** *to face God's wrath?*

This book is a collection of information mostly from Middle Eastern writings. The main evidence for this book is taken from the

Bible, the Dead Sea Scrolls, the epistle of Barnabas, and the ancient book of Jasher, all of which originated in the Middle East. If you are searching for information on the coming doom of this civilization, I think it would be foolish to look anywhere except the Middle East, unless you are looking up toward heaven. These dates will require looking at the biblical prophecies that were written in the greatest historical book of all time, the Bible. The Bible was inspired by God and written by men who lived in the Middle East.

We will take a serious look at NASA's prediction concerning the arrival of Asteroid 1999 AN 10. This asteroid, predicted to be as close as earth's satellites and expected to reach our atmosphere on August 7, 2027, could very possibly create great destruction and devastation to the surface of the earth. Some science observers say this asteroid is too erratic to predict its exact trajectory but that it will enter extremely close to earth.

This book will give you a brief history of the most prominent religions of our time and their doomsday prophecies. We will look at evidence for the impending holocaust that is presently manifesting around the globe. This holocaust will involve the entire seven billion-plus citizens of Earth.

The first five chapters will take you through several important religions of the world and the role they play in the last days. Some of these "religions" are not labeled as religious. However, according to the dictionary definition, they cannot escape the fact that they are religious. In chapter 6, we will examine six thousand years of mankind's ability to self-rule. In chapter 7, we will examine in detail this 7,007-year window of time on man's calendar, which is only seven days on God's.

The Dead Sea Scrolls reveal two new additional Old Testament historical books that were removed by religious men in the early days of the church. These books were part of the Bible during Jesus' time on earth, so by what or whose authority did men reduce the Bible down to as little as sixty books? Without a doubt we now have a total of at least seventy books in our Bible instead of the sixty-six present books.

Then, in chapter 8, we will reveal the key that unlocks the doomsday date. Furthermore, we will explore the Armageddon date. Chapter 9 will carry you back to Daniel's great prophecy. Most importantly, this entire book examines the words of Jesus Himself while He was on this earth and takes a look at the writings of His disciples and their predictions concerning these last days. Did you know that the early church leaders at the Council of Laodicea in AD 364 removed certain books from the Holy Scriptures that were considered part of the Bible during Jesus' time, plus many New Testament (NT) writings of the apostle Paul's? A look at these books reveals important facts to the understanding of a doomsday date. The Dead Sea Scrolls were discovered in caves only thirteen miles from the temple in Jerusalem. The Jewish temple scribes were using the Qumran caves to hide the temple library of Biblical manuscripts from the Roman Army. The Romans finally destroyed and burnt the temple in AD 70.

We know that the Middle East is referred to as the "cradle of civilization." History began in the Middle East less than six thousand years ago in the Garden of Eden. We know that Noah's ark also came to rest in the Middle East on the mountains of Ararat in Turkey. After the global flood, life restarted about 2316 BC, or 1,657 years after creation in the Middle East with eight souls—Noah and his immediate family. This has resulted in over seven billion of his descendants alive today. Accordingly, history will end in the Middle East when nations surround Israel with the intent to destroy her.

The Middle East will be the source of this civilization's holocaust. The infamous battle of Armageddon will take place in the Middle

East. Men from the Middle East destroyed the twin towers in New York City. I think this was a sign of the opening of the first seal. When the second seal is broken, Iran and ISIL will ride the red horse and peace will be taken from the earth. We are seeing warning signs of this coming destruction as Iran develops its nuclear program while ISIL (ISIS) establishes a new Islamic state for terrorists. We are witnesses to the beginning of the apocalypse! Consequently, this will bring war over the whole earth, *possibly* by the fall of 2015.

Christianity originated in the Middle East. We are seeing an influx of terrorism from the Middle East. Islam is the world's second-largest religion, also centered in the Middle East. Most Muslims live in the Middle East. The third world war will be about the Middle East. These Middle Eastern regions have big ramifications in the last days. The information found in this body of work came mostly from the authors from the Middle East. Need I say more?

If you are interested in the truth, it cannot be found kneeling at the altar of caveman worship or in some big bang fairytale or ancient Mayan calendar. However, the Aztecs may even be closer than the Mayans, for they have a doomsday prediction date. The bad angels who fathered the Nephilim built these Mayan and Aztec ancient cities before the flood. Are the Nephilim predicted to return at the end of time? Will there be a repeat of Noah's days, when the bad angels sexually mingled with the seed of the daughters of Adam as told in Genesis 6 and in Daniel 2:43? Could the Mayan date (December 21, 2012) be the birthday of the anti-Christ?

You will discover that man's time is only contained in a seven thousand-year window. God gave man a six thousand-year window to govern this earth by his own rules. Adam started God's countdown clock ticking about seven years after the creation. It is now counting six thousand years to the release of the wrath of God at the battle of

Armageddon, with an overall seven thousand years to the final great white throne judgment day of *all* of mankind. This includes everyone who has ever lived on the face of this earth.

This clock is ticking, and nothing will change or stop it from its accurate, appointed end of time. The wrath of God's judgment is extremely close to being poured out a second time. This time the earth's destruction will come by *fire*. God made the earth and all that is in it, so He can do with it as He sees appropriate. This is a judgment date that will occur at the end of the six thousand–year time clock God set for man.

In reading these writings, you will be exposed to some of the seven seals in Revelation 6, known as the four horses of the apocalypse. Could America be the Mystery Babylon destroyed in one day, as referenced in Revelation 18? Brace yourself for some very bizarre signs of the sun and moon. Finally, you will look at fourteen signs for a doomsday date for America, and the final chapter deals with a misunderstood Ancient Alien Theory, UFOs, abductions, and the Nephilim (giant human hybrids).

Of course, these dates are based on life being contained within a 7,007-year window and the AD portion of 2,014 years of the Gregorian calendar being accurate. So pull up a comfortable seat, get a good lamp and a cup of coffee, buckle your seat belt, and hang on for the next two hundred-plus pages that will truly change your life forever. Prepare yourself for the end of six thousand years.

CHAPTER 1

The Religious Atheist's Date with Destiny

In this chapter, one thing we will examine is what it takes to qualify any organization or personal belief as religious. But the question quickly arises, "How do I justify calling atheism a religion?" It is simple. Atheism is a philosophy or a belief system based on the claim that there is no supreme being higher than man. Atheists believe man created God and that if you can change man's reasoning process, you can remove God from existence.

Atheism is not based on facts. Atheism is believed by faith, and therefore it becomes religious in its nature. It is a faith-based belief. It is a philosophy, and they hope God does not exist but cannot prove His nonexistence. According to dictionary.com, religion is defined as "a body of persons adhering to a particular set of beliefs and practices." Atheism is a body of persons adhering to the nonbelief in God. Atheism is most definitely religious in its own right.

Are You an Atheist?

If you are an atheist, then I have a very important question to ask you. Do you know everything? You will say no, or you would be lying if you didn't. Well, we are going to pretend that you know half of everything that can be learned in this universe. I can assure you that you don't even know half of everything there is to know, even if you believe differently, but I will give you the benefit of the doubt. If so, then how about the half of knowledge you know nothing about? Have you ever stopped to think that God could be in the other half of what you don't know or don't want to know?

Take the English word *universe,* for example: "uni" means single and "verse" means spoken sentence. In other words we all live in one single spoken sentence. God said, "Let there be," and the universe plus all things that are within it came into being. Several spoken sentences over six twenty-four hour days produced the total creation. Nothing exists without the Creator, and He holds all things together in an organized and orderly system.

God expresses His anger toward religious atheists and unbelievers in the following verses in the book of Romans:

> But God shows his anger from Heaven against all sinful, wicked people who suppress the truth by their wickedness. *They know the truth* about God because He has made it obvious to them. For ever since the world was created, people have seen the Earth and sky. Through everything God made, *they can clearly see His invisible qualities*—His eternal power and divine nature. *So they have no excuse for not knowing God.* Yes, they knew God, but they wouldn't worship Him as God or even

give Him thanks. And they began to think up foolish ideas of what God was like. As a result, their minds became dark and confused. Claiming to be wise, they became *utter fools* instead. ... So God abandoned them to do whatever shameful things their hearts desired. As a result, they did vile and degrading things with each other's bodies. ... Since they thought it foolish to acknowledge God, He abandoned them to their foolish thinking and let them do things that should never be done. (Rom. 1:18-22, 24, 28 KJV)

Say unto them, as I live, says the Lord God, I have no pleasure in the death of the wicked; but that the wicked turn from his way and live. (Ezek. 33:11)

Big Problem for Unbelievers

If you are an atheist unbeliever, you are destined to experience the wrath of God coming to this earth within the next twenty-one years. Even if you believe God exists, it will not help you. There is a way to escape this coming holocaust. I know you don't believe in God or His coming judgment. You probably don't believe the historical Bible and its warnings of doomsday coming to the unbeliever. It has happened in the past and will happen again according to biblical documents.

I know your mind has been clouded with Darwinism and its bogus dating system, but you better look closer at the evidence. In about 2317 BC, God judged this entire world with a flood. The prophet Enoch recorded this warning in the Bible. Enoch warned of this coming flood just like the Bible is now warning of coming destruction by fire. The evidence of this global destruction can be widely found in the fossil record and in almost every civilization's recorded flood stories. Well over two hundred historical flood stories are found around the world today. Most unbelievers have dismissed those stories as myths.

Now you can dismiss these historical stories as myths at your own peril. The Bible warns that the natural man does not receive the things of the spirit, for they are foolishness to him. You must be born again in your spirit to ever understand the lie of the dark spirit world. These dark spirits are clouding the minds of unbelievers to the truth.

Man is made up of three parts. Man was originally made in the image of God. Man has a spirit, a soul, and a body, but they have all been damaged by the kingdom of darkness. In other words, the kingdom of darkness turned the light off inside man. The only way to turn the light back on is to have your damaged spirit experience a new birth. This is exactly what Jesus Christ offers an unbeliever. Only this new birth will enlighten your mind to the truth and exempt you from God's coming wrath.

The battle of Armageddon will destroy over seven billion earthlings within the next twenty-one years, more than likely you included. You have a choice being offered to you today. You can have your light turned on in your soul or continue to live in darkness. Jesus can rewire your lighting problem. Once He turns on the light in your inner being, you will be able to understand a very accurate historical book known as the Bible.

Famous Last Words

The bottom line for unbelievers is an internal lighting problem that blinds you to the truth. So you don't want God telling you anything. "No one is going to tell me what to do," are most unbelievers' famous last words. You have a darkened, rebellious spirit that needs some light. Only Jesus loves you enough to offer a fix to the lighting problem.

Your darkened philosophy is not based on facts. You cannot prove that God does not exist. By faith you *hope* God is not in that missing 50 percent of knowledge you don't know anything about, so I guess you might think you have less than a fifty/fifty chance, if you believe in chance. You believe these things by faith, making atheism a philosophy and truly a religion!

This darkness puts you in deep eternal trouble when Christ returns to judge the living and the dead. He is coming even if you refuse to believe what He says. Just because you don't believe in hell doesn't mean your appointment with destiny disappears. Just because you refuse to acknowledge God does not make God disappear or excuse you from His wrath.

God's Wrath

The wrath of God is being stored up for a judgment-day event coming soon to a city near you. The final book of the Bible vividly describes this judgment in a final seven years of mankind's life on this earth. The near future will not be good unless you repent of your ungodly life. This end is a set date, and nothing will stop God's wrath from being poured out on all *unbelievers*. You do have one option to escape. Atheism will bring you face-to-face with God's wrath, but Jesus has removed this wrath for the true children of the kingdom of God.

The answer to escaping God's wrath is in God's Son, Jesus Christ, who loved you by dying for all of your sins and making a way for you to escape this great judgment day. Jesus truly does not want you to perish and is throwing you a lifeline for a pathway to heaven.

Altered DNA

And Adam lived a hundred and thirty years, and begat a son in *his own likeness, after his image*; and called his name Seth: and the days of Adam after he had begotten Seth were eight hundred years: and he begat sons and daughters. (Gen. 5:3–4 KJV)

Adam lost his godly DNA and passed this altered DNA profile on to his children. This change in Adam was caused by instant death to his godly DNA and a following mutation that occurred in his flesh. We will examine this subject in chapter 5 and what resulted from it. The sin nature entered Adam's body changing his DNA. I have a complete book dealing with this very problem, coming soon.(page 264)

Escape God's Wrath with God's DNA

Mankind was created in 3973 BC, which was almost six thousand years ago. This first man and woman walked with God and had daily fellowship with God in the Garden of Eden. When they disobeyed their Creator, a death took place within them. They were children of God, and God was their only Father. The very DNA of God was in their physical bodies, just as your children have your DNA today. God's life and DNA can have nothing to do with sin. God and sin cannot coexist!

Sin Affected Adam's DNA

When sin entered Adam and Eve for the very first time, it affected their godly DNA, bringing darkness into their minds. God's DNA that was in their bodies instantly experienced death. God warned them,

"In the day you eat from the forbidden tree you shall die." Therefore, all of their billions of descendants who were born to them since their fall into sin were born into Adam's likeness and not in God's likeness as Adam was originally designed. They were born in Adam's darkened image with Adam's altered DNA profile.

Mankind began to quickly multiply on the face of the earth. The earth and its atmosphere were much different before the global flood in 2317 BC, with a canopy that filtered out all the deadly rays of the sun. The sun at creation was about 6% larger than today. Science has observed the sun is shrinking in, its solar diameter, about 1% per century or five feet per hour. Man once lived in a totally tropical climate, as evidenced by the prints of palm leaves that have been discovered at the top of all coal seams and under the ice cap at both the north and south poles. This is forbidden archaeology by Darwinists, and they would like to own your mind.

The Darwinists' big lie does not control everyone's thinking process. The Darwinists' thinking has been darkened by Adam's original DNA problem. Truly they cannot help their darkened thinking and will never be able to find their way out of this darkened world unless they seek the only avenue out.

Jesus is the only light switch to light up the darkened soul. This subject will be examined later in this book and will also be discussed in great detail in two future books titled *Forbidden History of the Ancient World as it was in the Days of Noah* and *The Book of Life Tracing God's DNA*, see the last page of this book. Check by late 2016 on zoebooks. org for these coming books.

God became disgusted with mankind and the efforts of the fallen angels to destroy His creation. We see the first historical reference to the global wrath of God in Genesis 6 of the Bible. Noah and his family escaped the great flood, which was a display of God's wrath. This global flood of judgment was sent because of the corrupted DNA manipulation done to both animals and mankind by these bad angels, as well as mankind's darkened participation.

God's judgment by a flood was cleansing the gene pool of these hybrids. This cleansing was necessary so pure humans could survive. The great deluge washed both human and animal DNA clean of this evil hybrid genetic engineering experiment caused by the fallen angels. Probably the only surviving hybrids from Noah's days are the mermaids found in the oceans today. (Watch the Discovery Channel's documentary entitled *Mermaids: The Body Found* and decide for yourself.) This cleansing event of Noah's flood shows God's ability to judge the universe He created. The next global wrath judgment is coming again very soon. This destruction will be with fire and not by water.

Secret Fix for Atheism/Avoid God's Wrath

The question is not if you believe there is a God. The Devil believes in God and trembles; in fact, he knows there is a God. The real issue is do you believe in His Son who gave His life on the cross to fix your bad DNA issue that you inherited from the first Adam? Jesus is the last Adam and has become the only intercessor between God and man. The secret fix is in His Son, who gave His life to fix this issue. This is the only way to remove the darkness from your mind. Your human spirit is the core of your being and a light to your soul. Your soul is your mind, your will, and your emotions. You have to have a rebirth take place in your human spirit to remove this eternal darkness.

Only Jesus Christ earned the right to bring a rebirth to your human spirit, so ask Jesus to come into your heart and create in you a new, sinless human spirit that is directly birthed from God. Only then will the light be turned on in your soul. Jesus will protect this new light from ever being turned off again by your sin. This is how Jesus saves you from hell and the wrath of God. God will become, at this new birth, your new heavenly Father, making you officially a child of God. Presently, all earthlings are not children of God but children of the first Adam—unless you have experienced a rebirth.

> Jesus was the true Light, which lights every man that cometh into the world. He was in the world, and the world was made by Him, and the world knew Him not. He came unto His own, and His own received Him not. But as many as received Him, to them gave He power to become the sons of God, even to them that believe on His name: which were born, not of blood, nor of the will of the flesh, nor of the will of man, but born of God. (John 1:9–13 KJV)

Once you become a child of God, you're always a child of God. This new birth that takes place within you is eternal life. This new life is a transfer of the DNA of God into your new human spirit by your new Father. New birth means new DNA, and the light is turned on again in your soul. Have you been re-fathered, which will write your name in the Book of Life? This is your alternative to the wrath of God being poured out on unbelievers on or before 2035. It happened historically in the past and is coming again very soon.

Jesus Saves You by Indwelling You

Jesus enters your body at this new birth, and your body officially becomes a temple of God. Jesus will set up residence within you, and the Holy Spirit will seal your newly created spirit into Jesus, never to sin again. All future sins will be committed in your soul and body but not in your newly created spirit that comes from your new Father. As long as you are alive on this earth, Jesus will be the gatekeeper of your new sinless spirit so no sin can penetrate Him to get to your newly created spirit. Sin can never completely turn off your light again, putting your mind, will, and emotions into total darkness. One-third of a born-again believer has become holy and sinless at his or her second birth; it is a gift from God to be born again.

I know this sounds farfetched to you. You have to believe it by faith. You believed in atheism by faith. This secret is known only among God's children. This secret that I have revealed to you is the only official process to fix this curse called atheism. Atheism is a terminal illness that only Jesus can heal. As long as you are breathing, you have a chance to escape this curse by willfully turning to Jesus. Atheism is a curse, for it will damn your soul to an everlasting punishment. Your future destiny and judgment are not eliminated just because you don't believe in hell or God. Your disbelief does not make your appointment disappear but makes it even more definite.

Could This Be Your Last Chance?

For some reading this book, it will be your last chance to accept the new lifeline God sent to you. You are drowning in a darkened, worldly life because your human ancestors lost God's DNA. The only begotten Son of God is the only source by which you can receive this new DNA birthright. Jesus is the last Adam and your last chance to escape (1 Cor. 15:45). This is a free gift Jesus made available for you. God truly loves you, and He is not mad at you unless you continue to disbelieve. This could be God's final offering to you today, for as death finds you so shall the final judgment. Then you will see the wrath of God!

Keeping the commandments of the entire Bible will not fix your DNA problem. Many seekers of the path to God go to the Bible and other religious writings to keep its rules, hoping to find favor with God and to get on the right path to eternal life. The Bible will not turn on your light but only point you to the light switch. Jesus can relight your soul (John 5:39–40). This new DNA of God is a must have to be able to go to heaven and escape the wrath of God. All born-again believers are family. Only the Spirit of Jesus can relight your soul and make you a family member.

We are body, soul, and spirit. When you receive *Jesus* in your *spirit*, your name is instantly written in the Book of Life. This happens only through Jesus Christ, the *only* begotten Son of God. Born twice and die once or born only once and *you will* die twice. Once you are born again, it is something that cannot be taken away from you. Once a family member, always a family member. God has no grandchildren but only sons and daughters. You must be born again, period.

Scientists can put a computer chip in your brain that will change your DNA and control your mind. This is not a farfetched idea today. Google "new mind control by computer chips". Research nanotechnology and their ability to alter DNA with a computer chip. If a scientist can do this DNA manipulation, then do you not think that the Creator of the universe entering your body cannot accomplish even greater DNA alterations? This is what Christianity is all about—the transfer of the DNA of God offered again to mankind through Jesus. This is what the first Adam lost in the Garden of Eden. The last Adam, Jesus, is only restoring to mankind what the first Adam lost!

A Diversity of Beliefs in Adam's Race (Rom. 5:12–21)

Most of those in Adam's race have not been rebirthed. They have human spirits that have sinned at least once, and they are all destined to the great white throne judgment. No matter how much you keep the commands of the Bible or other religious writings, it will not change your DNA; only Jesus can do it through the second birth. Many different ethnic groups exist within Adam's race. There are very religious people on one spectrum with the atheist religion on the other spectrum. But they still belong to the deformed spiritual race of Adam that lost the DNA of God back in the beginning. There are very good, moral people on one spectrum and evil descendants of Adam on the other. Who wants to be the best person who goes to hell?

However, they are all still sons and daughters of Adam totally separated from their Creator. They all will receive the same fate, possibly with some degree according to their works and the amount of truth given to them. The fate of all of Adam's descendants is the same if they have not been born again in their human spirits. They have one very sure date with destiny and an eternal separation from God.

Many so-called church members today are still just religious sons of Adam and never have truly been born into the kingdom. Do you remember your first car, date, job, or child? You should know your spiritual birth experience if you truly have been born again. If not, you may still be only a religious son of Adam on a religious church roll or in some religious organization but have not experienced the second birthday. No second birth, no passage into heaven. If you are not sure, then go to Jesus and secure your future now by being born again! It won't hurt if you are not sure.

In John's gospel he wrote,

> But as many as received Him, to *them gave the power to become the sons of God,* even to them that believe on His name: Which were born, not of blood, nor of the will of the flesh, nor of the will of man, but born of

God. And the Word was made flesh, and dwelt among us, (and we beheld His glory, the glory as of the only begotten of the Father,) full of grace and truth. (John 1:12-14)

Do You Have a Second Birthday?

If you are truly born again, you will remember your rebirth experience. You should know when Jesus Christ came into your life. God's true born-again children are not citizens of this world but only sojourners on this earth and ambassadors representing the kingdom of God to Adam's descendants. True believers possess God's DNA; we are the light of the world. God's DNA within us is the only light that can penetrate into this present kingdom of darkness.

The Power over Atheism

Note that only those who come to God and have been born anew in their spirits have received the new light. They alone will enter into His kingdom coming within the next twenty-one years. Which gate have you entered? Have you entered the wide gate of atheism or worldly religions that leads to destruction, or have you chosen the small gate that only a few will find? This road is narrow and not easy to travel. Many enemies lurk, and the narrow road is filled with trouble. If you choose the Jesus gate, you will receive light into your darkened soul.

Jesus makes this statement: "Enter by the narrow gate, for the gate is wide and the way is broad that leads to destruction and many are those who enter by it. For the gate is small and the way is narrow that leads to Zoë life [God's DNA] and few are those who find it" (Matt. 7:13-14 NKJV). Are you among the few that have found the light that is in Christ Jesus and become children of the kingdom? The indwelling of Jesus is our new DNA life! This is the only fix for atheism. The King and His kingdom are coming to earth in about AD 2035.

The Bible Consists of Seventy Books

After realizing the Bible consists of seventy books instead of the sixty-six books we have been allowed to have by religious men, I can now see clearly the six thousand years since Adam first sinned in 3966 BC. The end is here, and it is almost completed. Christ's earthly kingdom will end all human government. Christ shall appear in the sky, descending down to earth with all His angels, bringing an end to Armageddon. So be looking up, and don't be caught unaware!

The Antichrist King Is Coming by 2028

The Devil has taken human form and has had intercourse with some human female on this earth. It is like the fallen angels that produced the Nephilim in Noah's days. This union has produced a DNA half-breed son of Satan, which will be revealed as the Antichrist. He will be the one spoken of in the book of Daniel and the book of Revelation. Satan's DNA son, possessing the Devil's own spirit like Judas, will form a new global worldwide government after the financial collapse of most present governments.

This one-world government will destroy millions of the population through wars, famines, and sickness that will take place between 2021 and 2028. Destruction will come like pains in childbirth up to a final seven-year climax, 2028–2035, which will destroy billions before and during the battle of Armageddon in 2035. Wars and rumors of wars, many diseases, and famines will destroy billions of children of all races during these two final seven-year periods, with the most deaths coming in the final seven years.

Seven Years before Daniel's Seventieth Week

The first period of seven years will likely be before 2028. I truly hope I am wrong about this first seven years. The final seven-year period is from 2028 to 2035, described in Revelation 5–18. This is a time that has never existed before now and will never exist again. Over seven billion people are going to die within the next twenty-one years. God says that if this time is not shortened, no flesh would survive, but for the elect's sake this time will be shortened. I would guess several months will be taken off the final seven years so there will be surviving people to populate Christ's kingdom.

The Antichrist and his leaders are thinking they need to reduce the population to about 500 million. In Elberton, Georgia, the New World Order has posted their own Stonehenge, which is twenty-foot-tall granite stones. Carved on these stones are the ten commandments of the New World Order in twelve different languages. This stuff is real. One of their ten commandments is to "maintain population at ½ billion or 500 million."

Another sign is that Bill Clinton signed the Biodiversity Treaty, which states we need to reduce the global population to about one billion. What is going to happen to the other six billion? Satan has big plans for mankind in these next twenty-one years.

At Least Seven Billion People Will Die

There will soon be eight billion people on earth; that means over seven billion are going to be destroyed. They will be burned in gas ovens like the Third Reich. Search the web for gas ovens and concentration camps. Take notice as to who built them. That is exactly what we see in Revelation 5–18. Wake up, everybody—the end is here!

It appears that approximately AD 2035 is the end of the six thousand-year countdown from the time that Adam sinned. The great battle of Armageddon will take place about 2035. The Antichrist and the New World Order will be destroyed, and the gas ovens will be shut down by Jesus Christ, "King of Kings and Lord of Lords." Horrible days are coming on this earth for the atheists and all of Adam's natural descendants who have not been born again.

God's True Children Spared from His Final Wrath

However, the children of God will be delivered before the final seven years in an event known as the rapture in about 2027 to 2030 AD. The born-again believers will be removed from this earth before this final seven years of destruction occurs. The church, based in the United States, is keeping the one-world government from taking form. Once the church is removed, the prince who is to come (Dan. 9:26–27) will come on the scene. He will be the lawless one, the man of sin, the son of perdition, the Antichrist, the new world leader. I think he will be the literal Nephilim son of Satan. (This is just my opinion.)

According to Jasher 4:20, God removed the godly believers from the earth so they would not experience His wrath during the deluge. He removed the believers by allowing them to die of natural causes. Those believers remaining at the time of the flood were Methuselah and Noah and his family. When Methuselah died, the rains began to fall. Only eight believers were alive on earth to witness judgment day. Methuselah was the son of Enoch, and God had revealed to Enoch that when his son died the end would come. The Bible says in Genesis 5:24

that Enoch walked with God after he begot Methuselah. His son was the oldest man recorded in history at 969 years. The day Methuselah died the rain began to fall, and the fountains of the deep opened. Once flood waters started to destroy the unbelievers, they knew the end had come. They beat on the sides of the ark, wanting to get on board, but the Bible said God had shut the door. In the last days, sudden destruction will come again on all of mankind.

Atheist's Date with Destiny

The religious atheist's destiny with God is set. It is written in the book of the Living God and will take place just as it is written. It is coming soon to a city near you. Nothing can change this future—no, not even Obama, the guru of change. Only you can change your own destiny. Repent of your past unbelieving life and turn to Jesus; He will relight your soul. Join the kingdom of Jesus Christ and be spared from the wrath of God today!

Ambassadors of God, Be Looking Up

However, if you are an ambassador for God's kingdom, the King is coming to get His people. Lift up your heads and look up, for your redemption draws near. Don't let that day overtake you like a thief. The bride needs to get ready, for the marriage supper of the Lamb is at hand. But to my atheist friends, if you are breathing, you still have an opportunity to accept Jesus; however, if you want to stay where you are, then good luck! I have exposed you to the truth. Now it is in your hands, for my hands are now clean!

Only One Option to Escape

This could be your last *warning*! When we examine religious life in the Adamic race, we will find those who claim to be Christian, Hindu, Muslim, Baptist, Pentecostal, Church of Christ, Methodist, Catholic, Mormon, Jehovah's Witness, humanist, atheist, evolutionist, Satanist, occultist, etc., all will die. You have one option for an escape: come to God through His only begotten Son, Jesus Christ, the Way, the Truth, and Life.

Jesus offers to light up your soul, and it is your choice. Or you can follow the fate of all of the natural sons of Adam. You truly must experience a rebirth in your human spirit to escape judgment. Born once and you will die twice, born twice and die only one time. You will experience only physical death to your body.

Destined to destruction are those who have not had a rebirth in their human spirits. This destiny includes even children of Abraham, Jews and Arabs alike, who have not had a second birth. If you have not been born again, then you do not have the Son of God! I am sorry, but Mohammed is not the Son of God and he never claimed to be. His teachings *do not* overrule the teachings of Jesus.

Only Jesus Christ is the Son of God. If you are an atheist or just a religious person and you have not accepted Jesus as redeemer of your darkened soul, you will be doomed; Yahweh, not Allah, offers no other option! Allah offers other options, but are these options real? If you trust Allah instead of Jesus, then take his offerings and spend eternity with him. Myself, I am going to put my life in the nail-scarred hands of Jesus. I would rather spend eternity with Him than some other god.

> And the witness is this that God has given us eternal
> *Zoë life* and this *Zoë life* is in His Son. He who has the

Son has the *Zoë life* he who does not have the Son of God, *does not have the [DNA] Life of God.*" (1 John 4:11–12)

If your God has no Son then you are still in darkness!

The First Adam Chose a Path for You

Adam made a choice for you, but you can alter that choice. You cannot change it through any of the world's religions, being born of Abraham, or just by doing good works and keeping the Ten Commandments. You can only be changed through one person, the last Adam, Jesus Christ, the Son of the Living God. You must be born of God in your human spirit. You must be born from above with your new born-again spirit placed and sealed into Jesus. This is the only spiritual light that will light up your mind, will, and emotions. You can be sealed forever in Christ, by the Holy Spirit of promise.

In Him, you also, after listening to the message of truth, the gospel of your salvation—having also believed, you were *sealed in Him* with the Holy Spirit of promise. (Eph. 1:13NASB)

Twenty-One Years until the Kingdom

It is almost time for the thousand-year kingdom of Christ to set up on this earth. *You will not make it* to where Jesus is if you have not received Him as your redeemer and substitute for your sin. Maybe you don't want to be with Jesus. Then you have a much different destiny, but you have a choice, and as for me, Jesus is the only begotten of God.

Eternal life with Jesus is all about a rebirth in your human spirit and not about which religion you belong to or church you attend.

This statement will not be very popular among some religions, but it is a spiritual fact. If you trust your atheist religion, then all I can say is good luck. If you trust another religious belief system and you make it into heaven, then I will meet you there. As for me, I am going to choose Jesus.

The Natural Man Is Darkened

Read this entire book if you have eyes to see and you will understand God's plan for man. However, if you are only a natural man, a child of Adam, and have never been born again you will not be able to understand spiritual things. Your eyes and mind have been darkened and your ears have been deafened so you cannot see nor hear the truth (2 Cor. 2:12–16).

Hey, don't get mad at me! I did not do it to you. You were born this way and you have to do something to get out of that system, so don't blame me for your lack of ability to understand. For best results, get it fixed before 2028 or before you quit breathing.

I once was in the same condition as some of you who are reading this book until I realized I was in darkness. I turned to Jesus and had a rebirth in my human spirit. I became born of God with all my past forgiven, never to be the same again. Jesus now keeps my spirit from sin, lighting up my understanding forever. I now have a new life given to me that Adam lost in the Garden of Eden. My name is now written in the Book of Life.

If You Do Not Believe

If you do not believe in Adam and the Garden of Eden, if you do not believe in heaven or hell, if you do not believe that Jesus Christ is the

Son of God, then you are reading the correct book. The God of heaven and earth will open your eyes and heart to this truth. "Lord rebuke the spirits of darkness and may the veil be lifted from your eyes as you study!" All of Adam's children are darkened in their inner beings and just cannot understand spiritual things (2 Cor. 4:3–4). I am giving you the truth, and if you do not follow these directions, you will regret your choice for all eternity.

Quickly pray and ask God to open your eyes. Only the children of the kingdom that have been born of God—not of flesh or of the will of man—will be enlightened in these things. But you do have a choice, and if you have a better way than Jesus then take it and good luck. But I am warning you that Jesus is the only way (John 14:6)!

First Corinthians 2:7–16 says in part, "The natural man cannot understand this nor will the religious man see this; it will only be foolishness to them." Point made—if this is foolishness to you then maybe you have been deceived or you are not a child of the kingdom of Jesus Christ (1 Cor. 1:18–21). Become a child of God today by accepting Jesus Christ as your redeemer and you will not perish with the billions of Adam's descendants by 2035.

Everybody lives forever, but not everybody receives the DNA life of God. It is a matter of where you want to live for all eternity. The human spirit is eternal, and you can choose a new light or you can choose to go your own way and suffer the consequences of your decision.

Different Phases of Resurrection

At the end of Jesus' thousand-year millennial kingdom, everyone who has lived on this earth will be resurrected to an eternal body; this is called the second resurrection (Dan. 12:1–4). The first resurrection is in phases, and all who have a part in the first resurrection will receive eternal bodies likened to Jesus. Blessed are those who have a part in the first resurrection of such the second death has no power (1 Cor. 15:12–26). If you have part in the second resurrection, you will experience the second death that will never end.

Jesus was the first fruits of this first resurrection in AD 28. Next will be all the church saints who have died since AD 28, and this portion of the first resurrection will occur when all their graves open just prior to the rapture of the living saints in about AD 2027 to 2030. Then comes forth the seven-year tribulation saints in about AD 2035. The last ones to join the first resurrection family will be the believers during the kingdom and the Old Testament saints at the end of the kingdom. All from the first resurrection are names written in the Book of Zoë life (Rev. 20:10–15). Every person whose name is not written in the Book of Life will stand before the great white throne with a new eternal body and will face the second death in the lake of fire created for the Devil and his angels (Rev. 19:20). All unbelievers and all of the fallen angels and the bodies of the demon spirits will be resurrected. Everyone associated with the second resurrection will end up bodily in the lake of fire.

> Now when the thousand years have expired, Satan will be released from his prison and will go out to deceive the nations which are in the four corners of the earth, Gog and Magog, to gather them together to battle, whose number is as the sand of the sea. They went up on the breadth of the earth and surrounded the camp of the saints and the beloved city. And fire came down from God out of Heaven and devoured them. The devil, who deceived them, was cast into the lake of fire and brimstone where the beast and the false prophet

are. And they will be tormented day and night forever and ever. Then I saw a great white throne and Him who sat on it, from whose face the earth and the Heaven fled away. And there was found no place for them. And I saw the dead, small and great, standing before God, and books were opened. And another book was opened, which is the Book of Life. And the dead were judged according to their works, by the things which were written in the books. The sea gave up the dead who were in it, and Death and Hades delivered up the dead who were in them. And they were judged, each one according to his works. Then Death and Hades were cast into the lake of fire. This is the second death. And anyone not found written in the Book of Life was cast into the lake of fire. (Rev. 20:7–15 NKJV)

Jesus Is the Last Adam

This last Adam was created by God's DNA seed being placed in the womb of a young virgin named Mary. This last Adam was born with the full DNA profile of God. Jesus Christ was the *only* begotten Son of His Father, who was filled with all the fullness of God's life. The last Adam offered His perfect life as atonement for our sins. Jesus became the perfect offering that appeased the wrath of God, which had previously sent Noah's flood. This flood was the manifestation of the wrath of God's judgment. Armageddon will be the same.

CHAPTER 2

Scoffers Will Come
in the Last Days

One of the major signs that we are approaching the end of time and that we are in the very last days is the abundance of scoffers and mockers of God. These scoffers attack anyone who has a belief in the Creator. They make fun of anyone who believes this earth was once judged by a global flood. They ignore the evidence of intelligent design that is found in the fossil record and the genetics of life. Their theory, actually myth, of Darwinism must be taught as the undeniable gospel of truth. It has become blasphemous to even question these scoffers' doctrine of Darwinism.

If you want to be mocked and scoffed at, just question the principles of evolution. You will be labeled ignorant, stupid, and even evil if you have a belief that God even exists. They proudly laugh at the prophecies of Daniel and a coming judgment in the book of Revelation. Could the book of Daniel that was sealed until the end now be open? The following are only a few of many verses found in the Bible regarding scoffers and mockers.

The Coming Day of the Lord

Know this first of all, that in the *last days mockers will come* with their mocking, following after their own lusts, and saying, "Where is the promise of His coming? For ever since the fathers fell asleep, all continues just as it was from the beginning of creation." For when they maintain this, it escapes their notice that by the word of God the heavens existed long ago and the earth was formed out of water and by water, through which the world at that time was destroyed, being flooded with water. But by His word the present heavens and earth are being reserved for fire, kept for the Day of Judgment and destruction of ungodly men. But do not let this one fact escape your notice, beloved, that with the Lord one day is like a thousand years, and a thousand years like one day. The Lord is not slow about His promise, as some count slowness, but is patient toward you, not wishing for any to perish but for all to come to repentance. But the day of the Lord will come like a thief, in which the heavens will pass away with a roar and the elements will be destroyed with intense heat, and the earth and its works will be burned up. Since all these things are to be destroyed in this way, what sort of people ought you to be in holy conduct and godliness, looking for and hastening the coming of the day of God, because of which the heavens will be destroyed by burning, and the elements will melt with intense heat! But according to His promise we are looking for new heavens and a new earth, in which righteousness dwells. Therefore, beloved, since you look for these things, be diligent to be found by Him in peace, spotless and blameless, and regard the patience of our Lord as salvation; just as also our beloved brother Paul, according to the wisdom given him, wrote to you, as also in all his letters, speaking in them of these things, in which are some things hard to understand, which the untaught and unstable distort, as they do also the rest of the Scriptures, to their own destruction. You therefore, beloved, knowing this beforehand, be on your guard so that you are not carried away by the error of unprincipled men and fall from your own steadfastness, but grow in the grace and knowledge of our Lord and Savior Jesus Christ. To Him be the glory, both now and to the day of eternity. Amen. (2 Peter 3:3-18 NASB, also read Rev. 21-22)

And I heard, but I understood not: then said I, O my Lord, what shall be the end of these things? And he said, go thy way, Daniel: *for the words are closed up and sealed till the time of the end.* Many shall be purified, and made white, and tried; but the wicked shall do wickedly: and *none of the wicked* shall understand; but the *wise* shall understand. (Dan. 12:8-10 KJV)

You only have to spend one semester in any state-run college to discover these scoffers prophesied by Daniel in the Bible. They are scoffing, mocking professors who do not understand the things of God and are preaching their own wicked religious cult gospel message of Darwinism. They mock God's very existence and their scoffing is as described in the preceding Bible verses. These professors scoff at God and His six days of creation! "The fool has said in his heart, there is no God" (Ps.14:1). A fool is one who claims there is no God. This statement comes from God's written Word, not mine. God also calls them a den of snakes spitting out venom and poisoning the minds of our next generation!

These professors scoff at anything that does not line up with their own idea of the origin of the universe, which has become their own religion. They proclaim their faith-based worldview of their own evolutionary religious beliefs and label them as science. Like snakes ignoring their charmers, they refuse to listen to the other worldview, which is intelligent design.

> These wicked people are born sinners; even from birth they have lied and gone their own way. They spit venom like deadly snakes; they are like cobras that refuse to listen, ignoring the tunes of the snake charmers, no matter how skillfully the charmer's play. Break off their fangs, O God! (Ps. 58:3–6 NLT)

Darwinism Is a Cult Religion

Evolution has become a cult religion of the atheists. They believe the big bang totally by faith and their out-of-control imaginations run wild. After 170 years and millions of fossils that have been catalogued, the evidence they need has not fossilized! In her book *Godless*, Ann Coulter reveals that the so-called *gaps in the theory of evolution* are all there is; the whole theory in Darwinism is a gap!

This Is a Great Battle between Two Religions

These professors desperately try to fill our children's minds with their religious evolutionary doctrines. These religious beliefs, however, are labeled in the classrooms as scientific evidence and are now taught as fact. This is one of evolution's doctrines that is totally not of the truth! Coulter has accurately said our children must be baptized in the state-run religion of Darwinism.

Evolution is a religion of the atheists. They have ideas about the origin of the universe and the origin of life, but their ideas are without any true scientific evidence. For some strange reason, their evidence did not fossilize. The fossil record supports no transition fossils, and the fossils that should not be there are there. The fossils they need to be there have never been found.

The same science that should support Darwinism actually supports the creation view and intelligent design (ID). Intelligent design is found in the oldest layer of fossils known as the Cambrian Explosion. No transition fossils are to be found anywhere except in their minds.

Many scientific facts are available that prove creation and a very young earth. There is absolutely no evidence to prove the big bang theory and the teachings of evolution. Oh, they claim they have evidence, but when the evidence is scientifically examined carefully, a sickly pall hangs over all the evidence they put forth. When put to the test, it does not pass true scientific testing. Darwinism is still a theory in crisis supported only by your tax dollars, and they are still looking for evidence that is just not available. Darwinism and creation are both religious.

An example for the big Darwinism dud is the Sahara Desert. The Sahara Desert has a prevailing wind pattern. The hot air blows off the desert and kills the trees next door, and that new area becomes desert. This process is called "desertification" (*HBJ Earth Science* 1989, 277). After studying it for years, the scientific experts claimed the Sahara Desert is probably "about 4,000 years old" (see Potsdam Institute for Climate Impact Research in Germany, July 15, 1999, *Geophysical Research Letters*).

This means the Sahara desert began shortly after the flood of Noah's days in 2317 BC, according to true scientific research. When the water began to run off after the flood, lakes formed in low-lying areas and left sea creatures stranded. As the lakes dried up, we should have found fossils of sea creatures all over deserts. That is exactly what we find in the Sahara and also in many other deserts, with whale fossils singing "to God be the glory." These sea fossils are still being discovered in the deserts to this day. *Duh*, hello, there was a global flood in 2317 BC, and the Sahara should be about four thousand years old. You can find more information about this topic at the following websites.[1]

Darwinism Is a Religion, Not Science

The very first definition of the word *religion* at dictionary.com is as follows:

1. A *set* of beliefs concerning the cause, *nature*, and purpose of the universe.

---

[1]   http://www.british-israel.us/84.html
http://genesisministry.org/young-earth-evidence/
http://news.softpedia.com/news/Has-Sahara-Always-Been-a-Desert-47128.shtml
http://news.nationalgeographic.com/news/2011/12/pictures/111206-whale-graveyard-chile-fossils-science/

2. A personal set or institutionalized system of religious attitudes, beliefs, and practices.
3. The body of persons adhering to a particular set of beliefs and practices.

According to these definitions, evolution is a religion! By exercising faith in their religion, evolutionists have to believe in fairytales like the big bang myth. They have badly distorted archaeological thought in America with their fairytale myth of evolution. Evolution has become a most deceptive religion and is masterfully cloaked in a tax-paid smoke screen labeled as science.

However, evolution is not science. In fact, this battle between evolution and creation is not a battle between science and religion as most would have you believe. No! This is a war between two religions, and any dating methods that are associated with Darwinism cannot be honestly trusted. Millions and billions of years is a *myth*. There was no time before the creation week in 3973 BC. Time is only found in a certain window of seven thousand years that began with the sin of Adam and ends after Christ's future thousand-year government known as Christ's kingdom. Time is better explained in chapters 6 and 7 of this book.

These mockers from this theory of evolution are anti-God to their very core! Evolutionists cannot and will not accept the fact that the Bible has been proven to be full of true historical events and very accurate prophecies. The historical recordings of the Bible are accurately documented, and future events in prophecies concerning the end of time will take place as written. The Bible is the number one bestselling book in the world. Let me emphasize again: *no dates* associated with this evolution theory can be trusted at all! God has a more realistic time-frame of 7,007 years. Just look how our history has changed in the last 114 years.

Evolutionists make this following claim: "We cannot let religion get a foot in the door." Why? If the evolutionists let ID slowly ease a foot in the door, it will mess up their own religious belief system! Evolution is a faith-based religion like all others, but it has become a cult religion. Their "god" is man. Their belief is that God was created in man's mind and that man is actually the highest of all beings, and to even question the evolution theory has become blasphemy! To question Darwinism is the unforgiveable sin in our liberal, godless society. Darwinism is protected by the ACLU and our liberal court systems. Again, it has become holy blasphemy to question Darwinism. Darwinism is an indoctrination program and is not taught as theory but *fact*.

These evolutionists don't have the ability to read history properly and cannot understand why ancient civilizations were so intelligent. God created mankind as a fully intelligent being. The very first man, Adam, was created as an adult possessing the full DNA of God. The earth was Adam's kingdom, with everything subject to his full authority.

Adam did not speak caveman lingo with nasty bubba teeth shining between his lips! Adam spoke the Hebrew language very fluently. This is a far cry from the teachings of evolution and their so-called Neanderthal man. Ancient aliens did not genetically change Neanderthals into Homo sapiens, as the History Channel claims. Ancient aliens are nothing but fallen angels deceiving mankind. The skeletons of their hybrid children, the Nephilim, with elongated skulls are found in the fossil record around the world. Read the final chapter of this book. You have to watch this YouTube link by Trey Smith that uncovers Nephilim evidence of genetic evil. This is a must see

YouTube video revealing video evidence of Nephilim skulls discovered all around the world.[2]

Is Evolution Only a Fairytale for Adults?

This evolutionary, Stone Age thinking is literally a crime against our next generation and is crippling the scientific community of our time! There are still people living in this so-called Stone Age, even after six thousand years of development. Evolution is loaded with myths and unscientific theories that are only limited by the evolutionists' ability to dream and imagine. These unbelievable thoughts come from the distorted thinking of Darwinism, which has abandoned the truth altogether.

The true missing links can only be found somewhere between the two ears of an evolutionist! In fact, the whole theory of evolution is a missing link lacking common sense! Therefore, they mock the history of creation and rampantly scoff at the mighty Creator in these very last days. They are definitely one sign of the end of time.

Dictionary.com gives a revealing definition of this word fairytale: *"an interesting but highly implausible story; told as an excuse."* This definition is a mirror image of the theory of evolution, and atheists use it as an "excuse" to scoff at the existence of God. This definition of a fairytale fits like a glove on this theoretical hand of evolution. Evolution is a fairytale of myths, deceptions, and dreams limited only by their darkened thought processes. In fact, evolution does not even scientifically qualify as a true theory but only as a fairytale or myth!

---

[2]   http://www.youtube.com/watch?v=1zz8_MxcnzY

Many Myths in the Theory of Evolution

Anything that does not line up with the evolutionary belief system is sure to be labeled as a myth or it is just left out and ignored altogether. Evolutionists claim that their teaching is factually supported by a vast scientific community. Yet the science they claim actually supports an Intelligent Designer. It is true, according to a poll taken by Gallup on Darwin's two hundredth birthday (gallup.com/poll) that about 75 percent of post graduates believe in evolution and 40 percent of normal population. But that is not proof that this unfounded theory is correct! It just proves that a majority of educated people can be wrong. Plus, if you don't believe in evolution, you may not keep your job as a science teacher. It is pure propaganda, with no scientific facts to support it. None! These deceivers and scoffing liars have become the authors of the only real myth found in science today! Evolution is a real *myth*.

Here are just a few examples of the Darwinian deception. When the moon lander landed on the moon, there was a problem with moon dust. The problem was there was not enough dust discovered. They discovered less than one inch, less than ten thousand years of dust, and only 1/67 of that dust was meteorite dust. The extremely thick layer of moon dust that should have accumulated over billions of years was nowhere to be found. Plus, when they examined the moon rocks, they discovered they were not the same as earth rocks. If everything came from a big bang, they should be the same material. Duh, hello, is anybody at home in fairytale land?

At the North and South Poles, tropical plants are found frozen. Tropical plant imprints are found on the rock ceilings of all coal seams. The earth once had a tropical climate. Oil companies have discovered big trees under the ice caps and some as tall as 150 feet. Human footprints and dinosaur footprints are found in the same rock strata.

All fossils found in the oldest layer are fully formed and abundant in variety. This is known by scientists as the Cambrian Explosion, for which they have no answers.

After 170 years of digging, not one transitional fossil has been found to support their myth of macro evolution. If evolution was true, there should be thousands of missing links. These scientific facts are only a few discoveries available for one seeking the truth. But if you are a fool, then be careful not to choke to death on the missing moon dust.

The big bang is a *myth*; the evolutionary tree of life is a *myth*; the geologic column, invented by Charles Lyall in the 1800s, is a *myth*, and this systematic column can only be found in science textbooks; the cosmic soup or mud puddle from which life must have arisen is a *myth*; millions and billions of years is a *myth*. There are not enough pages in this book to list all of the myths of this religion called evolution or Darwinism. Simply stated, the complete theory is a *myth* still in search of evidence. They will never find it because it is not there.

The Sun Is Shrinking/a Scientific Observation

An article was written on the hourly shrinking of the sun by Russell Akridge, PhD, was posted on the ICR website, and this is only a portion of the article:

> The sun was larger in the past than it is now by 0.1% per century. A creationist, who may believe that the world was created approximately 6 thousand years ago, has very little to worry about. The sun would have been only 6% larger at creation than it is now.

However, if the rate of change of the solar radius remained constant, 100 thousand years ago the sun would be twice the size it is now.[3]

This shrinkage of the sun is a major problem for the theory of evolution and the Darwinian time machine. It is literally impossible for the earth and sun to be billions of years old, even millions of years old. This one scientific observation alone is undisputable evidence that Darwinism is a big fairytale from hell.

Many Good Scientists Don't Believe in Evolution

Please don't be discouraged because there are many good scientists who do not believe in this mythical theory called evolution. Michael Cremo has a great YouTube documentary on the lies of evolution and their forbidden archaeology. Reading the following great reference books will help to expose and disprove this evolutionary theory: *The Hidden History of the Human Race* by Thompson and Cremo, *Bones of Contention* by Marvin Lubenow, and *Forbidden History* by J. Douglas Kenyon. Also, there is a book that documents America's true past history by Richard J. Dewhurst titled *The Ancient Giants who Ruled America*. These great books provide an abundance of facts debunking this evolutionary theory and reveal that these evolutionists are like a pit of deadly vipers spitting deadly venom of lies that corrupt the truth! Dewhurst reveals the great cover-up by the Smithsonian, which is controlled by the Darwinists.

However, I do have an issue I would like to mention concerning these authors. While these books do significantly attack the very foundation of evolution, these authors still lean toward evolutionary

---

[3] http://www.icr.org/article/sun-shrinking/

dating. Nevertheless, these authors have some very good evidence revealing evolution's deceptive ways of altering the archaeological facts.

> For in *six days [3973 BC] the Lord made Heaven and Earth, the sea, and all that in them is,* and rested the seventh day: wherefore the Lord blessed the Sabbath day, and hallowed it. (Ex. 20:11 KJV)

God wrote this on a rock for Moses and the children of Israel. God doesn't stutter but was very clear when He spoke everything into existence in only six days. God did not put a date on the rock saying earth was made millions of years ago with a big bang.

Creation Was a Literal Six-Day Event

When we look in the original Hebrew text, the word for "days" is *yom*, which means literally "a twenty-four hour day." There was no gap between day one and day two. Each day was not a thousand years, and God did not use evolution to create all things. God made everything in six twenty-four hour days, but when did these six days occur? If you are looking for this creation date, which is about 3973 BC, you can find it like watermarks woven through God's entire document known as the Bible.

Christians Make Excuses for Evolution

Born-again believers do not have to make an excuse for millions of evolutionary years, like the gap theorists, etc. We only have to believe what the finger of God wrote in stone for Moses (Ex. 31:18). The Bible says by Adam death came into the world. If you believe the gap theory, then you have death before Adam, and you then have a real problem in your theology. You are putting death before sin, and that's a very big problem theologically.

> But now is Christ risen from the dead, and become the first fruits of them that slept. *For since by man came death*, by man came also the resurrection of the dead. For as in Adam all die, even so in Christ shall all be made alive. But every man in his own order: Christ the first fruits; afterward they that are Christ's at His coming. Then cometh the end, when He shall have delivered up the kingdom to God, even the Father; when He shall have put down all rule and all authority and power. Christ must reign, till He hath put all enemies under His feet. The last enemy that shall be destroyed is death. (1 Cor. 15:20–26 KJV)

Evolutionary Dating Is Bogus

Evolutionary dating has affected even the biblical theologians. They have created the day age theory, progressive creation, the gap theory, and everything in between to accommodate these evolutionary dates. You may not believe in evolution, but it will literally make you *doubt* the Creator and the six twenty-four-hour days of creation as written in God's historical Bible.

Evolutionary scoffers were wrong about the beginning of time, which began seven years after creation and the origin of man. They were wrong about the first doomsday of destruction (Noah's flood) predicted in the great historical Bible; surely you don't think they would have any idea about the truth of the end of time or the future of mankind. However, it is interesting to notice that even some of these scientists have their own doomsday clock, and it's about to strike midnight.

Evolutionists have this belief that man is getting bigger and better and smarter, but from all evidence we have been going downhill for roughly six thousand years of history. The teaching of evolution is *a* **sign** *that we have reached* **the end** *of time for man's government.*

> Sin whispers to the wicked, deep within their hearts. They have no fear of God at all. In their blind conceit, they cannot see how wicked they really are. Everything they say is crooked and deceitful. They refuse to act wisely or do good. They lie awake at night, hatching sinful plots. Their actions are never good. They make no attempt to turn from evil. (Ps. 36:1–4 NLT)

They Are Willfully Ignorant

The willful ignorance of these unbelievers was foretold in the Bible, and the source of their foolish thinking should not be surprising to us as born-again believers. We will discuss this subject in the following chapters in more detail. This distorted thinking problem goes all the way back to the beginning and the mutation that took place seven years after creation in a perfect man and woman.

Adam was made directly from the hand of God with super intelligence and advanced abilities (Gen. 2:7). God took the dirt with all seventy-two minerals and formed Adam's body from the soil. Therefore the body that was created from the soil has to be maintained with nutrition from the soil in order to keep it healthy. Then when the body dies, it returns to the soil.

God put His own DNA and glory in this creature called man. God created man just below Himself and above the angels who were to be ministers and servants to mankind, but Adam lost His glory. Jesus has returned God's DNA back to born-again believers. Christians are the only humans who know where they came from, where they stand, and where they are going after death.

Adam was perfect in all his ways until he took the wrong path in life by disobeying his Father and Creator and selling mankind into a slave market of sin. Adam decided through his free will to go his own way and do his own thing. Therefore, Adam's descendants were all born slaves with a slave mentality, causing them to progressively decline.

This decline was caused by a physical mutation that took place in God's perfect creation. This imperfection that entered Adam's DNA after he sinned caused a six thousand–year time clock to start ticking. This creation date is a far cry from the millions and billions of years that are written in science textbooks. The evolutionists are baptizing your children with million and billions of years into their religion of Darwinism. Invest in homeschooling or private schooling if you want to preserve your children.

The bottom line is that the teaching of evolution is a major sign of the end of time. It was foretold in the Bible and predicted by St. Nilus in about AD 400.

A Part of St. Nilus's Prophecy

And when they have achieved all this, these unhappy people will spend their lives in comfort without knowing, poor souls, that it is deceit of the Antichrist. And, the impious one! —he will so *complete science with*

> *vanity that it will go off the right path and lead people to lose faith in the existence of God* in three hypostases [the teaching of Evolution].[4]

Read more in chapter 14 about this prophecy or go to the web address in the footnote.

It is written in the Bible that "mockers" and "scoffers" will begin to fill the earth, challenging the existence of the Creator and His creation story. They are here; they are everywhere, like flies on cow dung, like gnats on a rotten banana. They have fabricated myths and fairytales as an excuse for the truth and labeled it science. Out of thin air they have created millions of years to stretch out their false teachings in an attempt to make them more believable. Only God controls time, and He has placed time in a 7,007-year window. God is all about the truth, and Darwinism is all about deception.

Hitler Arose Out of Darwinism

Hitler once said in *The Third Reich on War* on page thirty-eight, "If you tell a lie long enough and loud enough, and often enough, the people will believe it. They are more likely to believe a big lie than a small one." Evolution is a big lie straight from the kingdom of darkness and from Satan, the Father of Lies. Hitler was a disciple of Darwin's teachings.

> We do not wrestle against flesh and blood, but against principalities, against powers, against the rulers of the darkness of this age, against spiritual hosts of wickedness in the heavenly places. (Eph. 6:12 NKJV)

---

[4] http://www.traditioninaction.org/Questions/B249_StNilus.html

Our struggle is not against Obama and the physical government of man, but our battle is spiritual and we should pray for our president daily. The physical problem we have to deal with is the internal mutation that came from the first man. This mutation is the subject of chapter 5, and we will study how it vastly affects our thinking. We will examine this mutation in detail and see how it affects mankind in this very day in which we live. It will affect mankind through man's entire seven thousand–year window of time explained in chapter 7.

Evolution's Secret Formula to Help You Believe a Lie

For 170 years evolutionists have tried to brainwash the entire world by using their scientific dating methods, which are as bogus as three-dollar bills. They have a secret formula that will help you believe their big lie; it is known as millions and billions of years. Just look how much change has taken place in the last one hundred years, much less one thousand years. The six days of creation happened in about 3973 BC, and God made *everything* in six twenty-four hour days. Nothing but God existed before that time and archaeology should date artifacts within this six thousand–year time frame of history, but that will never happen. If they dated things this way, how different science would be today.

CHAPTER 3

A Brief History of Islam, Judaism, and Christianity

Note: Some of the resources about Islam, Allah and the Muslim religion, found in chapters 3 and 4 was taken from NCCG.ORG unless otherwise listed. A wealth of documented resources about Allah as the moon god can be freely studied at the following link on information concerning Islam.[5]

You may ask what this chapter has to do with doomsday. These religions of the Middle East will have everything to do with the coming doomsday in America and the infamous battle of Armageddon. This is only a brief overview to help you understand the importance of the Middle East and the history of these three religions that have originated from this region of the world.

Many religions are from different parts of the world. To name only a few: in India we have Hinduism and Buddhism; in East Asia we have Budhism, Taoism and Confucianism; in Russia we have the religion of atheism and humanism. In America we have Christianity, Darwinism, and every other religion that has been known to mankind. However,

---

5   http://www.nccg.org/islam/Islam01-Allah.html

there is no religion as volatile as the Islamic religion centered in the Middle East.

Christianity, Judaism, and Islam originate from the Middle East. Only one of these three major religions will provide you access to the true and living God, the Ancient of Days, the Creator and Designer of the universe, the maker of all things. This true God of all creation is also the designer of the seven thousand–year window of time and a six thousand–year doomsday clock that you will soon discover in future chapters. The true and living God has appointed a time that is counting down six thousand years until Armageddon and seven thousand years till the judgment day of all the living and the dead. At the end of six thousand years, the wrath of God will be poured out on an unbelieving religious people of this godless world. This is a day that nothing can alter or change.

This appointment with destiny was scheduled at the beginning of the seven thousand–year window of time for mankind. Only one of these three religions has the ability to provide you with the proper fire suit that will give you eternal Zoë life. Only one of these three religions will rescue you from the judgment and wrath of God. The other two religions will provide you a front-row ticket to a very hot seat in a very hot afterlife.

Of these three religions, you will be introduced to a couple of baby boys who were miraculously born in the Middle East, and their births truly have changed the entire world. You will discover a certain religion that in the last days will help you escape the battle of Armageddon. These last days are upon us, so keep looking up for the redemption of the born-again children of God. This redemption is known as the rapture of the church, which will occur about 2027 or 2028, with the latest possible date being in the fall of 2030!

Almost every person on the face of this earth is religious. In some way or another, they have some form of religious belief within them. Some worship a higher being, some worship created things, and others worship man. This worship of man is a belief that there is no higher being than mankind. In the state of Alabama, there is the worship of football coaches and teams. Others around the world worship things like cars, boats, bikes, sports heroes, the beauty of the human body, and the love of money—and the things money can buy have consumed many.

The following three definitions of religion are found on dictionary.com:

Re·li·gion—noun

1 - A set of beliefs concerning the cause, nature, and purpose of the universe. (Creationists versus evolutionists—battle of two religions)

2 - A specific fundamental set of beliefs and practices generally agreed upon by a number of persons or sects: (the Christian religion; the Buddhist religion, the Muslim religion, atheist religion, humanist religion, the evolutionist religion, Judaism religion, the Roman Catholic religion, etc.)

3 - The body of persons adhering to a particular set of beliefs and practices: (Jews, Muslims, Christians, atheists, evolutionists, Catholics, etc.)

As we examine this subject, we will not spend much time on all other religions of the world. We will only focus on the three religions originating from the Middle East: Judaism, Christianity, and Islam, plus a fourth atheist cult religion of Darwinism from America. Except for one, they are all truly bankrupt spiritually. They only worship different ideas and idols, abandoning Yahweh, the true and living God. Only those who worship a God who has a Son claiming to be the Creator of the entire universe have true access to heaven. No Son, no intercessor, no access!

These three religions claim to worship the same God. But Islam actually worships a different god even though they claim otherwise. Islam worships a god named Allah. Maybe you believe that Allah is god. If you are comfortable with Allah and you are willing to put your eternity in his hands, the decision is yours. You truly have the spiritual freedom to choose, but remember Allah is a god that has no son.

A Man Named Abraham

Islam, Judaism, and Christianity all have some reference to a man named Abraham found in the Bible. Christianity and the Muslim religion are the two of the largest in numbers in the world. Christianity and Judaism worship a God who is known by several names: YHWH, Jehovah, or Yahweh. He is also called El-Shaddai, Elohim, the God Most High, the Exalted One, etc., but never Allah. He was also called the God of Abraham, Isaac, and Jacob (whose name was later changed to Israel) (Ex. 3:14). This Jehovah God is the one and only true God. He is the God who inspired the writing of the Bible, the most popular, bestselling, most trusted book in the world.[6]

Christianity states that there are no other gods. Christianity claims that all other gods are false and are only created beings. Islam has the same claim on Allah. The world claims that there are many ways to get to God. Christianity claims that there is only one way to access the only God of heaven, and that is through His Son, Jesus Christ. In John

---

6   http://carm.org/what-real-name-god-yhwh-jehovah-yahweh

14:6 Jesus said, "I am the way, the truth, and the life. No one comes to the Father except through Me" (NKJV).

Judaism does not believe like the Christians. They only believe in the Old Testament part of the Bible but still believe that Yahweh is the God of Creation. They are different from Christianity in the way you are able to access God's favor and presence. Judaism believes in a works-based system, keeping the law given by Moses, and they do not believe in grace through Jesus Christ, the Messiah. Judaism is a belief that will get you the second death, even though they try to worship the true and living God. There is truly only one way to Him!

Judaism is under the old covenant of the past while Christianity is under the new covenant of grace given by Jesus Christ the Son of the Living God. In 28 AD the Jewish leaders rejected Jesus as Messiah and nailed Him on a cross. Christ is Christianity! *Americanlivewire.com* lists Christianity as the number one belief system in the world and the only system that operates under GRACE. Islam is the second largest and growing with a physical birth rate of eight or nine children per family, which is expanding their religion extremely fast. But Islam's god has no son. Christianity has Jesus and, by His innocent blood offering on the cross, became the only intercessor to the true and living God.[7]

Christians' access to their God Yahweh is not by keeping the Law or a set of rules as those in Judaism believe. It is not by killing the infidel and forcing others to believe in Islam as the Muslims believe. Christianity believes that Jesus Christ is the *only* intercessor who can get you into Yahweh's heaven! Jesus Christ is the only one offering eternal Zoë life, which is what you need for entrance into heaven.

Muslims believe in a different god named Allah, and they believe Allah is the one and only true god. In fact that is what the word Allah

---

[7]   http://americanlivewire.com/largest-religions/

means: only one god. Which one is the true God of creation? Both Muslims and Christians claim their God is Creator. I offer you a choice; you can pick Allah, who has no son as intercessor, or Yahweh, who has a Son named Jesus Christ. This decision is totally yours. I cannot make you believe in either one, but one thing I do know is true: *they are not the same "god," with an absolute **not**.* So with that we must take a deeper look into Islam and their claim to an earthly man named Abraham.

The Early Days of Abraham

According to historical records found in the Bible, the Dead Sea Scrolls, Jewish traditions, and the ancient book of Jasher: Terah, Abraham's father, served as an official in the courts of King Nimrod. Nimrod was the founder of Babel, Sumer, Assyria, and other cities of the Mesopotamian valley located in the Middle East. His stargazers and magicians warned the king that a threat to his kingdom had just been born to Terah, one of his officials. They were warning Nimrod to deal with this while this threat was still a baby. A similar incident happened two thousand years later with King Herod's attempt to destroy Jesus as an infant.

King Nimrod asked Terah to bring him his newborn son. The king offered to give Terah gold and silver and other wealth for his infant boy, named Abram. Bottom line the king offered to buy Terah's infant son. According to the ancient book of Jasher, Nimrod wanted to destroy Abram. But Terah refused to turn over his newborn son to the king. King Nimrod grew very angry and sent word to Terah that before the sun set he would destroy Terah's complete household if he did not comply. So Terah asked to have a few days with his family before he delivered Abram to Nimrod. God later changed Abram's name to Abraham. We will refer to him from this point on with his later name—Abraham.

Terah Deceives Nimrod

Terah devised a secret plan to save his son, Abraham. Terah was commanded to bring the infant Abraham to the king, but Terah instead brought a slave girl's baby boy who was born at the same time as Abraham. The king grabbed the infant by his feet and legs and slammed its head against the ground, crushing the baby's head until the slave's baby was dead. Nimrod was thinking all along that the infant was Terah's son, Abraham. Nimrod thought he was destroying the future threat to his throne.

After seeing the king's anger as he destroyed the infant, Terah feared that Nimrod would discover the deception, so Terah sent his wife, her handmaid, and Abraham to hide and live in a cave. According to the ancient book of Jasher, for ten years Terah fed and cared for them while in this cave. On Abraham's tenth birthday, Terah decided to send Abraham to live with his oldest grandparents, which would help to preserve his life. Terah knew Abraham would be out of Nimrod's sight and be well cared for living with Noah and Shem.

Abraham Goes to School

Abraham was now living with two of the eight people chosen to escape God's first doomsday judgment that came on the whole earth. According to all biblical sources, only eight souls had survived the wrath of God during the flood. Abraham, at ten years old, was in a learning environment with two of the godliest teachers who breathed air on the face of this earth. Scholars have wondered through the ages why Abraham was so full of faith in his belief in Yahweh. It is simple. He was homeschooled by Noah and Shem for forty years of his life, which produced a man filled with godly character as we find in the Bible narrative of Abraham.

This dangerous environment created by Nimrod had pushed Abraham into homeschooling with Noah and Shem. The first class was 101 in the six days of creation and God's ability to judge His own creation with the mighty flood waters that rose over fifteen cubits above the highest mountain. This flood had washed the surface of the earth clean of a very wicked Nephilim civilization. The pre-deluge longevity of life had caused the earth's population to be numbered at a minimum of one billion people and could have been as high as forty billion, according to Tom Pickett's math.[8]

I am sure they taught Abraham about the year they spent on the ark while the flood waters covered the face of the earth. Noah and Shem warned Abraham against the worship of false gods and about the evil Nephilim spirits that had roamed the earth since the flood. In fact, Noah had prayed for God to remove these demon spirits from the earth, and God did that very thing. However, in time Satan went before God and asked for some of these evil spirits to be restored back to his kingdom. Ten percent of these spirits were granted back to Satan, according to the Dead Sea Scrolls.

This was no accident that Abraham was now living with these two great men of faith, because all things will work together for those that are called according to God's purpose. God had planned for Abraham to be the father of the great nation of Israel. Abraham, as a young boy, learned to live by faith from Noah and Shem. He learned the ways of Yahweh his God from his oldest living ancestors.

---

[8]   http://ldolphin.org/pickett.html

Noah and Shem were still experiencing a long life caused by their genetic makeup that existed before the flood. Noah lived about 350 years after the flood and was able to spend quality time with a ten-year-old Abraham, who was the family line of Jesus the Messiah. However, I think a short time after Noah met Abraham, he placed his hands on Abraham's head and blessed him. Noah and Shem passed a godly blessing and anointing down the family line, as was their custom.

Forty Years with Melchizedek

For the next forty years Noah and Melchizedek (Noah's oldest son, Shem) became godly fathers to Abraham. It is recorded that Abraham left their presence shortly at age fourteen to visit his mother. But most of the next forty years of Abraham's life were spent with Noah and Shem, these godly men of faith. According to the Dead Sea Scrolls, the mysterious Melchizedek was the name given to Shem as the king and priest of Salem, which is now Jerusalem.

Abraham's earthly father was a pagan idol worshipper. You can see the wisdom of God in allowing this dangerous atmosphere, which caused Abraham to be removed from his idol-worshipping father's household. The infinite wisdom of God was seen in Noah and Shem's training of Abraham to become the father of a special chosen nation of the Hebrews. Through Abraham, God was going to create a nation that would display His presence and power to a pagan world. Hebrew was once the language of the whole earth. After the tower of Babel, it was a lost language until an angel came to Abraham and taught him Hebrew. His descendants, and eventually the entire Jewish race, adopted this language.

Shem was Noah's son, born one hundred years before the flood. Shem had assisted in the building of the ark, loading the ark, and feeding the animals while floating on the waters for a year as they waited for the judgment waters to recede. Shem had previously been with Methuselah, who had personally spent time with Adam. Abraham was blessed to be in the right place at the right time designed by God. He lived with Noah, who lived six hundred years in the evil antediluvian world filled with the evil giant hybrid beings. Shem lived one hundred years prior to the flood and five hundred years after the great flood, also making him very knowledgeable about both worlds.

Methuselah taught Noah and Shem about the creation, the fall of man, and the work of Satan. Noah and Shem had third-hand knowledge of the creation, and of course they lived through the flood experience on the ark for one year. Shem lived one hundred years with that ancient evil world filled with the Nephilim and Noah six hundred years in the old world. They knew the facts about the visible manifestation of some bad angels and their genetic activity among humans and animals. They saw the megalithic structures constructed by the fallen angels and their royal children in all their glory. What an encounter of godly men Abraham was honored to experience. No wonder Abraham became a man of great faith with a homeschooling classroom that lasted over forty years!

Just spending time with Noah had to be the highlight of Abraham's young life. I think as a young boy he was able to play in and around the ark, which was one and a half times the length of a football field (*wow!*). I am sure Abraham relived the stories told to him of the antediluvian world by his grandfathers and how this ark had saved both mankind and animals from the great flood. This had to be fascinating to him. Abraham would wander around the cages and living quarters in the ark and imagine or relive the story told to him by Shem and Noah. No wonder Abraham became so strong in his faith in God. He was told the purpose of the great flood was to destroy the evil giant civilization that had been created by the fallen angels and had taken over the world. God had preserved Noah and Shem and the original animal lines that God had created. He was preserving them from this first doomsday judgment on mankind and the earth. Jesus can preserve you from the next doomsday coming very soon.

Shem, who was the godly Melchizedek, had taught Abraham how to live by faith and the authority that a child of God has against the kingdom of darkness. He taught him that there was *only one true God*, named Yahweh. Noah and Shem taught Abraham about the prophecies of Enoch and future coming of the Messiah. This was the coming Messiah that was forecast by the prophet Enoch hundreds of years before the great flood. Noah had securely preserved all of Enoch's writings while on the ark.[9] The book of Enoch was later removed from the Bible by the Pharisees in AD 90 at the Council of Jamnia. Enoch revealed too much information concerning Jesus.

Abraham Was Taught about Demons

Abraham learned firsthand how to deal with the invisible evil spirits (demons) that torment mankind even to this day and how the demon spirits came out of the dead bodies of the giants who were half-human, half-angel hybrids. As the Nephilim died before and during the flood, their spirits became demons. The fossil record of today offers proof of the Nephilim giants that were once on this earth before the flood. Ancient writings provide evidence that demons and fallen angels are two totally different creatures from the kingdom of darkness.

These demon spirits, which came out of the Nephilim, invisibly cause sickness, fighting, wars, and depression, and anger, fits of

---

9   http://www.pseudepigrapha.com/faq/ShemMelchizedek.html;   http://en.wikipedia.org/wiki/Melchizedek.

rage, addictions, and constant thoughts entering the mind. They are constantly causing trouble among mankind. "They take no food and neither hunger or thirst. They cause offences but are not observed" (1 Enoch 15:10–11). Are not these stories of the origin and activity of the Nephilim spirits (demons) written in 1 Enoch 6 through 15 and the book of Jubilees written by Moses, both discovered in the Dead Sea Scrolls?

The Dead Sea Scrolls reveal a lot about demons, and you hear very little concerning them in the thirty-nine Old Testament books of the Bible until Jesus begins to cast them out and begins teaching about them in the gospels. The discovery of extra books makes forty-two Old Testament books, which is more than the thirty-nine books that religious men have allowed you to have. These three additional Old Testament books (1Enoch, Jubilees and Jasher) tell a much broader story of demons in the spirit world, the kingdom of darkness that Jesus confronted boldly in His time on earth. The book of 1 Enoch was part of the Bible during Jesus' days. *Who took it out?*

If you only read the sixty-six books we have in our English Bible, you will not learn much about demons until you reach the New Testament. Jesus dealt with demons and taught His followers how to deal with them. Why was so much information about early history missing in Genesis 1–12, and why was the identity of demons so vague in the Old Testament? Were these three missing Old Testament historical books removed from the Bible on purpose by the influence of demons on religious leaders during the early church period? The kingdom of darkness has definitely used the Pharisees, the Laodiceans, and the early Catholic Church to keep the Word of God away from the common people in past history. These are documented facts of history.

So it is no farfetched idea that these four missing books (three Old Testament and one New Testament) were removed from the Bible at different times by different religious groups. God restored them in the discovery of the Dead Sea Scrolls. *We have* at least seventy *books* in our Bible, not sixty-six. This number alone means incompletion. These missing historical OT books were canonical during Jesus' days. The question to ask is by whose authority were they removed from our Bible in the first place? Now put that in your pipe and smoke it.

There was and is an effort by the kingdom of darkness to keep mankind ignorant of God's true seventy books of His inspired Word. Are you one of Satan's religious puppets who keeps trying to hide and discredit these latest biblical books discovered in the Dead Sea Scrolls? A young shepherd boy discovered these missing biblical historical books, plus much, much more, in 1947 with the discovery of the Dead Sea Scrolls. God's Word will not pass away. Heaven and earth will, but not His Word; it will last forever.

Abraham's Visit to His Mother at Fourteen

At fourteen Abraham briefly visited his relatives, mainly his mother and her handmaiden. This was the first time he had been with his mother since his first ten years of childhood while hiding from Nimrod in the cave. I am sure that being away from his mother at this young age took both courage and caring grandparents. Homesick Abraham returned home to visit his mother, but now he was a different young man of faith than his pagan idol-worshipping father Terah and brothers.

Satan Plots to Destroy the Godly Line

Abraham's visit was in the spring, when the planting season had begun. He discovered his family was having trouble planting their crops. They had a problem with flocks of black ravens eating up their planting seeds before they could cover the seeds with soil. If the seeds had been covered and were sprouting, the birds would pull the fresh seedlings out of the loose soil. The birds were also destroying the fruit before it could ripen on the trees and vines.

A fallen angel named Mastema, or Satan himself, was sending the birds. Abraham was helping to scatter the seeds on the soil when he spotted the black bird cloud approaching. Before the birds could land on the soil and start consuming the seeds, Abraham ran toward the huge black cloud of birds and raised his hands and spoke. He commanded the black birds to turn back. Immediately the black cloud of birds obeyed Abraham's command and returned back from where they came (Jubilees 11:18–21).

History says Mastema *(another name for Satan)* sent them again and again and Abraham met them every time before they could land, sending them back to their source. Abraham, only fourteen, commanded the ravens seventy times while his family was planting the seeds. I would think the ravens finally ran out of gas, crashing to the ground with exhaustion and died, similar to the herd of pigs that drowned during Jesus' ministry. Fourteen-year-old Abraham was the victor, and the black ravens stopped invading his family's gardens.

This time spent with his oldest grandfathers, Noah and Shem, had changed Abraham's perspective on God and the spirit world. The faith and authority Abraham had learned saved his relatives from starvation. Then Abraham returned to live with Noah and Shem. He lived with them till he was fifty years of age. Then he moved back to live with his parents and had them moved away from Ur of the Chaldeans. They were headed to a new land close to where he had lived with his grandparents. He was headed to a land promised him by God, who changed Abram's name in his later years to Abraham.

Many Christians have wondered why Abraham was such a man of great faith. If you had been homeschooled for forty years with men God had selected to be survivors of a global deluge judgment, your faith would be changed also. First, you have the blessings and anointing of Noah and Shem on a ten-year-old boy who will become the father of the Jewish nation. Then Abraham spent forty years of his life with Noah and Melchizedek (Shem), men who saw the judgment of God and experienced God's grace in the flood. Abraham's faith was tested, only to become stronger. Abraham learned the prophecies of Enoch about the coming Messiah.

These historical events of Abraham's life can be found in the biblical history books found in the Dead Sea Scrolls and the ancient book of Jasher. Many other interesting events of biblical characters like Abraham can be found in these biblical books of history, such as Cain taking his sister Awan as his wife and Adam living in the garden seven years, one month, and seventeen days before he sinned. These events are written down for all believers and will help strengthen your faith in the mighty God of history and creation.

These historical books also tell us that Noah divided the earth among his three sons. They agreed to draw lots for different land areas and took an oath to obey the way the lots fell or become cursed. This happened during the days of Peleg, and Canaan was the first to disobey the lot. Canaan, the son of Ham, saw the Mesopotamian Valley (in the area we now know as Israel) and the land's productivity. The temptations were more than he could stand, causing a curse to come on his family line. He had settled in an area where the lot had fallen to Shem and his descendants.

Ham's blood genetics were pure, but his wife's bloodline was full of Nephilim DNA, and it was passed down to Canaan. Some of Ham's descendants did not disobey the lot and went toward Africa to the warm climate that Ham had won by the casting of lots. The Promised Land was thickly populated with huge giants by the time Joshua entered the Promised Land. This is the reason God said destroy all of them, women, children, and animals.

The Nephilim were doing genetic hybridization with animals, so God also wanted the animals destroyed in certain towns. God wanted them destroyed because they were remnants of the pre-flood Nephilim (giants) that made their way onto the ark via the three wives of Noah's sons. The total purpose for the global flood in Noah's days was to destroy the genetic hybrids' procreation accomplished by two hundred renegade angels. This was an effort to corrupt man's bloodlines so the Messiah could not come.

God had promised Abraham that he would become a great nation, but there was a problem. Abraham had no children, and he was eighty-five years old. God was testing his faith again. His wife, Sarah, could not bear children, so she decided to give her handmaid to Abraham and maybe God would give them an heir through her handmaiden. The slave girl's name was Hagar. Abraham did not complain about the deal, and Hagar conceived instantly and gave Abraham a son, who they named him Ishmael. Abraham loved the boy and Ishmael grew strong, and from his DNA came all the Arabic nations.

Then some angels visited Abraham and told him that Sarah was going to have a son the next spring. Sarah laughed because she was completely past childbearing age at ninety. The angels told Abraham that Ishmael would not be his heir but Sarah would have a son. Sarah conceived just as the angel promised and had a son, naming him Isaac.

Only the children of the promise are considered to be Abraham's children, for God had promised that He would return about that time the next year, and Sarah would have a son. (Though Abraham had other children, this does not necessarily mean Abraham's physical descendants are not children of God).

> And he said, I will certainly return unto thee according to the time of life; and, lo, Sarah thy wife shall have a son. And Sarah heard it in the tent door, which was behind him. Is anything too hard for the Lord? At the time appointed I will return unto thee, according to the time of life, and Sarah shall have a son. (Gen. 18:10, 14 KJV)

Both Jews and Arabs claim Abraham as their family line. We see this claim is very true being that Abraham had two sons, Isaac by his wife Sarah and Ishmael by the maidservant Hagar. Also in the Dead Sea Scrolls we find Ishmael is not the chosen seed.

For Ishmael and his sons and his brothers, and Esau, the Lord did not cause them to come to Him, and He did not choose them. Although they are children of Abraham, He knew them, but *He chose Israel* to be His people. He sanctified them, and gathered them from among all the children of men; for there are many nations and many peoples, and all are His, and over all nations God has placed *spirits in authority to lead them astray from Him.* (Book of Jubilees 15:30–31)

If you want to serve and worship the true God of Abraham, you must diligently seek Him with all your heart to avoid the deception of these bad spirits. Could one of these bad spirits be referring to Allah?

Ishmael had twelve sons and became the father of the Arab nation. No one is denying the fact that Abraham is the bloodline father of the Arabs, but Ishmael is the Arabs' spiritual father; Ishmael's twelve sons abandoned the God of Abraham and chose the god of the land, who was the supreme Allah. The descendants of Ishmael worshipped many other gods in the land, according to history.

Terah, Ishmael's grandfather, was a worshipper of Allah. Terah and his son Haran, Lot's father and Abraham's brother, had a shrine set up in Mecca that was full of idols. This shrine was a place of worship for all of the pagan gods, and these gods were worshipped by almost all the peoples of the Middle East.

Born a Muslim

The Arabs want desperately to make you believe that Muslims and Jews and Christians all worship the same God. If you pay close attention to this chapter, it will set this record straight once and for all. All of the Arabs in the Middle East are physically born into the Islamic faith, as Jews are physically born into Judaism.

Christianity is totally different than any other belief system. You are not physically birthed into Christianity, but you have to experience a second spiritual birth from above, and it is up to your free will and your own individual choosing when the Spirit of God calls to become a Christian. As Corrie Ten Boom once said, "a mouse born in a biscuit pan in your cabinet does not automatically make the mouse a biscuit." Being physically born into a Christian family does not make you a Christian, for God has no grandchildren. It is only a second spiritual birth in your human spirit that makes you a true child of Yahweh. You must be born-again!

Christianity is not a works-based religious system as all other religions are. It is a free gift and a grace system, not of works that none can boast. It is by the blood of Jesus Christ, the Lamb of God that takes away the sin of the world. This is how by your faith any person can become a Christian, even if your family is not Christian. You can be born a Muslim or born a Jew, and if you want you can become a Christian by being born anew in your human spirit.

Christians and Jews worship the same God, but the confusion among Christians is whether Jews, Christians, and Muslims worship the same God. Christianity is not a majority in the Middle East like Islam. Christianity began in the Middle East with the birth of their Messiah, as the Muslim religion began by a miraculous birth of a boy born in the Quraish clan in Makkah Province or Mecca Province. Today Muhammad's birthplace is the most populated province of Saudi Arabia, according to a 2004 census. (It had a population of 5,797,971.)[10]

Mecca is located in the Middle East and is the site of the revelation given to Muhammad of the Qur'an. It is also regarded as the holiest city in the religion of Islam. Today more than fifteen million Muslims visit Mecca annually.[11]

Birth of Jesus

The miraculous birth of two baby boys in the Middle East has literally changed the entire world. The birth of the first baby in Israel in 7 BC historically changed the world. A star appeared with a bright light pointing the way for wise men from the east as its glory shone over a barn or stable announcing the birth of Jesus Christ. This baby was born in a barn in an animal feed bin in a town called Bethlehem, located in the Middle East. The angel announced, "A King is born, a Savior is given. The Messiah has arrived." This miraculous birth event happened as follows:

---

[10]   http://en.wikipedia.org/wiki/Saudi_Arabia
[11]   http://en.wikipedia.org/wiki/Mecca

Then the angel said to her, "Do not be afraid, Mary, for you have found favor with God. And behold, you will conceive in your womb and bring forth a Son, and shall call His name Jesus. He will be great, and will be called the Son of the Highest; and the Lord God will give Him the throne of His father David. And He will reign over the house of Jacob forever, and of His kingdom there will be no end." Then Mary said to the angel, "How can this be, since I do not know a man?" And the angel answered and said to her, "The Holy Spirit will come upon you, and the power of the Highest will overshadow you; therefore, also, that Holy One who is to be born will be called the Son of God. (Luke 1:30–36 NKJV)

In the following chapter, we will discuss the second baby boy who formed the Muslim religion and his miraculous birth that affected the entire world. The other baby boy was Muhammad, and he was responsible for bringing the Arabs out of multiple-idol worship to the one and only supreme god of the Arabic people. He led them into worshipping only one god, Allah, who is the god of Islam.

Islam is the major religion in the Middle East, and Arabs worship a Middle Eastern Arabic god named Allah. They claim Allah is the supreme of all gods but historically have admitted that there are smaller, lesser gods. In other words, historically they worshipped 360 gods whose idol statues were kept in Mecca; Allah was the greatest of all these gods.

Archaeology proves Allah was around before Islam and Christianity. Allah was the most-worshipped god in the Middle East long before Muhammad. Muhammad stopped the worship of all these other pagan gods and stressed that all Arabs will worship only one god, for Allah is the supreme god and everyone is only to worship him.

Abraham's dad, Terah, and Abraham's brother, Haran, worshipped these multiplicities of idol gods, with Allah being worshipped at the center of their belief. If they were away from home, they were to bow toward Mecca, the center of idol worship in the Middle East. Worship of a god represented by the crescent moon goes all the way back to the Mesopotamian Valley, as revealed in archaeology.[12]

However, Allah was the main god, the greatest god of their day. Most people of the Middle East have always worshipped Allah as the greatest. According to archaeology, they have worshipped many idols as well. We must take a closer look at these deities. Therefore the birth of the prophet Muhammad and his mission was to stop the Arabs from all of this pagan idol worship and point them to only worship Allah.[13]

Muhammad's following grew very fast because he wasn't changing their basic belief in *Al-ilah,* only offering them power and the wealth of the infidels and virgins awaiting if they die in battle. The worship of the moon and other planets was very common for the Arabic people. The Qur'an did not have to explain who Allah was because they were already praying toward Mecca when Muhammad was born. Mecca was the center of pagan idol worship, housing a shrine full of idols. The Muslims worship a special black stone that fell from heaven, now housed in the Kabah. Millions of Islamic worshippers journey to Mecca once a year. Then they march around the Kabah seven times in an effort to be able to touch this black rock that fell from heaven.

According to historical archaeology, the Middle East has always been the center of worship of the crescent moon, and it represented the supreme god *Al-ilah,* who was the greatest of all gods. The moon worship was common for the Middle Eastern Arabs, like the common practice of the Egyptians was the worship of the sun god. Israel also had a problem worshipping the planets, moon, and stars. Many warnings can be found in the Holy Scriptures against planet worship, moon worship, and sun worship.

Abraham was truly the physical flesh-and-blood father of the Arabs and the Jews. The three major religions of Christianity, Islam, and Judaism have ties to a man in the Bible and Qur'an called Abraham. Abraham's father was worshipping idols housed in Mecca twenty-five hundred years before Muhammad was born. Muhammad was born into the worship of many gods housed in Mecca and Abraham's God was not found on that list of gods in Mecca. We have examined and discovered that they do not all worship the same God. Allah and Yahweh are not the same deity, and in the next chapter we will examine the Arabic god named Allah.

CHAPTER 4

Allah Has No Son

Could Allah and Yahweh be the Same God???

The real question to ask is which one of these two gods has a Son? That is the real issue in separating Yahweh from Allah. This one question in and of itself will show that they are not the same god. Muslims claim that Allah is the supreme god of all gods, and Christians claim Yahweh is the one and only true God. Muslims claim that Christians, Jews, and Arabs all worship the God of Abraham, but the Muslims never claimed that Allah came from the Jewish system of worship. Allah is and always has been an Arabic god. The Arab nations see no god greater and higher than Allah.[14]

If Yahweh is the God Most High, as the Jews claim, then Arabs claim He has to be Allah. According to Wikipedia and the Arabs, Allah means the greatest god. All Arabs and Jews descended from Abraham. In 2 Chronicles and 2 Kings, Solomon made this following statement while building the temple to Yahweh:

This must be a magnificent Temple because our God is greater than all other gods. But who can really build him a worthy home? Not

---

14   http://en.wikipedia.org/wiki/Takbir

even the highest heavens can contain him! So who am I to consider building a Temple for him, except as a place to burn sacrifices to him? (2 Chron. 2:5–6 NLT)

The Arabic people felt the same way about their god during the time of Muhammad and ever since the prophet lived. The supreme Allah was greater than all other gods and was worshipped by the Arabs like the Jews worshipped Yahweh. However, Allah definitely was not the God of Abraham but was worshipped by Abraham's father in Ur over two thousand years before Muhammad was born! This god of the Muslims once had different names, according to archaeology, and it was later changed to Allah. Evidence for this can be found at the end of this chapter. Allah means the greatest of all the gods. All Muslims worship Allah as the supreme God of all gods.

Do You Need Some Evidence?

Then take one or two clicks on Google and look at the discoveries in archaeology during the time of the Sumerians in Mesopotamia until the time of Muhammad; you will be shocked, and you are just a click away from the *truth* about Allah. In fact, the Middle Eastern people have always worshipped Allah, although with a different name, long before Abraham was born. The worship of a god represented by the crescent moon goes all the way back to Mesopotamian artifacts. This was the cradle of civilization. Each culture called Allah by different names, but he was never called Yahweh. Whatever name he was called, he was still worshipped by the symbol of the crescent moon as do the Arabs today.

Archaeology's artifacts prove without a shadow of doubt that the Middle East is and has always been the center of sun, moon, and star worship and is steeped in paganism with different idols. The crescent moon is a symbol of the great and supreme Allah. The crescent moon with a single star is used to represent Islam and is on their flag. The star is a representation of the daughters of Allah, and they are intercessors for their father. Yet Allah has no son.

Abraham Had Two Sons

Abraham had two sons: Ishmael, whose twelve sons worshipped Allah (the dominant god of the Middle East) and the god of his mother Hagar; and his second son Isaac, who worshipped Yahweh (the God of his father Abraham) and also the God of his much older ancestors Noah and Shem, who had survived the global flood.

The area in which Abraham lived with his two sons was a land of sun, moon, and star worship. There were two separate sons of Abraham who worshipped two totally different deities. **The God of the Bible is** *not the same* **god** *of the* **Qur'an**. They are totally two different gods, so which one is the true God of creation? The Bible and the Qur'an both state that their God is creator and the supreme God of the universe.

Islam tries extremely hard to make people believe that the God of the Bible and the God of the Qur'an are the very same God and that Muhammad's teaching trumps and overrules everything that Jesus taught. Islam says this is because Muhammad was the final prophet of all religions. Muhammad may have been the final prophet of Islam, but what Muhammad says has no authority over the teachings of the Bible. The Muslims' religious hatred and teachings against all other religions show they want to dominate and control worship to satisfy their own ideas as a religion and Sharia law.

Compare the Bible and the Qur'an

The God of the Bible is the God Most High, and His Son Jesus Christ is the only intercessor between Yahweh and man. For God so loved you, the reader of this book, that He gave His only begotten Son so that you should not perish but have everlasting life. This Bible had over forty prophets writing over a sixteen hundred-year period and never once did they overrule one another, but they all were in harmony concerning the coming intercessor, Jesus Christ. Jesus Christ is the *only* begotten Son of the Creator, who is Yahweh His Father. This is the Jewish God worshipped, not the Arabic god.

In Islam's ancient past history they worshipped the god named Sin who had the symbol of the crescent moon, according to many archaeological artifacts. The name of the god they worshipped was later changed to Allah, which means the supreme and only god in the Arabic language. Evidence for this can be found at the end of this chapter. Allah sent a final prophet with a mission to stop the Arabian people from worshipping all of these pagan idols. Allah is a jealous god and demands the nations of the earth to only worship him. Allah commissioned Muhammad as his final prophet to the world. I sincerely believe that Allah is worshipped as the supreme god of the Arab people.

Muhammad's Miraculous Birth

Muhammad was the other baby boy miraculously born in Mecca, a province of Saudi Arabia in the Middle East. Muhammad was born in about AD 570, almost six hundred years after Jesus Christ. As Muhammad's mother's womb dilated during his birth, a very bright light shone from the opening in her womb. It was told that the shining light magnified all the rooms in the palace. This light was announcing the arrival of a special baby who would be a prophet. At his birth, strange things happened in the palace buildings. Even the fire in the magician's lamp died down to a flicker. This miraculous birth of Muhammad gave authority to his claim as a prophet of Allah, and he has literally changed the world concerning religion.

We have a major problem because both gods claim to be the supreme Creator God. We have the God of the Bible, Yahweh, and the god of the Qur'an, Allah. Allah is an Arabic god worshipped by the Arabs; Yahweh is a Jewish God worshipped by the Christians and the Hebrew people. Yahweh has a Son, and Allah has three daughters. They all serve as intercessors for their own Father. As for me, I chose to worship Yahweh who has a Son named Jesus Christ. You have the freedom to choose either one as God or none of the above. It is an awesome privilege to be able to freely worship either one or none at all, but this choice has major consequences. As you make that choice, do it wisely.

You can research this yourself, and you will see what is available for the curious soul. The following is a reference in the Bible that will make you wonder about Muhammad's miraculous birth from a biblical perspective. Just what was the source of this light shining from his mother's womb? Make your own conclusion.

Bad Angel or Good Angel?

The following could be a couple of suggestions for the source of the light coming from his mother's womb:

> Suddenly, there was a bright light in the cell, and an angel of the Lord stood before Peter. (Acts 12:7 NLT)

> These people are false apostles. They have fooled you
> by disguising themselves as apostles of Christ. But I
> am not surprised! Even Satan can disguise himself as
> an angel of light. So it is no wonder his servants can
> also do it by pretending to be godly ministers. In the
> end they will get every bit of punishment their wicked
> deeds deserve. (2 Cor. 11:13–15 NLT)

If Satan can do this, then a good angel could do the same thing. Could Muhammad have been filled from birth with an angel of light? According to this Scripture from the Bible, Muhammad could have been possessed by an angel of light from his mother's womb. Could this indwelling light have been a bad fallen angel or a good angel? You decide. Could Muhammad be a prophet of darkness or a prophet of light, voiding out all of Jesus Christ's teachings? You decide. If this light came from a fallen angel, then Muhammad was a prophet of the kingdom of darkness. If this glorious light was from a good angel, then he was a prophet sent from God to correct some of Jesus' teachings.

If the angel producing the light in Muhammad's mother's womb was bad, then it makes the visions he received in the cave in Mecca anti-Christian and bad. Plus, all other teachings recorded in the Qur'an are anti-Christian or anti–Jesus Christ's prophetic teachings. If it was a good angel producing this light, then Muhammad's authority overrules all of Jesus Christ, the Son of the Living God's, and you can throw your Bible away for the Qur'an. The claim of good produces a real problem for Islam; all of Yahweh prophets have always been in harmony with all other biblical writers.

Should not Muhammad have confirmed all other biblical teachings? If he was truly a prophet representing Yahweh, his teachings would not be in conflict with biblical teachings. He was a prophet representing the Arabic god of the moon named Allah. The bottom line is that the Muslims practice moon god worship. Just observe and see what they will *possibly* do during the blood moon cycles coming on Passover in 2015.

You need to do a little research for yourself and examine the evidence so you can come to your own conclusion. I challenge you—research the Qur'an, the Bible, and the Dead Sea Scrolls. Then you decide which one is truly reliable. As for me, I am going to stick with the God who has a Son named Jesus. I think Jesus' teachings are for me; you decide for yourself.

In Islam you have only one prophet, Muhammad, proclaiming *himself* sinless while taking a nine-year-old little girl as his wife. Nobody is questioning that Muhammad truly was the last prophet of Allah, but Muhammad does not speak or prophesy for Yahweh or never claimed to. Allah is a god who has no son. Worship him if you like, but after you die, you cannot come back and change your god if you don't like the results. This is a most critical decision in life and will affect all eternity for you, so diligently seek the truth, for your eternal destiny depends on it.

Muhammad Received Angelic Visions

I am sure Muhammad received visions and angelic teachings while in a cave in Mecca. The question is about the angel who gave him the revelation, not Muhammad who received the visions. Mecca was the center of idol worship in the Middle East according to archaeology. Allah had chosen Muhammad to lead the Muslims out of this worship of many idols, which were only made from wood and stone. All of these idols were kept in a shrine in Mecca, and Muhammad was commissioned to lead these worshippers away from all these worthless idols.

You have this self-proclaimed prophet claiming his teachings overrule all other teachings, including Jesus, the Son of God. This is a ridiculous claim of the Muslims. Muhammad does not speak for Yahweh. Muhammad only speaks for Allah, the god of the Arabs. I am sure he would love to speak for Christians, but that will only happen to those Christians foolish enough to believe the teachings of Islam.

Cult Characteristics

Cults always begin with a self-proclaimed prophet. I question the taking of a little nine-year-old girl in the name of god. But who am I to question a prophet that cannot sin? Plus, marriage customs were different in those days. I am not a prophet and don't know the ways of a prophet. I am sure Allah makes special exceptions for his prophets and imams who cannot commit sins.

Now, again, with the Bible you have over forty prophets over about a sixteen hundred–year period from several different regions, all proclaiming the same message about Yahweh and Jesus Christ His Son. They all wrote very accurate history and prophecy for which archaeology provides a lot of proof today. I trust my soul to the nail-scarred hands of Jesus who died for my sin, not Muhammad. You also have this very same choice, so choose wisely if you are confronted with this choice.

Then you have the Dead Sea Scrolls providing much older documents that tell the same exact story. Which one do you want to entrust your eternal soul, the forty prophets over sixteen hundred years or a self-proclaimed prophet who himself wondered if a bad angel was speaking to him in the cave of Mecca?

Research it and see for yourself. However, after Muhammad's wife gave him assurance that it was truly Allah speaking to him in the cave, he accepted her counsel. Over the next thirty years, Muhammad established the Muslim religion of Islam. Since then many changes have been made and verses have been deleted in the Qur'an that Allah revealed to Muhammad. Some verses have been rewritten and others have been totally discarded from the Qur'an altogether. The Qur'an must be a work in progress even to this day.

Changing Allah's Words

These deleted verses were about Allah's wife, the goddess of the sun, and Allah's three daughters, Al-Uzza, Al-Lat, and Manat, whom Allah accepts as intercessors. The Muslims do not want you to know about Allah's three intercessory daughters. They cannot fool you into believing that the God of the Bible and the god of the Qur'an are the same god.

The God of the Bible has a Son, and the God of Islam has three daughters and a wife. You chose which one to believe and which one to entrust your eternal soul to. You will not be able to come back and change the choice you have made, for as death finds you so shall judgment.

Your soul and everlasting life depends on which one you choose! After you die and the virgins don't show up as Muhammad promised, it is too late. You cannot come back and change your mind or change your god. You will be doomed by your wrong choice for all eternity.

Respect for Women

The God of the Bible has a lot of respect for women and their rights as children of the heavenly Father. Don't be fooled by false teachings of men, putting men as superior beings and women as slaves or sub-beings. Jesus treated everyone as equal, and they have their proper positions in the family of God. Yahweh of the Bible teaches this very principle.

Long before the God of Israel was introduced to the population of the Middle East, the Arabian people were worshipping the moon. Israel was enslaved in Egypt with all its pagan worship while the Arab's commonly worshipped 360 different idols housed in Mecca two thousand years before Muhammad. The Arab's supreme god, Allah, needs some more research, so next we will take a closer look at him in archaeology.

Allah's Name

Allah is not a Hebrew or Greek name. Allah can only be found in the Arabic language and is only an Arabic name. If the Muslims want to worship Allah and follow the Qur'an, then it is their business. They were born with a free will to choose, as was all of mankind. If they want me to worship Allah then that is another issue. I do not choose Allah as my god, but I only choose Yahweh, who has a Son who sacrificed His life and paid my sin debt.

Allah is an Arabic god with an Arabic name. "Al" in Arabic is the definite article meaning the, and "*ilah*" was a term for one god or greatest god. They finally shortened "*al-ilah*" to Allah. Historically, the original name of their god was *sin* represented by the crescent moon (nccg.org/islam). Today he is called Allah and is represented by the same crescent moon. Could he be the same god? Allah is the supreme and only god worshipped by most Arabs.

Muhammad's Prophetic Mission

The mission of the prophet Muhammad was simple. Allah sent him to lead the Arabs toward the worship of only one god, and that god was Allah. Allah was the greatest of all gods to the Arabs. Allah was the only god in the world that was to be worshipped, and it was the mission of Muhammad to *make* the world that was full of infidels to worship and submit to Allah or die. The Arabic prophet Muhammad does not speak for or represent Yahweh the God of Israel. Yahweh has His own prophets, and Muhammad happens to not be one of them. Muhammad is the mighty last prophet of Allah, who is not the God of the Bible!

The Canaanites Worshipped the Moon

The entire Middle Eastern population was made up of idol worshippers until Joshua took the Promised Land from the moon-worshipping Canaanites who were living on the land divided to Noah's son, Shem; Shem's descendants were the rightful heirs to the land of Israel as described in the Dead Sea Scrolls, not the Canaanites, who were not descendants of Abraham. Dead Sea scroll 4Q181, which is a Genesis scroll, parallels the book of Jubilees, suggesting that Canaan was cursed because he defied his father's oath made when Noah divided the land (Jubilees 8). Noah had divided the earth among his three sons at the birth of Peleg. They all took an oath and drew lots for the land. Later Canaan, the son of Ham, decided he would defy the family oath and live on Shem's allotted portion. According to the oath taken by his father, Ham, this defiance brought a curse on the Canaanites. The land does not belong to the present-day Arabs but to the present-day Israelites.

Who Is Melchizedek?

Shem is the mysterious Melchizedek, king of Salem, found in the Bible. An added note: Shem was still alive during the time Israel was in Egypt. Shem lived to be six hundred years old and saw over ten generations of his descendants. Methuselah was the oldest man recorded before the flood. Noah was the oldest man after the flood, but Shem lived the longest and was the king and priest of Salem, which is now Jerusalem.

The Arabs had been told all their lives that Allah was the greatest god. Of all the idols the Arabs worshipped, the God Yahweh had never been on their list of gods. They never created an idol to represent Yahweh because they never acknowledged Him as God.

Any culture steeped in religious tradition is almost impossible to change. So leave the Arabs alone unless, like Jonah, God is calling you. Let them worship Allah, for they have freedom of choice like any other people or nation.

Yahweh, the God of Israel, sent the Israelites to live among this pagan region. They were to be a witness for Yahweh's existence. The nation of Israel was to represent the true Creator of the universe. Yahweh was the only true God and had just demonstrated His power to the Egyptians with the plagues and the parting of the Red Sea.

Egypt was the superpower of its day until it met the God of Abraham, Isaac, and Jacob. Until that meeting with Yahweh, it was a dominant world power. This superpower was drowned in the Red Sea and never was the same again.

Archaeology has uncovered that Ra was the sun god of Egypt. Sin was the moon god of the Arabs in the Middle East. They were being worshipped long before Yahweh, the God of Israel, was introduced to that region. Almost everyone in the Middle East worshipped Allah as the supreme god, and Allah was and still is the major god worshipped in the Middle East today.[15]

Ra the Sun God

For 430 years in Egypt the Jews were told about Ra, the sun god, and that he was the greatest of the gods. Now most of the Middle East had worshipped Allah for centuries before Muhammad was born. Egypt was a superpower and chose to worship Ra, the sun god. The Arabs, however, chose the worship of the moon. This worship of the moon historically goes all the way back to Mesopotamia and Sumerian archaeology, as verified on clay tablets. This is the reason God made several warnings to the Children of Israel about moon, star, and sun or planetary worship.

Google "archaeological articles on the moon-god." The following is only four of many articles available and is only a portion of each article (nccg.org/islam). They reveal what is available in the history of Allah, the god of Islam. You are just a click away from the real historical truth about Islam.[16]

1. The evidence reveals that the temple of the moon god was active even in the Christian era
2. We can endlessly speculate about the past or we can go and dig it up to see what the evidence reveals.

---

[15] http://nccg.org/islam/
[16] http://www.biblebelievers.org.au/moongod.htm

3. Archaeologists have uncovered temples to the moon god throughout the Middle East.

4. The Quraysh tribe into which Muhammad was born was particularly devoted to Allah, the moon god, and especially to Allah's three daughters, who were viewed as intercessors between the people and Allah.

Biblical Warnings to Israel Regarding Moon Worship

> And they shall spread them before the sun, and the moon, and all the host of Heaven, whom they have loved, and whom they have served, and after whom they have walked, and whom they have sought, and whom they have worshipped: they shall not be gathered, nor be buried; they shall be for dung upon the face of the Earth. (Jer. 8:2 KJV)

If there be found among you, within any of thy gates which the Lord thy God gives thee, man or woman, that hath wrought wickedness in the sight of the Lord thy God, in transgressing his covenant, And hath gone and served other gods, and worshipped them, either the sun, or moon, or any of the host of Heaven, which I have not commanded. (Deut. 17:2–3 KJV)

> And lest thou lift up thine eyes unto Heaven, and when thou see the sun, and the moon, and the stars, even all the host of Heaven, shouldest be driven to worship them, and serve them, which the Lord thy God hath divided unto all nations under the whole Heaven. But

the Lord hath taken you, and brought you forth out of the iron furnace, even out of Egypt, to be unto him a people of inheritance, as ye are this day. (Deut. 4:19–20 KJV)

CHAPTER 5

A Mutation Started/A Doomsday Clock

Historically, the rebellion of Adam against his Creator and his first sin in the Garden of Eden caused a mutation to take place within his body. The first sin, the mutation, and the loss of his godly likeness all took place in mankind when he sinned. At the time of this mutation, God began a six thousand-year clock counting down until Armageddon. When this clock stops ticking, it will bring an end to all human governments. This time frame to God was only six days. But in man's time frame, it is six thousand years.

> And He said to them, "You are from beneath; I am from above. You are of this world; I am not of this world. Therefore I said to you that you will die in your sins; for if you do not believe that I am He, you will die in your sins." (John 8:23–24 NKJV)

This chapter will provide a closer look at the origin of the first DNA manipulation of the human race by the fallen angels. Knowledge about DNA has increased in unbelievable ways as we approach the end of time. Knowledge has exploded since the last half of the twentieth century, which is a sign that we are in the very last days. Cloning, stem cell research, microchip technology—man's ability to manipulate our DNA is crazy. Scientific research has advanced to the point of having the ability to insert a microchip under your skin that could alter your mind and your own DNA.

Genetic Engineering by Renegade Angels

The fallen angels have had this DNA knowledge since creation. Sometime before the flood, they began an experimental evil genetic program to alter God's creation. This program began some twelve hundred years before the great flood during a time when the earth had a totally tropical climate. This earth was much different before the flood. All continents were connected with much more land than water. The water in the oceans today was once under the crust of the earth in huge storage chambers, and the crust had no fault lines.

During the flood, the fountains of the deep burst forth, and water gushed upon the earth for 150 days, giving us the fault lines around the crust of the earth and the vast oceans we have today. Psalm 136:6 says, "God stretched out the Earth over the waters." Psalm 24:1–2 says, "God founded the Earth upon the seas." Psalm 33:7 says, "God gathered the waters together as in a vessel, laying of the depths in storehouses." In Genesis it records that all the fountains of the deep broke forth in one day, and water issued through the fault lines for 150 days. Job 38 says, "God shut of the sea with doors, when it break forth, as if it issued out of the womb," using childbirth as an illustration.

> You placed the world on its foundation so it would
> never be moved. You clothed the earth with floods of
> water, water that covered even the mountains. At the

sound of your rebuke, the water fled; at the sound of your thunder, it fled away. *Mountains rose and valleys sank* to the levels you decreed. Then you set a firm boundary for the seas, so they would never again cover the earth. (Ps. 104:5–9 NLT)

Genetic Changes Began with the Mayan Calendar

An evil DNA program by the fallen angels was introduced to the world during the biblical time of Jared. Jared lived at the beginning of the Mayan calendar in 3114 BC, about 5,125 years ago. The Mayan civilization existed before the flood, and the Nephilim, who have been labeled Mayan, started building these massive Mayan temple complexes. The scientific community has misdated and mislabeled the Mayan civilization in an effort to protect the Darwinian legacy. The fallen angels were the fathers of hybrid beings and all of these evil DNA experiments. The population before the flood could have reached into the millions or even billions, due to the long five hundred- to nine hundred-year life spans and very large families.[17]

During this time, the Mayans were visited by a god (fallen angel) who came down from the sky. In fact, according to the Dead Sea Scrolls, the whole earth was visited by two hundred bad angels that descended and assumed human and animal forms and presented themselves to mankind as gods. Today they are referred to as ancient aliens. The Mayans called their god (fallen angel) Kukulcan, who appeared to them. Kukulcan was one of these two hundred bad angels that made a pact with each other to change God's creation. They knew they would suffer the wrath of God for their rebellious actions (1 Enoch 6:6).

---

[17]   http://ldolphin.org/pickett.html

Bad Angels and Daughters of Adam

This pact was to defile themselves sexually with the daughters of Adam, which produced the hybrid Nephilim. The Hebrew text does not say "daughters of Cain" or "sons of Seth," which is a false teaching from the religious kingdom of darkness. Many born-again believers have been deceived by this false doctrine. The original Hebrew text says "daughters of Adam." The phrase "sons of God" in the Old Testament always refers to angels. This is also abundantly recorded in the Dead Sea Scrolls, Genesis 6, 1 Peter 3:18-20, 2 Peter 2:4-5, and Jude 6-7. This mingling with the seed of Adam produced hybrid giants and undeniable evidence of these demigods, or Nephilim, can be found in the fossil record—for some reason bones don't lie like religious men.

So the fallen angel Kukulcan took a young Mayan woman as a wife and impregnated her. He built these great Mayan temples and pyramids for his hybrid royal son, who started a kingly line having elongated skulls with huge brain capacities and very large eyes that is found in the fossil record today. The Mayan leader Lord Pakal, as shown in stone art history, could be the royal descendant of Kukulcan. These Mayan temples found at Palenque were built by fallen angels. *All* of these pyramid cities were built by fallen angels before the flood, and today's science cannot find a place for them in their fairytale myth of history!

Scientists want to know how these Mayan temples were built. Who were they built by, and how were these huge granite stones being moved and shaped? How were they creating the statues and artwork we find on the stone walls still preserved today? The answer is found with very bad fallen angels that were cast out of heaven. One great example of the moving of these large stones can be found at the tomb of Jesus. A large stone was placed over the opening of His tomb. It is estimated that it would take up to twenty men just to roll the stone downhill only a few feet to cover the tomb's entrance. We are not talking about lifting the stone but only rolling the round stone downhill. Josh McDowell in the *Resurrection Factor*, part 3, states that fifteen men could not move the stone.[18]

But this stone that covered Jesus' tomb was lifted and removed uphill from the tomb, which would have been impossible for humans. As recorded in the gospels, this was no human that lifted this stone. I contend that fallen angels were moving and shaping huge fifty-ton and larger stones. The bad angels constructed all these unbelievable pyramids and cities before the flood during Noah's days. According to the Dead Sea Scrolls, fallen angels constructed thirty-six cities for their half-breed children, the Nephilim.

> And, behold, there was a great earthquake: for the angel of the Lord descended from Heaven, and came and *rolled back* the stone from the door, and sat upon it. His countenance was like lightning, and his raiment white as snow: And for fear of him the keepers did shake, and became as dead men. (Matt. 28:2–4 KJV)

> The first day of the week cometh Mary Magdalene early, when it was yet dark, unto the sepulcher, and sees the stone *taken away* from the sepulcher. (John 20:1 KJV)

Jesus Is Not in the Tomb

John uses a different Greek word for the stone being removed. The other three gospel writers used the general word *apokulio* for rolling the

---

[18] http://www.bethinking.org/bible-jesus/intermediate/the-resurrection-factor-part-3.htm

stone away. This term means "to roll off or away," but John used the Greek word *airo* which means to lift up and carry away from the tomb. This is exactly what the angel did, and then the angel sat on it. John noticed more details about how this huge, round stone was removed from Jesus' tomb. John noticed there were no marks on the ground as if it had been rolled away.

The other gospel writers, more focused on the body of Jesus, assumed it was rolled away because it was round. They noticed it was away from the tomb and not just the opening but did not pay much attention to the details of how this huge stone was removed. However, John noticed. That is the reason he used the Greek word *airo* instead of *apokulio*.

Angel Architects of Pyramids

The bad angels were moving these giant stones and were building these ancient pyramid cities. These angelic beings and their hybrid children are labeled as ancient aliens who genetically started the human race. The kingdom of darkness and the History Channel would have you believe they were aliens from another planet not in our solar system. This fallen angel intervention was all a designed effort by these bad angels to destroy God's creation and stop the coming of the godly seed, the Messiah. It was an all-out war from these bad angels to destroy God's creation.

This evil DNA manipulation was revenge against God for passing irredeemable judgment upon all the fallen angels. They became jealous because God offered grace to mankind and not to them. They wanted forgiveness from the Creator for their evil misdeeds, and it was not available. The judgment was final for angels because they were heavenly eternal beings. Are not this evil DNA manipulation and angels seeking redemption abundantly found in two missing historical books discovered in the Dead Sea Scrolls? These once biblical books are known as 1 Enoch and the book of Jubilees.

Adam Lost God's Likeness

Adam was created in God's image and according to God's likeness. Adam was clothed in a radiant glory light and did not know he was naked. But Adam lost his godly DNA in one disobedient act in 3966 BC, and it changed his genetic makeup forever. The glory light was gone, and he tried to clothe himself with fig leaves. A genetic mutation began to form in Adam's body after this loss of his godly DNA. Not only did he lose his DNA likeness of God and his eternal state, but in one act he surrendered his earthly kingdom that God had created for him. This all took place seven years, one month, and seventeen days after the creation. (Jubilees 3:15-21)

Man's loss of his godly DNA was known as Adam's loss of Zoë life, and sin brought instant death to his godly DNA. This death of Zoë life created a void in Adam's body. This void in Adam's body was replaced with a mutation known as the sin nature. This nature became a part of Adam's altered DNA profile. Adam's DNA was then passed down to all of mankind except for Jesus, who was *not* born of Adam but born of God. From this mutation God assigned man seven thousand years. This mutation started mankind a six thousand–year time clock ticking down to the battle of Armageddon.

Only One God with the Big G!

I need to say this and make it very clear! There is only one God with a capital G. There are many deceptive gods with a small g and the one God has total authority over all of them, period. Only the Judeo-Christian deity is truly The God. He is the God of Abraham. Now the Muslims are correct in saying there is only one God. But the problem for them is that it is not Allah, even though they believe differently. Abraham never worshipped a god called Allah. The true God has several names—Elohim, Yahweh, El Shaddai, El Elyon, Adonai, and Jehovah—only to name a few, but Allah is not one of those names. The only way to get to Yahweh is through Jesus Christ, His only begotten Son, and the Bible is the final word from God not the Quran (Koran).

The true God gives His born-again children eternal Zoë life. The Book of Life is Zoë (which is my next coming book). The tree of life is Zoë. The river of life is Zoë. You must have Zoë life to live eternally with Yahweh and His Son Jesus Christ. The only begotten Son of God came to restore this Zoë life that Adam lost. No one else offers this wonderful gift or comes even close. It is your choice to choose eternal Zoë life or eternal separation from Jesus. You can spend eternity with Allah, Buddha, Krishna, or any other deity of your choosing. You have a free will, so you can choose. You can be deceived also, but you cannot change gods after death. You will be stuck with your choice. May the God of Abraham open your eyes and hearts to the *truth*!

Is 2035 the End of Man's Ability to Rule?

Heaven and earth shall pass away, but God's words shall never pass away, as demonstrated in the Dead Sea Scrolls. I truly believe God has allowed us to look upon His calendar but not His time clock. No one knows the day or the hour of the return of Christ. I do not have any secret revelation that my fellow Christians cannot know if they study God's Word for what it says. Our real purpose is to tell about this new life to be had in Jesus Christ and spread the gospel about His kingdom until this world is over. We all must seek the help of the Holy Spirit and ignore the traditions of religious men. Plus you must study all seventy books of the Bible and not just the sixty-six books.

What Caused This Mutation?

Mankind was duped by a powerful, deceitful fallen angel who came from heaven to earth. This bad angel was Lucifer, who was also created by the same Creator that made the first man. Neither mankind nor the bad angels were created bad, but both were given *free will*. They made some bad decisions, and they were previously warned that these rebellious decisions would bring instant death. This instant death was not total death as we know it but the death of God's DNA likeness and image, as originally given to Adam at creation. Adam was created perfect; he had God's own DNA and was clothed with the glory of God.

In fact, Adam and Eve died the moment they sinned, but it was the godlike dimension of life within them that died. This glory life was the radiant likeness of God; it was God's DNA, which was instantly snuffed out! Gone! Disappeared! Adam contained God's own DNA. Oh, they were still alive in body, soul, and spirit, but now they were without God's perfect DNA likeness. Man was originally created to have this perfect DNA likeness of the Creator, but this mutation took place in Adam and Eve's fleshly bodies. This mutation became known as the sin nature, and it became a part of mankind's fleshly DNA profile to this day.

What Replaced God's DNA?

The sin nature is found in man's fleshly DNA, and it affects the soul and spirit. As long as this flesh is breathing, it will contain this mutation. If allowed, the body you live in will eat you to death, smoke you to death, drink you to death, and drug you to death if you don't contain it. Romans 7:24 says, "O wretched man that I am! Who shall deliver me from the body of this death?" (KJV).

Only the new birth in our human spirits can give us hope! Jesus came to give us Zoë life and give it to us abundantly! Jesus came to download God's DNA back into the children of Adam but only to those who would be willing to surrender their lives to Jesus Christ, the last Adam, the genetic DNA Son of God. Jesus came into this world to restore to mankind what the first Adam lost in the garden.

> Therefore do not let *the Sin Nature* reign in your mortal body, that you should obey it in its lusts. (Rom. 6:12)

> O wretched man that I am! Who will deliver me from the body of this death? (Rom. 7:24)

> Knowing this, that our old self was crucified with Him, in order that *our body of this Sin Nature* might be done away with, so that we would no longer be slaves to *the Sin Nature*; for he who has died [been crucified with Jesus/death to your old human spirit] is freed from *the Sin Nature*. [Receiving a new born-again human spirit that is not married to your body or flesh like the old human spirit or the old man was.] (Rom. 6:6–7)

The DNA of God

> For as the Father hath *Zoë life* in Himself; so hath he given (His DNA) to the Son to **have Zoë life** in Himself. (John 5:26)

I have a new book titled *The Book of Life Tracing God's DNA*. It will soon be available at www.zoebooks.org in the future. This DNA of God is described in one old Alexandrian Greek noun called Zoë, meaning God's life, God's image, and God's likeness. When Adam sinned, Zoë life died and sin mutated his whole being. He was never to be the same again. Then Adam passed on this mutation through the male seed. This was a mutation in the flesh. Because of this mutation from perfection to sin, God allotted man a seven thousand-year window of time (or seven days on God's timetable) to allow this mutation to run its course.

On God's eighth day, He will make all things new like the original creation or better. On the eighth day as described in Revelation 21 and 22, a new heaven and earth will appear, similar to the original Garden of Eden except this will be the garden of the earth put back to an original tropical climate as originally designed (watch Dr. Kent Hovind—Garden of Eden DVD). Only six thousand years of the seven thousand were given for mankind's self-rule. God's seventh day is the final thousand years for Jesus' kingdom on earth as described in Revelation 20.

After the fall of man, Adam remained only a fraction of the original design. He was damaged because he was now missing the DNA of God; in other words, he lost the Zoë life. What was once Zoë life was now replaced with a sin nature! It was at this point that the doomsday time clock began ticking toward Armageddon. Before man sinned there was no need for time, but after man's fall God inserted a seven thousand-year window of time for this mutation in man.

> So this I say, and affirm together with the Lord, that
> you walk no longer just as the Gentiles also walk, in
> the futility of their mind, being darkened in their

understanding, *excluded* from the (Zoë) Life [DNA] of God because of the ignorance that is in them, because of the hardness of their heart; and they, having become callous, have given themselves over to sensuality for the practice of every kind of impurity with greediness. (Eph. 4:17–19 ASV)

Because God's children are human beings—made of flesh and blood—the Son also became flesh and blood. For only as a human being could He die, and only by dying could He break the power of the devil, who had the power of death. Only in this way could He set free all who have lived their lives as slaves to the fear of dying. We also know that the Son did not come to help angels; He came to help the descendants of Abraham. Therefore, it was necessary for Him to be made in every respect like us, his brothers and sisters, so that he could be our merciful and faithful High Priest before God. Then He could offer a sacrifice that would take away the sins of the people. Since He Himself has gone through suffering and testing without sin, He is able to help us when we are being tested. (Heb. 2:14–18 NLT)

The Law of Moses was unable to save us because of the weakness of our Sinful Nature. So God did what the law could not do. He sent his own Son in a body like the bodies we sinners have. And in that body God declared an end to the Sin Nature's control over us by giving his Son as a sacrifice for our sins. (Rom. 8:3 NLT)

> You must have the same attitude that Christ Jesus had. Though He was God, He did not think of equality with God as something to cling to. Instead, He gave up his divine privileges He took the humble position of a slave and was born as a human being. When he appeared in human form, he humbled himself in obedience to God and died a criminal's death on a cross. (Phil. 2:5–8 NLT)

Adam basically put the human race into slavery and surrendered his earthly kingdom to (Lucifer) Satan, the King of Darkness. Satan had taken Adam and Eve as his captive slaves. They were hostages and slaves to the King of Darkness! God, the Creator, knew these things would happen and planned to become a part of His own creation in order to *rescue* these hostages from captivity. Later, God would send Jesus, His Son, into the world. Jesus would not be born of the seed of Adam as all the rest of mankind. However, He would be born of a woman. God reached into Mary's side and placed His own DNA seed into Mary's womb, leaving her still a virgin. This is in contrast to when God reached inside of Adam, took a rib, and made Eve, who received God's DNA though Adam's DNA rib.

The Last Adam was created by natural human birth in the womb of a *virgin*. The first Adam was God's Son and contained God's own DNA until he sinned. Jesus was the Last Adam, full of God's DNA being created in Mary's womb. Through Mary God became a part of His creation to rescue the hostages Satan had taken captive. God was offering Jesus as the Lamb without blemish. Jesus purchased mankind out of this slave market of sin with His offering of His precious, innocent blood, which He willing gave.

Both Adam and Jesus were DNA sons of God, full of *Zoë life (God's DNA)*. Remember in the Garden of Eden when Adam sinned? This is when Adam lost Zoë life. God created Jesus in order to have a Son with His own DNA. Jesus was both fully man and fully God. Had Jesus committed only one sin, He would have ended up like Adam! Jesus came to earth to restore mankind to this DNA likeness of God that Adam once had.

Jesus reestablished a brand-new race of the children of God, which is called the kingdom of God or the kingdom of His dear Son. Jesus started this new race possessing again the Zoë *life* of God, but this time God's DNA likeness was given only in their human spirits, with the ability to obtain it fully in the flesh through the same free will that got Adam in trouble in the first place. In John 10:10 Jesus said, "I come to *give* you Zoë life and *give* it to you abundantly." The whole Christian life is described in this one verse.

We receive God's spiritual DNA when we experience our rebirth in our human spirit. This DNA likeness of God becomes a part of our new human spirit. We then have a choice as to whether we want it also in our bodies and souls. Once you have been born from above, you still have a choice; however, God has given you everything pertaining to Zoë life and godliness (2 Pet. 1:3–4). You can live holy by the power of His indwelling presence and the anointing of the Holy Spirit, or you can continue to live in sin, which will get you an early trip ticket to heaven, if you are a child of God.

> Seeing that His divine power has granted to us *everything pertaining to (Zoë) life* and godliness, through the true knowledge of Him who called us by His own glory and excellence. For by these He has granted to us His precious and magnificent promises, so that by them

you may become *partakers of the divine nature,* having escaped the corruption that is in the world by lust. (2 Peter 1:3-4 NASB)

This spiritual DNA will flow from our spirits into our flesh, if we mature properly in our souls. We need to fill our minds with the Zoë words of the Living God. This DNA will also put away or disable the mutation received from Adam, and we can be filled again with Zoë life abundantly. What an awesome thought—a Christian being filled to all the fullness of Christ (becoming a partaker of the divine nature, the very DNA of God)! Then we will look like Jesus, act like Jesus, and do the works Jesus did. This is Christ's intended goal of the Christian's life in Christ, but first we must die to self.

Always carrying about in the body the dying of Jesus, so that the Zoë life of Jesus also may be manifested in our body. For we who live are constantly being delivered over to death for Jesus' sake, so that the Zoë life of Jesus also may be manifested in our mortal flesh. (2 Cor. 4:10-11)

For in this earthly body we groan, earnestly desiring to be clothed upon with our body which is from Heaven: If so be that being clothed we shall not be found naked. For we that are in this earthly tabernacle do groan, being burdened: not that we would be unclothed by losing this earthly body in death, but further clothed upon, *that this mortal body might be swallowed up or consumed with Zoë life* [which is the life of Jesus]. (2 Cor. 5:2-4)

If Christ is in you, though the body is dead because of the Sin Nature, yet the spirit is full of Zoë life because of the indwelling righteousness of Christ. But if the Spirit of Him who raised Jesus from the dead dwells in you, He who raised Christ Jesus from the dead will also give Zoë life to your mortal bodies through His Spirit who dwells in you. (Rom. 8:10–11)

Then said Jesus unto his disciples, If any man will come after me, let him deny himself, and take up His cross, and follow me. (Matt 16:24)

And He summoned the crowd with His disciples, and said to them, "If anyone wishes to come after Me, he must deny himself, and take up his cross and follow Me. (Mark 8:34 NASB)

And he said to them all, If any man will come after me, let him deny himself, and take up his cross daily, and follow me. (Luke 9:23 KJV)

Old Adam Flesh

Only a new born-again believer has the ability to crucify the old Adam flesh by the power of God's indwelling presence. You can put this mutation to death, but there is a problem. As long as this old Adam flesh is breathing air, the mutated sin nature can come back to life. You actually have to die to the flesh every day to have any success in rendering the sin nature powerless and dormant, but all things are possible to him who believes.

This mutation, which is the sin nature, cannot be totally eradicated as long as this body is pumping blood. This mutation is only in the flesh but affects your whole being. This mutation has the ability to send your whole being into eternal damnation if you do not receive Zoë life through Jesus Christ. Even though we as children of God have the ability to die to self and make the mutation dormant, it is still lurking about like a dead battery waiting to be recharged and looking for any avenue to produce sin that will bring the mutation back to life. (Read James 1:12–15.)

> Blessed is the man that endures temptation: for when he is tried, he shall receive the crown of Zoë life, which the Lord hath promised to them that love him. Let no man say when he is tempted, I am tempted of God: for God cannot be tempted with evil, neither tempts he any man: But every man is tempted, when he is drawn away of his own lust, and enticed. Then when lust hath conceived, it brings forth sin: and sin, when it is finished, brings forth death to the Zoë life in the flesh. (James 1:12–15)

The crown of life is referring to Zoë life in the flesh during this life. The mutation feeds on sin, and by committing sins you give new life to the mutation in your Adam flesh. If you recognize what is about to happen and that temptation is at work within you trying to produce life to this old mutation, you can abort it before it reaches the birth of sin and kills the Zoë life within your flesh. Living in sin will remove any anointing you have accumulated in your fleshly body. Read these verses in James very carefully.

If this sin nature comes to life, it will destroy any godly DNA that has been resurrected in your body. Just as one sin destroyed Adam, one sin will destroy your fleshly Zoë life. However, as born-again children of God, sin cannot touch your Zoë DNA in your human spirit because it is shielded by Jesus. This is grace. God commands us to be holy for He is holy. God would never require a born-again believer to do something that was impossible to obtain. But through His indwelling presence, all things are possible for anyone who believes.

Your godly DNA is sealed inside of Jesus, who has entered your body at your rebirth. Nothing, I mean nothing, can penetrate Jesus that indwells you. Nothing can destroy this godly DNA that has been placed inside of you. You have become the temple of God. If you have been born again, one-third of you has become total holiness for all eternity. It is the other two-thirds (body and soul) that you have to truly deal with daily.

Jesus saves us every day from sins that would cause DNA death in our human spirits. I am working on a new book titled *Tracing the DNA of God in Humans*. This new book deals with the death of God's DNA in humans plus life struggles within believers. It will soon be available at zoebooks.org maybe in 2016. *Forbidden History of the Ancient World as it was in the Days of Noah* is another great book giving you the true, accurate history unblemished by this evolution fairytale that distorts our history today. Check with *zoebooks.org* in late 2016 for an update on these new books.

If you have been born again, you are the temple of God (1 Cor. 3:16) and your innermost being has become the new holy of holies in this temple. Your new sinless human spirit has been sealed in Jesus in you by the Holy Spirit. The indwelling Jesus has become your veil around your holy of holies, and nothing can enter to tarnish your new spirit. No sin can enter into the holy of holies in your human spirit, which is the *core* of your being. This godly DNA sealed in you will keep your spirit safe until the day of redemption. At such time God will redeem your whole being: body, soul, and spirit. This is a brand new godly DNA life known as Zoë life, which is the true church of Jesus Christ. Remember, the day of redemption is at the end of this six thousand-year time clock! The rapture of God's children will be about seven years earlier.

Jesus Births a New DNA Race

The establishment of a brand new race of God's children with His own DNA within them was the beginning of the church. Qualifications to enter this race will require a new birth in your human spirit (John 1:12–13). This is accomplished only by Jesus entering your body during the new birth process. The Holy Spirit baptizes you into Jesus' death, crucifying your old human spirit (Rom. 6:3–4). Then He places a newly created spirit man inside of you during this first baptism. His Spirit gives Zoë life (God's DNA) to your new human spirit.

One of the benefits of this godly DNA will be to escape the wrath and judgment of God when the six thousand–year time clock quits ticking, marking the end of man's government. God will remove all who possess Zoë life from the earth before His wrath is poured out on all unbelievers. He removed the believers in the days of Noah before the flood, as it was written in the ancient book of Jasher 4:20.

The battle of Armageddon is an event foreseen by John at the end of the six thousand years (Rev. 19). Jesus will return to earth and put an end to this war, or no one would be alive to populate His kingdom, which will last a thousand years! At the end of Christ's kingdom, man's allotted seven thousand-year window of time will come to an end.

Then we enter eternity as described in Revelation 21-22. Time shall be no more.

This brand-new race was to be a spiritual kingdom during man's time of rule. However, exactly 2,007 years after Christ was resurrected, there will begin an earthly, physical, governmental kingdom, ruled by Jesus and His saints, who will govern mankind for one thousand years during the seventh day of God's timetable. This event will be the golden age and is still in the future. But about seven years before the end of man's government, Jesus promised to remove the church. This event is known as the rapture, coming very soon to a city near you!

You may be a son of Adam and have never been born again. It is never too late to join this new race established by Jesus. It is available for those who are tired of this life's struggle and are looking for something that is real or looking for the high from which you will never have a hangover. Christians are to submit to all governmental authorities and cause them no problems because God has placed them in office. The world is full of things that are phony among religions, but government is established by God. The final battle will be Jesus with His holy angels against the kingdom of darkness and all unbelievers.

The mutation of the sin nature hinders and distorts your thinking process. Give yourself an inside advantage today; surrender your life to Jesus, and be spiritually born again. Escape the destruction that is about to come on this earth! You can alter this mutation, if not totally reverse it, by surrendering your life to Jesus.

This is a little insider trading per se: let Him be the Redeemer of your soul. Jesus said we must become like little children to come to Him. Come and enter this new race by childlike faith and be changed in the twinkling of an eye. You must do it before the six thousand-year clock stops ticking. Next we will take a look in detail at this six thousand-year time frame.

CHAPTER 6

A Six Thousand–Year Countdown to Armageddon

One Thousand Years = A Day

> But do not let this one fact escape your notice, beloved, that with the Lord one day is like a thousand years, and a thousand years like one day. (2 Peter 3:8 NASB)

It appears that God has a period of six days, or six thousand years, for the race of Adam to govern and rule on this earth; this period began with Adam's first sin in the garden, and these six thousand years are divided into three distinct two thousand–year periods. To God, these are two-day periods on His time table dealing with mankind. First is the two-day period of conscience from Adam to Abraham, second is the Mosaic Law from the covenant God made with Abraham to Christ's crucifixion, and third is the church age of grace from the crucifixion to the rapture.

> Remember the former things of old: for I am God, and there is none else; I am God, and there is none like me, Declaring the end from the beginning, and from

ancient times the things that are not yet done, saying,
My counsel shall stand, and I will do all my pleasure.
(Isa. 46:9–10 KJV)

Three Equal Covenants of Two Thousand Years Each

This six thousand–year period appears to be broken down into three
equal divisions or unconditional covenants the Creator makes with
man. He did make other covenants, but we will only be looking at
these three specific covenants. These three covenants equal six days to
God but six thousand years for man. This predetermined time period
is broken down by God into three two-day periods with a day being
one thousand years for mankind.

To mankind these are three two thousand–year covenants or six
thousand years of allotted time for man's government. The Adamic,
Abrahamic, and church-age covenants form those three divisions. Each
covenant has an exact period of two thousand years each or two days
under God's time table, which equals six thousand years on man's time
clock. From Adam's sin to Armageddon is exactly six thousand years
or six days to God.

> God that made the world and all things therein, seeing
> that He is Lord of Heaven and Earth, dwells not in
> temples made with hands; Neither is worshipped with
> men's hands, as though he needed anything, seeing He
> gives to all life, and breath, and all things; and hath
> made of one blood all nations of men for to dwell on
> all the face of the Earth, and *hath determined the times
> before appointed*, and the bounds of their habitation.
> (Acts 17:24–26 KJV)

The first period with Adam began not at creation but when Adam sinned. This first covenant lasted two thousand years, and then God made a second covenant, which began with Abraham. This second period is two days for God but two thousand years for Abraham and his descendants.

This second period was specified in Hosea 6:2 as two days. Daniel told of the final 490 years of this two thousand-year covenant in the great prophetic and historical book of Daniel. Daniel prophesied about the close of this covenant and about the crucifixion of Christ. Then the angel told that his book would be sealed. The book was sealed unto the last days, which are now.

Days five and six, or the third two thousand-year covenant, is made with Christ's followers known as the church, not the religious establishment, for religion has been on the earth since before Noah, but this covenant is with the church of His only begotten Son.

The Kingdom of God Will Become Physical

The church of Jesus Christ is the beginning of the government of Christ's kingdom. His kingdom is now a spiritual kingdom but will become a physical kingdom within the next twenty-one years. Christ and a host of angels will overthrow the Antichrist and his evil one-world-government. Then for one thousand years Christ will rule in His coming kingdom with His resurrected saints. This will be God's seventh day.

Breakdown of the Six Thousand Years

The six thousand years will look like this: two thousand years for Adam, 1,993 years for Abraham, with seven years still in the future.

This final seven years is reserved and will take place prior to the end of human government, as recorded in the book of Revelation. These two periods total two thousand years or two days for the Abrahamic Covenant. Then the last two thousand years will be for the church.

Learn when Christ was crucified and add two thousand years to it, and you will know the year of the beginning of the tribulation period. The end of time is: 2,000 +1993 + 2,000 + 7 + 1,000 = the end of time. The Bible says we don't know the *day* or the *hour*, but it does not say anything about knowing the year. Do not get sidetracked by this and lose focus on preaching the gospel about Christ's kingdom.

There is a warning; we are not to sleep so that His coming will take us like a thief in the night. We know that it will take place in the fall of the year at the feast of trumpets. I personally think that in the fall of 2028 (if the AD side of the Gregorian calendar is accurate), Christ will remove His church. This will not be any later than the fall of 2030; I know this time without a doubt will take place before 2030 ends.

Snatching Away of the Church

The rapture should come before the close of 2028; don't be caught not watching. Christ's second coming to rule and reign will be about 2035 or no later than 2037 for sure. Lift up your heads and look up, for your redemption draws nigh.

Searching for These Covenants in God's Word

Now we will look for these three covenants in God's Word and see what we can find. According to the book of Jubilees in the Dead Sea Scrolls, we find that Adam lived in the garden seven years, one month, and seventeen days before he committed the first sin. Adam sinned when he disobeyed his Creator. This event started a six thousand-year countdown to Armageddon and the first two thousand-year period allotted to mankind.

This first period began with Adam's first sin and ended with God's call to Abraham. God created a new nation with Abraham. He established a covenant for the children of Israel. In fact, according to God's time clock, Two days was exactly two thousand years from Adam to Abraham. The generations are listed in the Bible; add them up for yourself. I think God is allowing us to see His calendar of all things in these last days. No one knows the day or the hour of Christ's return. Let us see if we can find this covenant in the Bible.

The Second Covenant

We should find something about Abraham's two days or two thousand years after Adam's sin. If my theory is correct, there should be evidence of God making a second covenant. This second covenant was with Abraham, which will last two thousand more years before a third and last two thousand-year covenant is made with the church.

There should be evidence of three covenants separated by exactly two thousand years each. We have added up the years from creation according to the Bible and find the making of a covenant with Abraham to be approximately 2,018 years from the creation, give or take a few years, due to the rounding off of eighteen generations listing everyone's age. At one time in the ancient past a child was considered one year old at birth—they did not count from zero to one. So 2,018 minus 18 with children being counted one at birth equals 2,000 minus 7 years in the Garden of Eden equals 1,993.

There were eighteen generations rounded off, which could equal seven to nine years added back to 1,993, which would be two thousand years. God said it was two days or two thousand years between Adam and the Abrahamic Covenants according to historical records; I think it is exactly two thousand years or the first two days of God's six thousand–year program for man and his government. God keeps good time, and we don't need to doubt the eyewitness.

The second of three covenants began two thousand years after Adam sinned; I personally think it was exactly two thousand years or two days on God's timetable. This first period began in Genesis 2 and will last for two thousand years up to Genesis 12. I don't believe man has kept perfect time. God's time clock has never missed a beat and keeps perfect time. Also, notice we only have approximately twelve chapters in our present sixty-six books of the Bible covering one-third of human history. Why so few chapters on this era of human history? Could some history books of the Bible be missing, and were they found in the Dead Sea Scrolls?

Additional History Books Discovered

Thankfully we had the wonderful discovery of the Dead Sea Scrolls in 1947 that corrected this missing history. Two missing historical books of the Bible were found in the scrolls that were part of the Bible during Jesus' time on earth. Another historical book covering this period from Adam to Abraham outside of the Dead Sea Scrolls makes three. The Ancient Book of Jasher has been researched and appears to be authentic. Ken Johnson Th.D has the best translation of Jasher. I am not saying that this book of Jasher is part of the Bible, but it does look promising. These books cover this first covenant or first two days (two thousand years) and the early life of Abraham, revealing where he learned to be such a man of faith. I am saying the two historical books found in the Dead Sea Scrolls are part of the Old Testament.

Dead Sea Scrolls

The Dead Sea Scrolls are a collection of 972 texts discovered between 1946 and 1956 at Khirbet Qumran in the West Bank. They were found in caves about a mile inland from the northwest shore of the Dead Sea, from which they derive their name.

The texts are of great historical, religious, and linguistic significance because they include the earliest known surviving manuscripts of works later included in the Hebrew Bible canon, along with extra-biblical manuscripts which preserve evidence of the diversity of religious thought in late Second Temple Judaism.

Biblical Books Found

There are 225 biblical texts included in the Dead Sea Scroll documents,

Listed below are the sixteen most represented books of the Bible found among the Dead Sea Scrolls in the 1970s, including the number of translatable Dead Sea texts that represent a copy of scripture from each biblical book:

Number of Biblical Book Found in D.S.S.

Psalms-39 copies

Deuteronomy-33 copies

1 Enoch-25 copies (Enoch was the third most popular)

Genesis-24 copies

Isaiah-22 copies

Jubilees-21 copies (Jubilees and 1 Enoch were removed from our English Bibles by the Pharisees at the council of Jamnia in AD 90.

Exodus-18 copies

Leviticus-17 copies

Numbers-11 copies

Minor Prophets-10 copies

Daniel-8 copies

Jeremiah-6 copies

Ezekiel-6 copies

Job-6 copies

1 & 2 Samuel-4 copies

Sirach-1 copies

Tobit Fragments[19]

To this day a majority of the scrolls have not been assigned to any particular book. Esther and Jasher are two books that have not been

---

19   http://en.wikipedia.org/wiki/Dead_Sea_scrolls

identified, but forty of the Old Testament books have been assigned, like Isaiah and Genesis. The scrolls uncovered two very popular books that were canonized in the Ethiopian Christian Bible—which were not affected by the Romans or the Pharisees. All of the scrolls are pre-Christian around the second century BC.

These two historical books discovered in the Dead Sea Scrolls were the book of 1 Enoch and another book by Moses named the book of Jubilees. These great books were part of the Bible during Jesus' time; they, with the *Ancient Book of Jasher* by Ken Johnson, fill in all of the missing historical blanks during this first two thousand–year period of man's history. They were removed by the Pharisees and the church of Laodicea, two not-so-reputable groups. I believe we are also missing one New Testament book, the epistle of Barnabas. These four books can be easily purchased on Amazon.

Old Testament Covers Second Two Thousand–Year Period

The rest of the Old Testament and the four gospels cover this second two thousand years, which is the period from Abraham until Christ's sacrificial death. God begins this second covenant for the second two thousand years, which will bring us all the way up to the life and time of Jesus. The last 490 years of this second covenant is recorded in Daniel 9, revealing the seven final years of this covenant, which will not be fulfilled until after the third two thousand–year covenant will be completed in about AD 2028 or no later than AD 2030.

This second covenant is broken into two parts, with a reservation of the last seven years for a special time described in the book of Revelation. The third two thousand–year covenant is sandwiched in the split before the last seven years can be fulfilled. The last seven years of this second two thousand–year covenant is reserved and extended to the end time so that 144,000 Jewish evangelists can be sealed by God for the end-time ministry as seen in the book of Revelation. They will do in seven years what the nation of Israel did not do during the first 1,993 years of that second covenant.

Trying to come up with an accurate year count during the time between Abraham and the church is virtually impossible with man's timekeeping. The Jewish calendar is basically accurate from creation up to the first three thousand years, and after this time there are several big questions that would need to be answered. We will use the Jewish calendar to establish the first two thousand–year period from Adam to Abraham.

This second period from Abraham to Jesus' death is very difficult, but any way you count it, it is no more than 2,018 years. Another way we count the years, it is no less than 1,844 in man's feeble efforts to keep time; it is so close to the number two thousand you have to truly wonder at my theory of the end of time, knowing God is a better time keeper than man. In fact, man has made inaccurate records of timekeeping during this second two thousand–year period or this second covenant. I think God has allowed us to see in His window of 7,007 years of time. I haven't done anything to deserve this revelation. It is available to any believer willing to believe God's written Word. It is just grace and God warning the world of the impending doom.

The Third Covenant

Moving forward about 3,993 years after Adam sinned and we find ourselves in AD 28, dealing with one year for the zero year that occurs due to switching from BC to AD. What happened in AD 28? The Lord Jesus Christ was crucified and purchased us out of the slave market of sin. He is the Lamb of God, which takes away the sins of the world. Some say this seven thousand–year theory should make unbelievers extremely frightened. But if you are an unbeliever, you are blinded to the truth by the spirits of the kingdom of darkness. However, some believers do not agree with this crucifixion date. Many think Jesus died as late as AD 34.

Selecting a Calendar

We are going to use the Gregorian calendar for the last covenant of the church because we are counting two thousand years from the crucifixion. God keeps better time than humans, and nobody knows the day or the hour of Christ's return except the Father!

The Jewish calendar is basically accurate for the first covenant, and the Gregorian calendar is basically accurate for the last two thousand-year covenant of grace. The middle two thousand years is tough and is anybody's guess except God, but the second two thousand years is there, and it exists on God's time clock even if it is not on ours. Let us make reference to these three covenants equaling six thousand years for man's government.

The Beginning of the Church

The church began the year Christ was crucified, which is the year of Pentecost in AD 28. The beginning is recorded in the book of Acts. The church age will end two thousand years later with the rapture of the church in AD 2027 to 2030. But there will be a final seven years of testing, which will look similar to the horrors found in the book of Revelation. This will not be Daniel's seventieth week, which is the final close of the Abrahamic covenant. This period will be the last seven years of the church age immediately before the seven years of tribulation. Doomsday preppers had best be fully prepared by the end of 2021. I hope I am wrong about this final seven dark years for the church age.

Christ's crucifixion was the first year of the final two thousand-year covenant. I believe AD 34 was not an accurate starting point as some believe, and there is proof Jesus was crucified earlier in AD 28, starting the third covenant. We know a final seven years still remains for the Abrahamic covenant. Historically only 1,993 years have expired of this second two thousand–year covenant (see Daniel's seventieth week recorded in Daniel 9).

So AD 28 is short of the second two thousand years by seven. What do we find in history for proof of a third two thousand-year covenant? None other than the New Testament, which is located between the Old Testament (1,993 years) and the book of Revelation (the final seven years). This final seven years for Israel was foretold in Daniel 9. The fulfillment of these final seven years is described in detail in the book of Revelation 4–16. At the end of the last seven years, God will pour out His wrath upon the earth like the days of Noah, except this time it will be by fire and not by water.

> Come, and let us return unto the Lord: for he hath torn, and he will heal us; he hath smitten, and he will bind us up. After *two days* [the Abraham Covenant the second two thousand years] will he revive us: in the *third day* he will raise us up, and we shall live in his sight. (Hosea 6:1–2 KJV) (This third day is Christ's thousand-year kingdom spoken of in Revelation 20.)

No One Saw the Third Covenant/Days Five and Six

Most of the Old Testament writers never could see this two thousand-year church age or days five and six on God's time table. They could not see the church but only the coming kingdom, which is God's day seven or Hosea's third day found in Hosea 6. This is the reason so many people thought the first time Jesus came was to deliver them from the Roman Empire. They tried to usher in the kingdom by putting Jesus on a colt and by spreading palm leaves in His path, declaring Him as King. But the religious Pharisees put an end to that and had Jesus nailed to a cross by the Roman army.

Then the earth, after six thousand years or six days of turmoil and labor, will enter the seventh day of rest, ushering in the millennial kingdom. The Abrahamic covenant is recorded in the biblical Old Testament. The final two thousand–year covenant begins at Pentecost and ends sometime after the rapture. Then the Antichrist will sign a seven-year peace agreement with Israel. All of the events of the end of time are recorded in the Bible.

These last two thousand years have a starting point, and it begins with the year of the crucifixion. This starting point was the beginning of the church age, the third of three two thousand–year covenants. This covenant in the New Testament began with the resurrection of Jesus, the event of Pentecost as described in the gospels, and the beginning of the church as described in the book of Acts, and ends with Revelation 3.

The last seven years are described in Revelation 4 to 16, with 17 and 18 describing the one-day destruction of Mystery Babylon, which is possibly America. This destruction in 2028 will usher in the final seven-year tribulation period. The Antichrist will rescue Israel from Islam. He will sign a seven-year peace treaty with the Jewish nation.

A Final Seven Years for the Church Age

The final two thousand–year covenant with the church occurs between 1,993 years of the old covenant (Abrahamic Covenant) with the children of Israel and Daniel's seventieth week, which is the final seven years of that covenant. This final two thousand–year covenant with the church also appears to have a final seven-year period from about 2021 until 2028. This will be a time of testing and some dark days for the church. It will be open season on Christians around the world as economies continue to collapse. You will either stand for your faith in Jesus and be put to extreme testing or deny your faith in Jesus Christ, hoping to escape martyrdom. The Christian to the NWO will be like the Jew to Hitler.

This time is designed to test the church in America as never before with the face of martyrdom as Christians die for their faith. Many will deny their faith and desert their Savior! This last seven years of the church age will be a time when many will be deceived into thinking we are in the tribulation and the rapture is not going to take place. But the true born-again believer must never stop looking up. Death and destruction await many in America during this time. A Christian's faith will be tested as never before. I truly hope I am wrong about these final dark days for the church age.

These final dark seven years of the church age is not Daniel's seventieth week but will have a lot of the same characteristics with the fall of America's economy and the deaths of thousands of Americans. America must fall before the New World Order can set up a one-world global government that will be operating at the time of the return of Christ. I think the destruction of America will usher in the Antichrist.

The first covenant was with Adam and was the age of conscience. With the second covenant, God birthed a nation through one man named Abraham and gave them the Mosaic Law. This covenant is missing a final seven years. In the third covenant, we entered the age of grace with the church of Jesus Christ. This final seven years of this second covenant foretold in the book of Revelation brings an end to human government and ushers in Armageddon.

Overview of Six Thousand Years

Many a Bible scholar has attempted to add up the chronologies found in the Bible. If you start at creation, you will find six thousand years ending about AD 2021, with some rounding off of genealogies. At one time, a child was considered one year old when born; basically, he was two on his first birthday so that can affect an accurate count according to when that was.

In this book I have taken a different approach based on three equally divided covenants of two thousand years each. Then we work from the crucifixion date, allowing two thousand years for the church. That is the reason we spent so much time on Jesus' birthday date discovery.

Let us add it all up one more time; at age seven Adam sinned, beginning the six thousand–year countdown or God's six-day countdown for man. This Adamic covenant is the first two thousand years. The second covenant was with Abraham, so 1,993 years plus seven years at the end of man's government equals two thousand years and the battle of Armageddon. The third covenant was with the church, so two thousand years begins at AD 28 and goes to 2028 with another economic downfall possibly coming in late 2015. Around 2021 to 2022 we will enter a final dark time of testing for the church. Could this time be the collapse of the American republic? This will end in about 2027 to 2030 with the rapture of the church and the destruction of Mystery Babylon.

Then will come the last seven years of the Abrahamic covenant recorded in Revelation, which ends or equals six thousand years for man's government or six days on God's timetable. This will be the conclusion of man's rule and Satan's rule over the earth. Satan knows his time is short so he will step up his attack on all born-again believers.

The Nephilim in the Last Days

Will Satan again fill the earth with the Nephilim as in the days of Noah? Will the Antichrist be a Nephilim? Will the ten toes of Daniel's statue or the ten kings of the revived Roman Empire all be Nephilim rulers? Will the battle of Armageddon be between Christ and the Nephilim rulers headed up by the son of Satan? The answer is yes, according to the prophecy of Daniel 2:43. There are reports of many children being seen all over the world with strange-looking eyes and a presence of evil about them. Once they reach maturity, they will all wear sunglasses to hide or cover their strange-looking eyes. The present Nephilim have been genetically engineered to look like modern humans as much as possible.

The Second Coming/Day of the Lord

This time of two thousand years for the church will come to a close in fall of 2028, or no later than 2030, considering the Gregorian calendar's accuracy. Then the second coming of Christ could be in the fall of 2035, or no later than the fall of 2037. Jesus Christ comes to earth after Daniel's seventieth week comes to an end, which is the final seven years of tribulations described in the book of Revelation.

> For yourselves know perfectly that the day of the Lord so cometh as a thief in the night. For when they shall say, Peace and safety; then sudden destruction cometh upon them, as travail upon a woman with child; and they shall not escape. But ye, brethren, are not in darkness, that that day should overtake you as a thief. Ye are all the children of light, and the children of the

day: we are not of the night, nor of darkness. Therefore
let us not sleep, as do others; but let us watch and be
sober. (1 Thess. 5:2–6 KJV)

Watch therefore, for ye know neither the day nor the hour wherein
the Son of man cometh. (Matt. 25:13 KJV)

After six thousand years comes to an end at Armageddon, the
final seventh day or the thousand-year reign of the Lord begins. Since
we now see the biblical signs of the end, what kind of life should we
be living? Will you be ashamed when Jesus appears in the clouds to
call out His church? Or will you cry out for the rocks and mountains
to fall on you when God's wrath is poured out on the earth during
the day of the Lord at the end of the great tribulation? Jesus will then
close it out with a one-thousand year kingdom on earth as foretold in
Revelation 20, in which true righteousness and a perfect government
will rule over Adam's descendants who have survived the seven years
of horror coming to a city near you.

God's Stimulus Package

The ultimate stimulus package will be issued for those who are true
believers who survived Armageddon. Satan will be locked away for one
thousand years. This thousand-year kingdom is just like one day to God
but will be one thousand years to us earthlings. Survivors' children will
live to be nearly one thousand years of age like Methuselah, similar to
the beginning of creation. This earth will receive a remodeling job for
the kingdom of Christ, and the Nephilim will be removed from the
earth again as during the flood. The resurrected born-again believers
will not fight in Armageddon but will be on this remodeled earth and
help Jesus rule and reign in His kingdom.

Look at God's time pattern of six days for human government and the seventh day for Christ's kingdom, a perfect divine government. One of the reasons for Jesus coming to earth the second time is to set up His kingdom and to judge the people who are still alive on this earth who have survived Armageddon.

But here are some questions about those that populate the earth during the kingdom: will man still have their mutated bodies with their sin nature, even though they will be living without Satan's influence? How about the other bad angels and demons? Will God start fresh again like the Garden of Eden? Even with Satan locked away, will the natural descendants of Adam still have a problem with their inherent sin nature? They will not be able to blame the Devil for a core DNA problem when this mutation raises its ugly head. It will be interesting to see how Jesus deals with it. All of the saints from the church covenant will be there in new glorified bodies like Jesus.

You Decide

I know I have just set some dates and repeated myself several times, but only God in heaven knows the day and the hour. Notice I did not specify a day or an hour. I did not even specify a certain month. I only want to make you aware of the time, so do not be distracted from the real purpose in life. Share about this new life that can be had in Jesus. I take full responsibility for this theory, and I am going to label it the theory of David. If it is wrong, I am the one to blame. I have found most of the evidence for this theory of David in the Bible, the Dead Sea Scrolls, the epistle of Barnabas, the ancient book of Jasher, and the observation of world events.

I have seen the seven thousand-year theory among older theologians but not in detail like this. I am sure many of the same faith have figured this timetable out long before me. I wanted to put my theory of David in writing for the church in these very last days, and that is one of the reasons for this book.

I have not had a dream or a visitation from God, and no angels have appeared to me. However, I believe the Holy Spirit has guided me in my studies of the Word of God and in the writing of this book. Many guessed 2012 to be the end, but just like Y2K, 1988, etc., nothing happened! If I am wrong, all I have to say is, *"Come, Lord Jesus!"*

Foolish religious leaders during the early church who were influenced by the kingdom of darkness removed several books from our Bible. These books were removed by the Pharisees, an anti-Christian group, in the Council of Jamnia in AD 90 after the fall of Jerusalem. Don't you know Jesus had a real problem with the Pharisees? The Council of Laodicea in AD 364 removed some books. John had some bad things to say about the Laodiceans, the seventh church in the book of Revelation. Who gave any person the authority to remove these very popular biblical books discovered in the Dead Sea Scrolls? Both groups cast doubt on the removal of certain books of our Bible. We have at a minimum of seventy books in our Bible, not sixty-six. I am not concerned about the religious whining of certain overly religious church leaders of today. I am only concerned for the truth and my Lord's kingdom.

This seven thousand–year theory is present like a watermark or hologram found in these seventy books or documents of the Bible today. *Come on, man,* sixty-six books is not all; sixty-six books is not the whole story. This Laodicean council even removed Ephesians, Romans, and Philippians from our Bible. They cut the Bible down to sixty books, but the truth is we have a minimum of seventy books in the Bible. The main evidence for a seventy-book Bible, instead of sixty-six can be found in the discovery of the Dead Sea Scrolls in 1947. Dismiss these extra historical biblical books at your own peril.

Sixty-Six Books Is Not the Whole Story

Six is the number of incompletion and the number of man. The Bible is not a book of man but a book inspired by the Holy Spirit. Seven is the number of completion, and seven is a perfect number. There are a minimum of seventy books in our Bible, not sixty-six, as overly religious men would have you believe. You must look closely to see these things. Only the Spirit of God is the ultimate *canon* of books for our Bible. He and only He can guide you into all truth. If this bothers you then you have a much deeper problem than what I have just exposed.

It is written in 1 Corinthians 2:14: "The natural man receives not the things of the Spirit for they are foolishness to him" (KJV). The number seven is a perfect number and is one of the emphases of this book. The number of books in our Bible should be divisible by seven in both the Old Testament and New Testament.

Back to the Six Thousand Years or God's Six Days

Now that I have gotten this sixty-six-book thing off my chest, mankind has six thousand years and then we enter into Christ's rest, which is the final one thousand years. A maximum of seven thousand years has been given for man to live on the earth before it is totally destroyed and we move on to a new earth that will be much nicer than this one (Rev. 21–22).

I think Hosea 6:2 is a very compelling passage for a seven-day theory set by God for earth and man. You must study it in *context*, so here it is again to help you understand it.

> After two days will he revive us: [speaking of the Jewish people] in the third day he will raise us up, and we

shall live in his sight. (Hosea 6:2 KJV) (The third day is the thousand-year kingdom or God's seventh day in His overall program for mankind. The two days Hosea refers to is the two thousand years of the second covenant. This is the time from Abraham to Christ explained on the Hosea chart in this book.)

Don't forget, seven days is God's timetable, while seven thousand years is the timetable for mankind. This complete text is in a Jewish, Mosaic Law context. Thus, a seven thousand–year window of time has been set for man.

> For a thousand years in thy sight are but as yesterday when it is past, and as a watch in the night. (Ps. 90:4 KJV)

> But, beloved, *be not ignorant of this one thing*, that one day is with the Lord as a thousand years, and a thousand years as one day. The Lord is not slack concerning his promise, as some men count slackness; but is longsuffering to us-ward, not willing that any should perish, but that all should come to repentance. But the day of the Lord will come as a thief in the night; in which the heavens shall pass away with a great noise, [this will truly be the Big Bang] and the elements shall melt with fervent heat, the Earth also and the works that are therein shall be burned up. (2 Peter 3:8–11)

CHAPTER 7

A Seven Thousand–Year
Window of Time

God that made the world and all things therein, seeing that He is Lord
of Heaven and Earth, dwells not in temples made with hands; Neither
is worshipped with men's hands, as though He needed anything, seeing
he gives to all life, and breath, and all things; And hath made of one
blood all nations of men for to dwell on all the face of the Earth,
and *hath determined the times before appointed*, and the bounds of their
habitation. (Acts 17:24-26 KJV)

> And God said, Let there be lights in the firmament of
> the Heaven to divide the day from the night; and let
> them be for signs, and for seasons, and for days, and
> years. (Gen. 1:14 KJV)

When Did Time Begin?

Time has a beginning, and I firmly believe the Bible is accurate in
describing time and history. The creation week occurred about 3973
BC, and according to God's historical bookkeeping, there was nothing

but God before that date. The countdown for seven thousand years of time began seven years after the creation week in the Garden of Eden about 3966 BC. God has a right to tell this story as it happened, since He and the angels were the only eyewitnesses to the event. God tells this creation story in the first chapter of Genesis and in the Dead Sea Scrolls. Angels dictated the creation event to Enoch and Moses to be written down for future generations.

The question is not what do you speculate happened at creation and which Hebrew words mean what; the question is do you believe what God has *said*? If not, then do you have any other eyewitness to this *event*? If you do not have an eyewitness then you do not have a credible witness. Only the *fool* has said in his heart, "There is no God." Now, either you can reveal to everybody that you are a *fool* or you can believe the only eyewitness account of the origin of the universe. It truly is your choice because the Creator did give that freedom when he created in you free will. Either you believe God or bottom line you are a *fool*. This is the end of the discussion. Just be a *fool* if you want, or believe the only eyewitness account!

God created *all things*, and without Him nothing came into existence. You can read the eyewitness creation account in the first chapter of Genesis and in some historical books found in the Dead Sea Scrolls or just declare that you are nothing but a *fool*, beginning your endless speculations about something you know nothing about. Nothing existed except God before 3973 BC. Billions and millions of years are nothing but smoke and mirrors for a big bang fairytale for *fools*.

Fairytales for Adults

The big bang fairytale is a *fool's* attempt to explain something he knows nothing about. Some late scientists declared that all matter in the universe more than likely started no bigger than a dot on a page or no bigger than an atom. The dot began to spin extremely fast. It then exploded into a big bang, causing the stars, sun, and planets to form. And they call this science? This is how the leading evolutionists try to explain what they claim happened in their imaginary time frame of twenty billion years ago.

All matter no bigger than a dot on a page? Can you believe that someone cut down a tree to make sheets of paper to print this nonsense, and they even took tax dollars and put it in a book only to label it as *science*? If you believe that this nonsense is science, I have some ocean front property in Tennessee you would be very interested in buying.

You have a choice to believe a fool's adult fairytale, or you can believe the eyewitness account that God recorded in history. News flash—some of these scientists have now met this only eyewitness and have discovered the truth. They wish they could come back and *warn* their students and buddies! But they cannot get a weekend pass, and no transportation is available for them. You see, they have died and met the only eyewitness, and there is no coming back to correct or change the path they chose while breathing God's atmosphere on this earth. Warning, as death finds you so shall the final judgment.

God Set a Time Clock for Man

According to God's record after the fall of man, He allots six thousand years for man's government or man's ability to rule himself. Then God allots the final thousand years for Christ's perfect government. This allotted time began when Adam sinned in about 3966 BC. According to my calculations, 5,993 years later should be about AD 2028, which will start the final seven-year countdown and then after these final seven years, which is the end of the six thousand-year countdown. This will be the battle of Armageddon, as revealed in the last book in the Bible, the book of Revelation.

It is all coming to an end, and we are about to see the final seven years of man's corrupt government unfold before our very eyes that will make Hitler look like a virgin Sunday school teacher. This final seven years will complete six thousand years of man running the show. I have come to this conclusion after discovering the six thousand years of allotted time for man's government. Notice that the end wasn't in 2012 with the end of the Mayan calendar, but it is amazingly close and will be approximately less than twenty-one years later from now, around AD 2035 following the last seven years recorded in the book of Revelation.

Time only exists within this *seven thousand–year window*. Before Adam sinned there was no need for time because it was all perfect. After the seven thousand years are completed in about AD 3035, there will be time no more. You can pull off your watch and throw away your cell phones, for Jesus will make all things new on the eighth day of God's timetable. We are just going to be there, and there is no need to keep time, for we will be there for all eternity.

God's Time and Man's Time Differ

The seven thousand years of time for man is only seven days on God's timetable. Six days for man, and the seventh day is for His Son to rule this earth as He comes with His holy angels to end the battle of Armageddon (Rev. 19). Then, after one thousand years of Christ's kingdom, on God's eighth day He makes all things new (Rev. 21–22). But on this seventh day of God's timetable (Rev. 20), Jesus will have everyone beat their weapons into plow shares, for there will be war no more for one thousand years (Isa. 2:7 and Mic. 4:3).

At the beginning of Jesus' reign, He will totally *redo* this earth back to a global tropical climate again! He will rule His earth in righteousness and holiness. King Jesus will return this earth to the Garden of Eden conditions and human genetics will exist again when a seventy-five-year-old man will only be a boy. The mutated sin nature will not be removed from Adam's natural descendants. Satan will not be able to tempt mankind because he will be imprisoned in a pit for a thousand-year period. Mankind will realize this sin nature inherited from Adam is a really big problem and he can't blame the Devil. This sin nature is a mutation in your very flesh inherited from the first earthly man named Adam. Christ was not a descendant of Adam but was the Son of God.

Armageddon

The destruction of this earth and the final battle between light and darkness, which is *World War* IV, will take place in AD 3035 after Satan is loosed from his prison for a short time. In about AD 2035, the surface of this earth will be destroyed by fire during World War III, known as the battle of Armageddon. Jesus Christ and His holy angels will end this battle, and the earth will undergo some major renovations like it did during Noah's flood. However, after World War IV in 3035, this earth will be replaced with a newly created earth that will exist for all eternity.

> Wail, for the day of the Lord is at hand! It will come as destruction from the Almighty. Therefore all hands will be limp, every man's heart will melt, and they will be afraid. Pangs and sorrows will take hold of them; they will be in pain as a woman in childbirth;

they will be amazed at one another; their faces will be like flames. Behold, the day of the Lord comes, Cruel, with both wrath and fierce anger, to lay the land desolate; And He will destroy its sinners from it. For the stars of Heaven and their constellations will not give their light; the sun will be darkened in its going forth, and the moon will not cause its light to shine. "I will punish the world for its evil, and the wicked for their iniquity; I will halt the arrogance of the proud, and will lay low the haughtiness of the terrible. I will make a mortal rarer than fine gold, a man more than the golden wedge of Ophir. Therefore I will shake the heavens, And the Earth will move out of her place, in the wrath of the Lord of hosts and in the day of His fierce anger. [Could this be describing your future?] (Isa. 13:6–13 NKJV)

We have lots of scientific evidence today of that first renovation by water. However, during its future second renovation the surface will be destroyed by nuclear war and fire from heaven. The Bible says, "If those days are not shortened, not one soul out of billions would survive to populate the kingdom." (Mark 13:19-20) God promises that those days will be shortened during the final seven years.

No One Knows

Therefore, no one knows the day or the hour of Christ's return but stay focused on the gospel of His kingdom. There will be a few survivors to populate the kingdom after the valley of judgment that even the ultra-serious doomsday preppers will not escape. During this time Christ will send forth His angels to gather all living people, and you cannot hide from angels. Christ will judge the living people who have survived an end time period of hell on earth as described in Revelation 4–18.

This will take place within the next twenty-one years; billions of people will die on this earth. The end of time is upon us, and if you want to survive, you must be born again. A rebirth in your human spirit is the only way to survive. Even then your body of flesh may be destroyed.

Only One Way to Escape

Jesus is the way, the truth, and the new life; trust in Him today and be born again. Escape the coming wrath of God, as it is about to be poured out on an unbelieving population. Be a part of the church that will be changed in the twinkling of an eye. Be a part of that group or new race of people who will be changed into a glorified eternal body, never to die. What a wonderful promise of grace, getting something I truly don't deserve. It is a gift from God made possible only through Jesus.

Jesus made the following statement concerning His coming:

> When the Son of man shall come in his glory, and all the holy angels with him, then shall he sit upon the throne of his glory: And before him shall be gathered all nations: and he shall separate them one from another, as a shepherd divides' his sheep from the goats; [Note: This event will take place at the end of the final seven years.] And he shall set the sheep on his right hand, but the goats on the left. Then shall the King say unto them on his right hand, Come, ye blessed of my

Father, inherit the kingdom prepared for you from the
foundation of the world. (Matt. 25:31–34 KJV)

He will gather the remaining humans who have survived the
horrors of the Antichrist in one location and divide them like sheep
and goats. Those who pass His judgment will enter into His kingdom
with Him, and those who don't pass will go into eternal punishment.
They will be cast alive into eternal punishment. The ones who pass
His judgment will enter His kingdom and live under this earth's
first perfect government. Jesus will genetically change the survivors.
They could possibly live for hundreds of years or have children that
could live nine hundred to one thousand years as in the beginning of
creation. All on this present earth will be newly renovated. Christ will
begin a divine government that will last one thousand years.

Whose Kingdom Will Survive?

This millennial kingdom of Christ will all take place within less than
twenty-one years. The next twenty-one years will be a time like has
never been on the earth and never will be again. You are going to
witness the entire world economy collapse. Islam is going to attempt to
take over the world but will be defeated by the Antichrist and his one-
world government, which will be the revival of the old Roman Empire
(presently called the club of Rome). Rome will rise to power as the two
feet and ten toes of the statue of Daniel's vision come back to life.

The United States and Canada will become one nation and
government. One of the Antichrist's ten kings or presidents will take
control, but America will not be the superpower it once was. America,
or Mystery Babylon, will be destroyed in one single day as Sodom and

Gomorrah in Bible times. America will become powerless to stop what is coming on this earth.

All of this overspending is a master plan to bring America down from within. You just cannot survive spending more than you take in. Riots in the world's streets will be rampant. Gangs will murder at will and steal your goods. If you live in America, possibly your end may come before Daniel's final seven years, and it will be as it was in the days of Lot, who lived in Sodom and Gomorrah.

Beam Me up, Scottie

Christians, be looking up, for your redemption is at hand. If you have never been born again, you must try it, for I know you will like it. If you choose to reject Christ, then all I can say is *good luck!* If you live in America, begin to look up for heavenly fire. Destruction is coming, for God's wrath comes very soon for the *scoffers* and the unbelievers!

Understanding the Time

The key in knowing the exact year is finding out the year Jesus was crucified and adding 2,007 years to that date to know the year of the battle of Armageddon. According to the Gregorian calendar, if the AD portion is accurate, 2028 should begin the final seven years, but no later than 2030.

Jesus' Second Coming

Immediately after the tribulation of those days shall the
sun be darkened, and the moon shall not give her light,
and the stars shall fall from Heaven, and the powers

of the heavens shall be shaken: And then shall appear the sign of the Son of man in Heaven: and then shall all the tribes of the Earth mourn, and they shall see the Son of man coming in the clouds of Heaven with power and great glory. And he shall send his angels with a great sound of a trumpet, and they shall gather together his elect from the four winds, from one end of Heaven to the other. (Matt. 24:29–31 KJV)

Be Ready for His Coming

But as the days of Noah were, so shall also the coming of the Son of man be. For as in the days that were before the flood they were eating and drinking, marrying and giving in marriage, until the day that Noah entered into the ark, And knew not until the flood came, and took them all away; so shall also the coming of the Son of man be. (Matt. 24:37–39 KJV)

Could Lot's Days Be America/Mystery Babylon?

Likewise also as it was in the days of Lot; they did eat, they drank, they bought, they sold, they planted, they built; But the same day that Lot went out of Sodom it rained fire and brimstone from Heaven, and destroyed them all. Even thus shall it be in the day when the Son of man is revealed. (Luke 17:28–30 KJV)

Could it be that as the rapture is taking place, flaming meteorites will be coming from God on certain cities and they will be totally destroyed that same day? This is the prophecy concerning Lot's days, and my calculation about the year is AD 2027–2028. As God's children are ascending, fire will be descending, likened to the ancient cities of Sodom. Could the prophecy in Luke, which describes the days of Lot, and the prophecy in the book of Revelation 17–18, which describes a mysterious city called Mystery Babylon, be talking about America? I truly think so!

CHAPTER 8

The Key to Doomsday Date

Knowing the exact year Christ was crucified and the start of the third two thousand-year period allows us to count forward 2,007 years to find the date of the battle of Armageddon with accuracy and count backward four thousand years to the creation of the universe in 3973 BC.

We have learned that six thousand years was set for the completion of man's government after Adam sinned. We have learned that this period was divided evenly into three two thousand-year segments. According to my calculations, the church started in AD 28, so we need to subtract four thousand years from 28 to get the date of the Creation week, which was about 3973 BC.

Calculating the date of the creation is easy. The concept of time as we know it can be calculated by using God's method. God sees days and not years, for all of time is contained within seven days to God. But to man it is not that easy. One day is as a thousand years to God, but a thousand years is a thousand years to man.

We have to convert God's days into years, so seven days equals seven thousand years—six days for man's government and the seventh day for His Son Jesus Christ or one thousand years appointed for the kingdom of Christ. To properly calculate time, you have to ignore man's dating methods. Most of mankind is choking to death from the smokescreen of millions and billions of years put forth by Darwinism.

Could everything have developed in six thousand years? Just look at how things have developed in the last 114 years. Open your eyes—only 150 years ago we were still in the Civil War, and we are talking about six thousand years. We have been so deceived by this Darwinian doctrine that has created billions of years out of thin air that it makes us doubt the only eyewitness account of creation. Darwinism is not science, but the big lie from the spiritual kingdom of darkness. You truly have to have help to believe Darwinism, and the kingdom of darkness is ready to help you believe.

There is an appointment set in the heavens. This appointment is set for the wrath of God to be poured out on the unbelievers; during this time the second destruction of the surface of this earth will take place. Before the first destruction, God used Noah to warn the people of the coming global flood. This second coming destruction will be by fire and not water. Today God is warning us in the Bible and through world events. He is trying to warn the mass population, but they are not listening.

Earth's Water Source for the Flood

From creation until the global flood in 2317 BC, most of the water in the oceans was stored in underground subterranean chambers, which were located under the crust of the earth. The Bible tells us that the fountains of the deep were opened and water gushed out upon the earth for 150 days, creating the global flood, and this release of the subterranean water created all the fault lines and the vast oceans we see around the globe today. Earth could have had very small mountain ranges with much more land surface, and the higher mountains did not arise until after the flood. This is the reason hundreds of structures and cities are found underwater around the world.

Some Christian scientists think an ice meteor came crashing into earth with tons of ice crystals collecting around both poles. These poles were a part of earth's tropical paradise, and much more land was inhabitable before the flood. Earth was tightly stretched over a vast underground water supply. The impact created a crack in this tropical earth's surface and caused the crust to split around the globe in probably less than a day.

The subterranean waters were under great pressure from the overbearing rock and soil, as oil is today. The water had to supersonically spray into the atmosphere when the meteor or asteroid struck the earth. Our earth is the only planet with fault lines observed in our universe.

If you are interested in learning more about these creation theories put forth by several Christian scientists, I refer you to a very scientific based book titled *In the Beginning* by Walt Brown, PhD. Also, DVDs *The Hovind Theory* and *The Garden of Eden*, which were created by Dr. Kent Hovind, can be watched on YouTube free or purchased from Creation Science Evangelism. Both men are extremely hated by the Darwinists. Brown and Hovind put forth compelling scientific evidence for the Creation and flood event ideas. God's judgment came on mankind with a global flood, and the creation event took place less than six thousand years ago, according to the hard scientific evidence.

Been Judged Once

This first judgment of destruction came true, as predicted in the Dead Sea Scrolls, during the days of Noah. Both the prediction and destruction are recorded in the old writings of Enoch and the preaching of Noah before the flood. It rained for forty days and nights, and the water under the crust of the earth gushed forth for 150 days, until the waters rose about fifteen cubits above the highest mountains. Even today we find fossilized clams on the tops of the highest mountains. When mountain climbers first reached the summit of Mt. Everest, they took pictures of the sea fossils, namely huge fossilized clams, which they discovered at the very peak of the mountain. Clams are not good mountain climbers. The last time I looked, I did not find feet or legs or wings on a clam (duh). How did they get there?

The Bible predicts that the next destruction will be with fire. In this nuclear age in which we live, it can be accomplished, but not till that appointed time. This appointment date is six thousand years from the first sin of Adam. To find this date, we must look at the one who set this appointment date with destiny.

Finding a Year Date, Not a Day

God alone knows the day and the hour but He warns us in His written Word with different signs and prophecies. He doesn't want you to be dumb concerning this appointed time; stay focused on life and the purpose you were placed here for. The end is a very important date. To discover the end of this six thousand–year time clock, you must first figure out the exact year of Jesus' crucifixion. So when was Jesus crucified? We have dates from AD 27 to 34, and most scholars agree on AD 30. I think AD 28, but just in case I am wrong, it is no later than AD 30.

We know that the church of Jesus Christ began the same year Christ was crucified. So two thousand years after Christ's crucifixion should end the church age. Before the wrath of God is to be poured out on all unbelievers, God's children must be removed from the earth in an event known as the rapture of the church. Then the seven years of God's wrath and destruction designed for the unbelievers will take place as foretold. These seven years are the tribulation period and will close out the Abrahamic Covenant. This final seven years will end the six thousand years of man's ability to govern.

At Minimum Seven Years until Armageddon

Daniel foretold of these final seven years of the Abrahamic Covenant. This remaining seven years is also foretold in detail in the book of Revelation. God's seventh day is described in Revelation as the last one thousand years of a seven thousand–year program for man. The first six thousand years are for man to govern himself, and the last one thousand years are for Christ to govern man under a divine government during the millennial kingdom. Then comes the final judgment day when Adam's natural descendants from all time will stand before the great white throne.

The tribulation period will begin two thousand years after Christ's crucifixion. During this last seven years, over seven billion people will be destroyed, partly by the Muslim holy wars as Islam tries to take over the world. My theory is that these holy wars will take place between 2015 and 2028, but Islam will be defeated by the Antichrist, Satan's Nephilim son. Satan has big plans to reduce the population to a much more manageable one half billion people within the next twenty-one years.

America's Stonehenge

Go to Elberton, Georgia, and you will find the ten commandments of the New World Order carved into twenty-foot-tall granite stones. The commandments are listed in eight modern languages and at the top of these monuments, in four ancient languages. The stones are nineteen feet, three inches tall and weigh 237,746 pounds each. These six granite monuments are called the Georgia guide stones or by some, "America's Stonehenge."

If you will notice what is written on the stones, the first commandment of the New World Order is to maintain population under 500,000,000. A lot of people will have to die to accomplish these numbers; roughly about seven billion will have to be eliminated from planet earth. This is serious stuff, and life on this earth is about to change forever. What is about to come on this earth never has been and never will be again. Bodies will be consumed as they stand on their feet before they can fall to the ground.

The Key to This End Date

Calculating the death of Christ is very simple. First, we have a discovery in archaeology that concerns Herod the Great, the King of Judea. We know from archaeology that Herod died in March of 4 BC. We also know that Herod killed all of the male children two years old and younger as he tried to eliminate the future king of the Jews. Christ's birth was at least in March, 6 BC. Knowing He was born in the fall of the year should put His birth at the end of 7 BC.[20]

> Now when Jesus was born in Bethlehem of Judaea in the days of Herod the king, behold, there came wise men from the east to Jerusalem, saying, Where is he that is born King of the Jews? We have seen his star in the east, and are come to worship him. When Herod the king had heard these things, he was troubled, and

---

[20] http://en.wikipedia.org/wiki/Herod_the_Great

all Jerusalem with him. And when he had gathered all the chief priests and scribes of the people together, he demanded of them where Christ should be born. And they said unto him, In Bethlehem of Judaea: for thus it is written by the prophet, "And thou Bethlehem, in the land of Juda, art not the least among the princes of Juda: for out of thee shall come a Governor, that shall rule my people Israel." Then Herod, when he had privily called the wise men, inquired of them diligently what time the star appeared. And he sent them to Bethlehem, and said, Go and search diligently for the young child; and when ye have found him, bring me word again, that I may come and worship him also. (Matt. 2:1–8 KJV)

And being warned of God in a dream that they should not return to Herod, they departed into their own country another way. And when they were departed, behold, the angel of the Lord appeared to Joseph in a dream, saying, Arise, and take the young child and his mother, and flee into Egypt, and be thou there until I bring thee word: for Herod will seek the young child to destroy him. When he arose, he took the young child and his mother by night, and departed into Egypt: And was there until the death of Herod: that it might be fulfilled which was spoken of the Lord by the prophet, saying, Out of Egypt have I called my son. Then Herod, when he saw that he was mocked of the wise men, was exceeding wroth, and sent forth, and slew all the children that were in Bethlehem, and in all the coasts thereof, from *two years old and under, according to the time* which he had diligently inquired of the wise men. (Matt. 2:12–16 KJV)

Herod had asked the wise men to report back to him so he could also go and worship the newborn King. However, he did not want to worship but destroy Jesus while He was still an infant. The wise men were warned in a dream, telling them to go home a different way and not to return to Herod.

The Rage of King Herod

I guess Herod fumbled around and finally realized that the wise men were not coming back. They had betrayed him. He grew furious and made a last-ditch effort to kill Jesus. Herod gave the order to kill all male children. There was a time factor involved. Herod knew it had been at least two years since the wise men had entered his courts, so he had all male babies two years old and younger in Jerusalem and all the surrounding areas killed in his effort to destroy the future king of Israel. But an angel had warned Joseph to flee to Egypt, so he took Mary and baby Jesus and fled to Egypt and stayed until Herod's death.

Christ Birth Was in 7 BC

Again, according to archaeological discoveries, Herod's death was in March of 4 BC. If you add the two years from the time he had talked with the wise men and learned of this new King being born to the 4 BC discovery of Herod's death, it equals March of 6 BC. I believe Jesus was born in the fall of 7 BC and died thirty-three and a half years later in the spring of 28 AD.

If you add a year for the change of BC to AD (for there is not a zero year), you will come up with 28 AD. I know all the arguments for a later date, but I have an inner spiritual reason to favor this date above all others and all arguments. I know that I am not infallible and I could be wrong. If so, it is no later than AD 30. If AD 28 is correct, add two thousand years for the church age and seven years for the tribulation, and you will end with the battle of Armageddon. The end is immediately upon us; whether the church age ends in 2028 or 2030, the end is here. Then the antichrist will be revealed.

Christians, seeing this time is short, it would be a good idea to store about fourteen years' worth of nonperishable foods for your families. Then we need to spread the gospel about the coming King and His kingdom for the next fourteen years as we wait for our Lord to redeem us as He promised. There will be trying times before the rapture. The second seal will be opened, and my theory is that Islam is the red horse and that they will take peace from the earth sometime between 2015 and 2028.

> And when he had opened the second seal, I heard the second beast say, Come and see. And there went out another horse that was red: and power was given to him that sat thereon to take peace from the Earth, and that they should kill one another: and there was given unto him a great sword. (Rev. 6:3–4 KJV) (This great sword I think is Iran developing a nuclear weapon.)

Description of the Rapture

> Behold, I show you a mystery; we shall not all sleep, but we shall all be changed, in a moment, in the twinkling

of an eye, at the last trump: for the trumpet shall sound, and the dead shall be raised incorruptible, and we shall be changed. For this corruptible must put on incorruption, and this mortal must put on immortality. (1 Cor. 15:51–53 KJV)

Unbelievers, the decisions you make while you live will seal your destiny after you die for all eternity. All born-again believers will be removed from this earth before God's wrath is unleashed. Consider giving your heart and life to Jesus, the only one who can truly save you.

How to Know the Antichrist

The Antichrist helps Israel defeat Islam, which has been trying to destroy Israel. He will make a firm peace agreement (Dan. 9:27) with the nation of Israel for this final seven years. When the peace agreement is signed, the Old Covenant time clock begins to click off the final seven years as the world marches toward Armageddon. The one-world ruler that signs that seven-year peace agreement with Israel is the Antichrist!

We Don't Know the "Day"

We truly don't know the day or the hour of Jesus' return to rapture all those who are in Christ. We possibly could know the season and maybe the year He will redeem the church. We truly don't know the *day* or the *hour* when He will come to the earth as conquering King. Only the Father in heaven knows the *day* and the *hour* of the returning events of His Son Jesus Christ. But don't live in fear. Instead live in excitement and share Christ with a lost and doomed world.

Birth Date Speculations

Look very carefully—Jesus was possibly born in the seventh Jewish month, which is October in the Georgian calendar of 7 BC. This is two years before Herod's death in March of 4 BC. I know how God loves the perfect number seven. Maybe Jesus was born in 7/7/7 BC. In other words, maybe Jesus was born in the Jewish seventh month and seventh day in the Roman year of 7 BC.

Jesus was then crucified thirty-three and a half years later in the spring of AD 28, which is after the sixty-nine weeks (483 years) of Daniel's prophecy. This leaves seven years for the seventieth week of Daniel described in Revelation 4–18.

CHAPTER 9

Planning for Global Domination

According to the biblical prophecies, there will be a one-world government functioning at the time of the Messiah's return. We presently have three groups planning a global world takeover. They have been putting things in place for years for their one-world governments. World War III will be fought over this very subject as well as the destruction of the nation of Israel.

The following is a description of these world-planners in general but not with great detail. If you are looking for more information about these organizations, the Internet and your local library can provide you with more detailed information pertaining to each of these groups. This chapter is designed to make you aware of their existence and their long-term planning for a takeover.

1. United Nations (the New World Order or NWO)

The United Nations is planning a one-world government. Everybody knows them as peacekeepers, but in the end days they will become the godless aggressors. They are extremely powerful, having no shortage of funds available for their end goals. They hope to take control of the world without firing one shot.

The United Nations and the money families of the world are planning a New World Order and a cashless society, coming soon to a city near you. The United Nations of Islam is group number two, and the third group is the workers' unions run by state capitalism, which is nothing but good old-fashioned communism. These three will be jockeying for world power and control once America falls. The Obama administration may be the straw that breaks the camel's back. However, this Affordable Care Act will be more like a tree instead of a straw. We will be at twenty trillion debt by 2016 if something does not change.

The American economy is being blown up like a hot air balloon, with a government-fabricated false recovery created by cooked books, plus the printing of billions of new dollars. I think it will crash big time by September 2015. At such time it will be a depression, not a recession: millions will lose all their savings and retirement accounts. Try to continually run a private business on borrowed money and see how long you will survive. Oh, you can have new cars and big houses and wear nice new expensive clothing and most will think you are doing quite well while. All along no one knows that you are living on borrowed money and are cooking the books like our present elected officials. There has to be a payday someday, and mark my words it is coming very soon. I have been told that FEMA has built over six hundred prison camps across the United States which are to maintain order during a collapse because our prisons are overfilled now. I have not seen these camps and don't even know if they exist. I am not a conspiracy theorist, but it sounds very strange and scary considering the state of our government and our national debt. I think at the most America has about fourteen years, this being 2014, but it could be a lot less.

The New World Order I think will be in power when Jesus comes back to this earth. The following document is available on the Internet and the address is listed below. This is only a portion of the article, and thanks to Dr. Lorraine Day for all the research and time put into the publishing of this document!

The following is a link to an article which everyone needs to read and educate themselves about their future plans:[21]

The Council on Foreign Relations (CFR), the Trilateral Commission, and the Bilderbergers are just three working groups of the New World Order.

2. The United Islamic Nations

The second organization with aspirations to rule the world is Islam. Islam is divided into two separate groups—the Sunnis and the Shiites. They believe in the coming of a Muslim Messiah to bring world peace, but first they have to hasten the coming of their messiah, Imam-Al-Mahdi. They must first cause massive bloodshed and turmoil around the entire world by instigating such chaos that it will hasten their messiah's return.

President Mahmoud Ahmadinejad never claimed to be Islam's messiah but only John the Baptist of Islam. He claims to be the forerunner of Islam's coming messiah, and he must prepare the way, by creating worldwide bloodshed. The twelfth imam is to return and set up a global Islamic kingdom that they claimed will bring peace.

This twelfth imam is to rule the world and help install Islam by force as a world religion and Sharia law, destroying all other governments. The Middle East is the focal point of the world. They believe they must kill millions of infidels to bring this much-awaited

---

[21] http://www.goodnewsaboutgod.com/topics.htm#politicaltruth

twelfth Imam. They cherish the thought of martyrdom and don't care about this world's opinion.

Words from Iran's Former Leaders

Iran's former president, Mahmud Ahmadinejad, sees the joining with China as the catalyst for a new world order. He added, "The order and the systems dominating the world at present are worn-out and corrupt. Under the present conditions, the world needs a humane and fair new order. Iran and China can have fruitful cooperation in the interest of humanity to define and establish this order." In his speech, the Iranian president stressed increasing cooperation between Iran and China in order to bring about both countries' vision of the new world order.

In Ahmadinejad's view, the new world order to be established by Iran and China is aimed at replacing the current world system of many different governments with one based on justice and rule of law. Yeah, right![22]

3. Workers' Union/State-Run Capitalism

This group for global takeover has been around for years. They, following the Third Reich, have had plans for world domination, but the United States was always in the way of their goal. This group is just old-fashioned communism. The USSR has been planning on taking over the world since the defeat of Hitler; it began with the Soviet bloc nations. After the German trial of East and West Germany, it revealed just how evil this communist system could be. The wall eventually came tumbling down, but their goal is still there.

---

[22] http://henrymakow.com/2013/02/is-china-part-of-the-new-world.html

In modern times they have changed their names to hide their goals. They have worked tirelessly for years as government employees and school officials gained control of the education systems in an effort to slowly gain control of the youth in America. They are now known as social justice or progressivism instead of communism. They are the left wing of the Democratic Party, which has hijacked the old party.

The United States has to collapse into economic chaos before this one-world government can rule. They have to change the Constitution by doing away with America's bill of rights. They must destroy the foundation on which America was formed, which are God-given rights to man. They must do away with the Judeo-Christian heritage.

The Third Seal—Famine

The *black* horse of *Russia* is one of the four horses of the apocalypse and will begin to exert her power. The black horse rides out after the red horse of Iran and ISIL has taken peace from the earth. As allies they will assist each other in war. They will cause worldwide famine and massive inflation; a loaf of bread will cost a day's wages.

War and inflation is the third horse of the apocalypse or the third seal of Revelation. Could all four horses of the apocalypse begin to ride over the earth before the last seven years begin and before the rapture of the church takes place? If America is Mystery Babylon and meets her destruction by 2028, the four horsemen will ride over the earth within the next fourteen years.

The Antichrist will arise to power out of Europe and stop Russia, China, and Islam from setting up their version of a one-world government. The Antichrist comes to Israel's rescue, helping to save them from destruction posed by Islam and state capitalism. The

Antichrist and his ten kingdoms will sign a peace treaty with Israel for seven years, the last seven years described in the book of Revelation.

The country located directly north of Israel is Russia, the old Soviet Union. According to Zechariah this black horse is riding out of the north and will cause a great shortage of food.

> When the Lamb broke the third seal, I heard the third living being say, "Come!" And I looked up and saw a black horse, and its rider was holding a pair of scales in his hand. And a voice from among the four living beings said, "A loaf of wheat bread or three loaves of barley for a day's pay. And don't waste the olive oil and wine." (Rev. 6:5–6 NLT)

Runaway inflation makes money worthless. That in turn becomes an excuse for the rigid controls over buying and selling. We see this in Revelation 13 when, under the reign of Antichrist, the whole world is subjected to enormously restrictive population control by retina (forehead) or fingerprint (right hand) scanning for commerce. Possibly literal microchips could be inserted in your foreheads or hands, so that "no one can buy or sell without the computer chip of the beast." We have read the last book in the Bible; we know the outcome of the battle of Armageddon.

CHAPTER 10

Daniel's Prophecy of One-World Dictators

The book of Daniel was sealed until the end of time, and now that time has arrived. History has recorded five one-world rulers since the global flood. Biblical prophecy predicts a sixth future one-world ruler before the seventh and final thousand-year kingdom of Jesus Christ comes into power. The following is a list of these six *one-world global governments*: King Nimrod of the Mesopotamian valley (2100–1960 BC), King Nebuchadnezzar of Babylon (605–538 BC), King Darius of Medo-Persia (538–331BC), Alexander the Great of Greece (331–168 BC), and the Roman Empire (168BC–538AD). A sixth future global government led by the Antichrist will come into power on or before AD 2028. It will originate out of the old Roman Empire. This empire very possibly may be the present existing organization known as the club of Rome.

A Dream of Global Rulers

Nebuchadnezzar, the king of Babylon, had a dream and was very troubled. He searched his entire kingdom for someone who could interpret this dream but could find no one. Finally a Hebrew slave by the name of Daniel, who possessed the Spirit of the living God, was found. Daniel prayed to God to give him the same dream and the interpretation of the dream. God gave a vision of this same dream to Daniel. A statue was seen in the dream, and it represented five kingdoms that would each rule the known world as a one-world government.

These governments were represented in the statue of Nebuchadnezzar's dream. Babylon was the head of gold on the statue. Nimrod, the first global ruler, was not represented in the statue because he was already in past history and all other kingdoms were future to the present king of Babylon. The stone striking the feet of the statue is Jesus Christ, the seventh and final one-world ruler. You can read the whole story in the prophetic book of Daniel 2 found in the Old Testament of the Bible.

Nimrod's global kingdom was recorded in the ancient book of Jasher, and this statue in Nebuchadnezzar's dream was prophecy dealing with Babylon and the one-world governments that were to follow. After the great deluge of 2317 BC, Nimrod ruled all of the descendants of Noah from 2100 BC until he was defeated by King Chedorlaomer in 1960 BC, ending Nimrod's global empire.

The book of Daniel tells a story of King Nebuchadnezzar, who was troubled by a dream he had and was seeking someone to help him understand its meaning. Nebuchadnezzar was king of Babylon. This was only his second year to be king, and he was proud of what he had accomplished. He was the second one-world ruler after the great flood of Noah's days.

The First Global King

The beginning of all civilizations after the flood was located in the Middle East in the Mesopotamian valley. The Bible calls it the plains of Shinar, but it can be better translated Shumer or Sumer. The Sumerians, as they were known, were at the center of all trade and commerce, and Nimrod was their king. Nimrod had other cities that he had settled in that area. Babel (later known as Babylon) and Assyria were once Sumerian cities. King Nimrod was the first one-world ruler after the flood for a time. If there were any other kings on earth, they were subject to Nimrod the mighty hunter. Nimrod was born to Cush, and Cush was a son of Ham, who was one of Noah's sons.

Nimrod and the Sumerians were black in color, and many references in archaeology call them black-headed or black-faced people. This first one-world ruler was a black man, and some speculate that the last one to govern will be as well. Sumer was predominately a black community.

The Sumerian culture was hidden until archaeologists dug up these cities. They stand as evidence that the great historical Bible is the true history of the world and are the Words of the Living God. Then archaeologists found thousands of clay tablets revealing that this great Sumerian civilization of ancient biblical times truly did exist.

Babel Becomes Babylon

Babel later became Babylon and was ruled by King Nebuchadnezzar; Babylon became the second one-world power. These kingdoms were located in the Middle East in the Mesopotamian Valley. We find in history that the first three one-world dictators were located in this area of the Middle East.

According to the dream interpreted by Daniel, there would be five additional global world powers after Babylon. Two dictators are still to come in the future. They would rule the known world, and the dream revealed these kingdoms to Daniel and it was recorded for us who will live in the last days. Historically, Daniel's prophecy was very accurate, for the first world power of Nimrod had already been defeated long before the time of Daniel. Next will be Islam's attempt to try to rule the world.[23]

History Is in Daniel's Predictions

King Nebuchadnezzar, the statue's head of gold, described him as the present one-world dictator, then Medo-Persia as the chest and arms of silver, then the Greek Empire as the waist and belly of bronze. The fourth world government in the dream was the Roman Empire, and it was described with two legs of iron. Now the last global human empire is represented by the two feet and ten toes. It is still to come in the future, a revived Roman Empire led by the Antichrist (666). I think it will be the modern-day club of Rome. The final kingdom was the stone not made with hands that strikes the statue and destroys all human governments that will never rise again. Jesus Christ's kingdom is the seventh and final kingdom, ruling the globe for one thousand years from approximately AD 2035 to 3035.

Like Napoleon, many have tried to become a world dictator, but all have failed, except those listed in Daniel's prophecy. Five global rulers are now collecting dust in the archives of history. Hitler is one of the latest dictators who actually tried to rule the world. His efforts to establish the Third Reich that was to rule the global world for one thousand years was crushed at the end of World War II. Communism

---

[23] https://www.youtube.com/watch?v=sv5UzALN080

had plans of world domination but was blocked by the United States during the Cold War.

The Final Human Government

The last one-world government in history was the Roman Empire. The feet and ten toes of Daniel's statue is a future revival of Rome and is a sixth one-world government that shall be in place when Christ returns to earth. This resurrection of the old Roman Empire was foretold by Daniel. It will consist of ten kings, as represented by the feet and ten toes of Daniel's statue. They were made partly of iron and partly of clay. This one-world government will be in control of all governments in the entire world during the time of Christ's return. It will be like the Third Reich on steroids.

A quick overview of one-world global dictators that have ruled the world looks like this: Nimrod at Babel; Nebuchadnezzar of Babylon; Darius of Medo-Persia; Alexander the Great of Greece; the Roman Empire. Still to come are the Antichrist of the revived Roman Empire and finally the seventh, Jesus Christ, the stone not cut with hands, which strikes the statue, grinding it to powder and ends all human rule forever in about AD 2035 at the battle of Armageddon.

> But there is a God in Heaven that reveals secrets, and
> makes known to the king Nebuchadnezzar what shall
> be in the latter days. Thy dream, and the visions of
> thy head upon thy bed, are these; as for thee, O king,
> thy thoughts came into thy mind upon thy bed, what
> should come to pass hereafter: and he that reveals
> secrets makes known to thee what shall come to pass.
> But as for me, this secret is not revealed to me for any

wisdom that I have more than any living, but for their sakes that shall make known the interpretation to the king, and that thou might know the thoughts of thy heart. Thou, O king, saw, and behold a great image. This great image, whose brightness was excellent, stood before thee; and the form thereof was terrible. This image's head was of fine gold, his breast and his arms of silver, his belly and his thighs of brass, His legs of iron, his feet part of iron and part of clay. Thou saw till that a stone was cut out without hands, which smote the image upon his feet that were of iron and clay, and break them to piece. (Dan. 2:28-34 KJV)

And whereas thou saw the feet and toes, part of potters' clay, and part of iron, the kingdom shall be divided; but there shall be in it of the strength of the iron, forasmuch as thou saw the iron mixed with miry clay. And as the toes of the feet were part of iron, and part of clay, so the kingdom shall be partly strong, and partly broken. And whereas thou saw iron mixed with miry clay, *they shall mingle themselves with the seed of men:* but they shall not cleave one to another, even as iron is not mixed with clay. And in the days of these kings shall the God of Heaven set up a kingdom, which shall never be destroyed: and the kingdom shall not be left to other people, but it shall break in pieces and consume all these kingdoms, and it shall stand for ever. (Dan. 2:41-44 KJV)

The Nephilim Are Here

The sixth global kingdom will be made up of ten kings. This is the club of Rome's plan in dividing the continents into ten regions or kingdoms. The United States and Canada are to be one, for example. The club of Rome has already divided the globe into ten kingdoms; it has not happened yet, but it is in the plans. This statement was made in Daniel 9:43: "They shall mingle themselves with the seed of men." It was in the days of Noah, for the Nephilim ruled the earth. Could these ten new kings be Nephilim kings?

The Nephilim were ruling the earth during those days, and this is a reference to the fallen angels mixing with the seed of men again because they know their time is short. Could it be that these ten kings will be the hybrid Nephilim as in the days of Noah? Be on the alert for black-eyed children, for they are the Nephilim that are already here on earth today; avoid them at all costs, and do not take them in. Their eyes are solid black with no white at all. Go to YouTube and look for black-eyed kids and children with night vision or cat eyes.

Jesus Christ is the stone cut without hands, and He will strike the statue at His second coming, in all of His glory will destroy the sixth and last human global government; in fact, it will end all human government forever. At such time Christ will set up a seventh world kingdom that will rule the global world for one thousand years, which was the dream of Hitler and his Third Reich. The old Roman Empire was the only government that came close to a thousand-year reign, lasting from 168 BC until AD 538.

Man's ability to govern himself will be gone forever, but at the end of the one thousand years of divine government mankind, influenced by Satan, will try one last time to rule. Satan will be loosed out of his prison and will go forth all over the earth (Rev. 20). They will attempt to create war once more but will not succeed. This will be the end of time in about AD 3035.

Satan's Last Stand

Satan will gather a great army that is tired of the rule of Christ. They will gather together to take back the earth from this righteous Judge and King. They will come to fight the resurrected Lord of Lords and King of Kings. Fire will come down and instantly consume them all, plus the atmosphere and the earth. This earth will be destroyed and leave its orbit, going out in space, never to be inhabited again. This truly is the end of this present earth, never to be remodeled again but replaced with a new heaven and earth straight from the Creator of all things.

John said in Revelation 21, "I saw a new atmosphere and a new Earth for the first Heaven and Earth were passed away." God has remodeled the surface of this old earth during the flood and will do it again after the battle of Armageddon. The earth will not get a third renovation after 3035. This will be the end of the seventh day on God's timetable and will usher in the eighth day. God will make all things new like in the original six days of creation. Then John, in his vision of the future, saw a new earth. He saw a holy city descending out of heaven called the New Jerusalem. He tells us how large the holy city will be—the same physical size as the moon. This holy city was coming down to earth, but it wasn't round like the moon; it was a cube. John describes this city in the Bible in Revelation 21. Everyone needs to read the entire chapter; here are the first five verses:

> And I saw a new Heaven and a new Earth: for the first
> Heaven and the first Earth were passed away; and there

was no more sea. And I John saw the holy city, New Jerusalem, coming down from God out of Heaven, prepared as a bride adorned for her husband. And I heard a great voice out of Heaven saying, Behold, the tabernacle of God is with men, and he will dwell with them, and they shall be his people, and God Himself shall be with them, and be their God. And God shall wipe away all tears from their eyes; and there shall be no more death, neither sorrow, nor crying, neither shall there be any more pain: for the former things [the seven thousand years of time] are passed away. And he that sat upon the throne said, Behold, I make all things new. And he said unto me, *Write: for these words are true and faithful.* (Rev. 21:1–5 KJV)

This is what is known as heaven or a place where the children of God shall live for eternity. Surrender your heart to Jesus today and live forever with Him. The alternative eternity without Jesus looks very bleak.

CHAPTER 11

White Horse of America/ Mystery Babylon

Beginning of the Apocalypse/Seven Seals

The opening of the first seal was described in Revelation 6. The four horsemen of the apocalypse are described in the sixth chapter of the book of Revelation. Many scholars ascribe the horsemen of the apocalypse as occurring within the final seven years known as the tribulation period. The four horsemen are symbolic descriptions of separate events that will take place in the end times. The first horseman of the apocalypse is described in verse 2: "And I saw, and behold a white horse: and he that sat on him had a bow; and a crown was given unto him: and he went forth conquering, and to conquer" (KJV).

I personally think one of the four horsemen began to ride on 9/11. The white horse is America, and the first seal of the apocalypse has been opened. The first seal opened September 11 in the year 2001 with the attack on New York City. The white horse represents America, and George Bush was president. He was bent on conquering the terrorist network Al-Qaeda. He rode into Iraq as conqueror. Next he was given a crown in reelection as president. The second seal will probably quickly follow, opening around 2015, as the red horse of Iran and ISIL begins to ride with a great sword (a nuclear weapon) and will take peace from the earth before the rapture of the church expected in AD 2027 to 2030.

Some of the horrors of the end times will come while the church is still awaiting the rapture, and possibly four of the seven seals will be opened before the church age comes to a close. I think global war will bring in the Antichrist and the other horsemen of the apocalypse. The first horseman began to ride with the attack on New York City and the destruction of the twin towers.

The church in certain parts of the world is and has been going through horrors of unbelievable persecutions of Christian brothers and sisters. The world hates the church of Jesus Christ because we are right and they are wrong. The Devil has helped the world swallow Darwinism and the ancient alien theory—with an attitude of no one is going to tell us what to do! They don't want anything to do with a God who demands righteousness. Plus, unbelievers and a lot of Christians have believed the big lie of millions and billions of years.

The Church in America Has Become Complacent

Here in America we have become complacent, and many in the church believe and are hoping that the rapture of the church will take place before things get really bad. I truly do not think this will happen and many trials will come upon the church, especially here in America. Before Jesus comes in the clouds to redeem His saints, our faith is going to be tested as never before. We are approaching troublesome times, with other nations not hiding their plans to destroy us.

If the prophecy in Revelation 18 is truly the United States as Mystery Babylon, then doomsday for America is upon us. Change, change, change is what the populace has voted to have, but the change coming is more than they ever bargained for. The battle of Armageddon or World War III is coming to a city near you. Whether this one-hour destruction of America comes by 2028 or by 2035 at Armageddon, it is coming within the next twenty to thirty years at the most, and some nuclear destruction may be here by 2021 if not as soon as the fall of 2015. The doomsday preppers are getting ready for the end of this great nation. As fire destroyed Sodom, it is coming to Mystery Babylon; whether before the tribulation (2028) or at the end of the tribulation (2035), it is here. Your faith is about to be tested as never before.

I am convinced that the prophecy of the days of Lot is talking about America. As God's people leave America, fire will fall in one hour; if so, then 2028 is the days of Lot. There won't be evolutionists walking around after the rapture saying what has happened to the Christians, for total destruction follows the removal of God's people. The four horsemen found in Revelation 6 will possibly take place before the last seven years of tribulations begins, spoken of in Revelation 4–16. I truly hope I am wrong about all events leading up to 2028. The four horsemen could all ride before the church age comes to a close. This will be a time from the crucifixion of Christ until the rapture in about 2027–2028.

The church will be tested severely in these end times. They have become lukewarm like the church of Laodicea as they have departed from the Word of God, seeking those preachers to tickle their ears with philosophy. This is not true of all churches, for some have kept the faith and are watching, but the greater part of the church of the end times is described in Revelation 3:14–19 as the Laodicean church. This is another sign of the end of time.

The testing of our faith is upon us; our true colors will begin to show, and many will reject their faith to satisfy the God of their stomachs and the desires of their flesh. They have never denied the desires of the flesh, giving it anything it desires in the land of plenty; they have never had to truly do without. People in America will be in trouble as they see these things coming on the earth in these last days; their hearts will fail them for fear. Self-discipline and self-control need to be a part of your survival kit for America's coming doom. Americans have not been confronted with such troubles that the end time will bring, and those who have been pretending to be godly will be exposed.

If you try to go two or three days only taking in water, your flesh will scream to high heaven and you will see how much the body is in control of your life. Consult your doctor first, and then I challenge you take the test if you do not have any medical issues; again you must consult your doctor before trying any fast. In fact, you can go easily twenty-one days without food and not die; some have gone forty days and did just fine, but only under medical advice. Most people think that if they miss one meal they are about to die. The human spirit should be in control, not the body. The body should be submissive and obedient to your human spirit, not to your soul, which is your mind, will, and emotions. When you fast without food, it seems to free up your spirit to commune with God; His voice becomes much clearer during a period of fasting.

Man is a spirit housed within a body. The soul is imprisoned by bars of bones. The soul too can cause lots of problems if in charge because it wants to feed the flesh to keep it quiet. Your body is like a big school bully and will try to control both your soul and your human spirit, if possible. The flesh will demand food or alcohol or drugs as it has always been given in your life and will drive your mind crazy with cravings. The body does not care if you die as long as it gets what it wants when it wants it. The body will eat you to death, drink you to death, drug you to death, and smoke you to death if left to itself. You must control the desires of the body with your inner being.

You need to have seasons of fasting to prepare yourself for what is coming. Always consult with your doctor before beginning a fast. I suggest storing about fifteen years of nonperishable foods for the survival of you and your loved ones as we wait and look for our coming Redeemer and the rapture of the Church in about 2027–2028.

Mystery Babylon

Is America the unnamed nation called Mystery Babylon found in Revelation 18? Read Revelation 17 and 18 and you will see the fate of the country in which we live. People get real mad when I suggest this. Pull your heads out of the sand and smell the coffee. We have been the greatest nation on earth, but all nations throughout history have met their doom, and America will be no exception. Destruction is in the air for America, and I am not the only one smelling it. The life of a nation like the United States is about two hundred years; we are now 236 years old.

Could it be the doomsday of America is when the red horse of Iran begins to ride? Or could it be when the third seal is opened and the black horse goes forth from communist Russia? I believe that Revelation 18 could take place before 2028, which is the beginning of the last seven years of Revelation. Just because it is toward the end of the book of Revelation doesn't mean it will be after the Rapture, but I hope I am wrong and we escape. Not all events in Revelation are in chronological order. Maybe, just maybe, the third and fourth seals will not be opened until the last half of the tribulation period.

Likewise also as it was in the days of Lot; they did eat, they drank, they bought, they sold, they planted, they built; But the same day that Lot went out of Sodom it rained fire and brimstone from Heaven, and destroyed them all. Even thus shall it be in the day when the Son of man is revealed. (Luke 17:28–30 KJV)

When the son of man is revealed, could this be talking about when He is revealed in the clouds to take the born-again believers from this earth? The same day that Lot went out of Sodom, fire consumed Sodom instantly. Could it be America is Mystery Babylon and will be destroyed instantly as the church is leaving this earth? As the church goes up, the fire comes in and destroys America in one hour. America has been the stronghold of the Christian faith as the Middle East is the stronghold of Islam.

Could it be as in the days of Lot, when God's children were leaving Sodom and Gomorrah, fire was coming in for total destruction of gay lifestyles of nonbelievers and bestiality as they went after flesh of a different kind?

> And the angels which kept not their first estate, but left their own habitation, he hath reserved in everlasting chains under darkness unto the judgment of the great day. Even as Sodom and Gomorrah, and the cities about them in like manner, giving themselves over to fornication, and going *after strange flesh*, are set forth for an example, suffering the vengeance of eternal fire. Likewise also these filthy dreamers defile the flesh, despise dominion, and speak evil of dignities. (Jude 6–8 KJV)

The white horse of America at 9/11 was the breaking of the first seal. The apocalypse has begun, and economic collapse of the entire world is around the corner. It is about to get more intense. The second seal is next, and the red horse from a country east of Israel is preparing to ride with a great sword (nukes); when we look at the map, Iran is directly east of Israel and Islam is represented by a red flag. Russia has possibly already secretly armed its partner with nuclear weapons, even though it is developing nuclear technology itself.

The two and maybe four horsemen of the apocalypse will ride during a period of twenty-seven years prior to the final seven years of the tribulation period before Armageddon and the end of man's government. Many scholars have always put the four horsemen within the last seven years, but I think this is a mistake. The church will be faced with faith-testing trials before the rapture takes place. This will especially be true for the church in America and their self-centered attitude. It is possible that Revelation 17-18 could and most possibly will take place during the next fourteen years, prior to the final seven years recorded in the book of Revelation.

When John wrote Revelation over nineteen hundred years ago, the new Babylon was a mystery and was sealed up and would not be revealed unto the end. Read the following passages, then the entire two chapters in the Bible, and tell me if you don't believe America is the Mystery Babylon revealed in the end times. Then you just don't want to believe and are deceiving yourself.

Mystery Babylon Destroyed in One Hour

Mystery Babylon will be destroyed in one hour. It will either be by nuclear weapons or by fire falling from heaven like in Sodom. On August 7, 2027, could this be the event from heaven as a big asteroid, not a meteorite, enters into our atmosphere, according to NASA? Read the following Scripture found in the Bible and make your own decision. Plus read the fourteenth chapter of this book on the fourteen reasons or signs for a 2028 date.

> For all nations have drunk of the wine of the wrath of her fornication, and the kings of the Earth have committed fornication with her, and the merchants of the Earth are waxed rich through the abundance of her delicacies. And I heard another voice from Heaven, saying, *Come out of her, my people,* that ye be not partakers of her sins, and that ye receive not of her plagues. For her sins have reached unto Heaven, and God hath remembered her iniquities." (Rev. 18:3–5 KJV) (Could this be the rapture?)

> How much she hath glorified herself, and lived deliciously, so much torment and sorrow give her: for she says in her heart, I sit a queen, and am no widow, and shall see no sorrow. Therefore shall her plagues come in one day, death, and mourning, and famine; and she shall be utterly burned with fire: for strong is the Lord God who judged her. And the kings of the Earth, who have committed fornication and lived deliciously with her, shall bewail her, and lament for her, when they shall see the smoke of her burning, standing afar off for the fear of her torment, saying, alas, alas, that great city Babylon, that mighty city! For in one hour is thy judgment come. And the merchants

of the Earth shall weep and mourn over her; for no man buys their merchandise any more. (Rev. 18:7–11 KJV)

The merchants of these things, which were made rich by her, shall stand afar off for the fear of her torment, weeping and wailing, And saying, Alas, alas, that great city, that was clothed in fine linen, and purple, and scarlet, and decked with gold, and precious stones, and pearls! For in one hour so great riches is come to nothing. And every shipmaster, and all the company in ships, and sailors, and as many as trade by sea, stood afar off, And cried when they saw the smoke of her burning, saying, What city is like unto this great city! (Rev. 18:15–18 KJV) (Could this be describing America with a female president?)

And Babylon, the glory of kingdoms, the beauty of the Chaldeans' Excellency, shall be as when God overthrew Sodom and Gomorrah." (Isa. 13:19 KJV)

The show of their countenance doth witness against them; and they declare their sin as Sodom, they hide it not. Woe unto their soul! For they have rewarded evil unto themselves. (Isa. 3:9 KJV)

And as it was in the days of Noah, so shall it be also in the days of the Son of man. They did eat, they drank, they married wives, they were given in marriage, until the day that Noah entered into the ark, and the flood came, and destroyed them all. Likewise also as it was in the days of Lot; they did eat, they drank, they bought, they sold, they planted, they built; But the same day that Lot went out of Sodom it rained fire and brimstone from Heaven, and destroyed them all. Even thus shall it be in the day when the Son of man is revealed. (Luke 17:26–30 KJV)

And spared not the old world, but saved Noah the eighth person, a preacher of righteousness, bringing in the flood upon the world of the ungodly; And turning the cities of Sodom and Gomorrah into ashes condemned them with an overthrow, making them an example unto those that after should live ungodly. (2 Peter 2:5–6 KJV)

CHAPTER 12

Red Horse of Iran and the Twelfth Imam

The second seal is next to open with the second horseman of the apocalypse getting ready to ride as described in verse 4:

Another horse, fiery red, went out. And it was granted to the one who sat on it to take peace from the earth, and that people should kill one another; and there was given to him a great sword. (Rev. 6:4 NKJV)

Directly east of Israel is Iran. The red horse will ride and take peace from the earth. The rider of the red horse was given a great sword (the nuclear bomb). This seal will open around 2015 and no later than 2021. The opening of this second seal will be an effort by Islam in a move toward world domination. They believe it is their destiny to bring world chaos and dominate the entire world for Islam.

Islam, in these last days, will be guilty of the slaughter of millions of infidels, and the Shiite branch of Islam will be the radical terrorists that will bring about the doomsday of our existing civilization. This third world war will be fought by these three groups that are planning for world domination at the end of time, coming soon to a city near you. Watch these Islamic radicals as they prepare for their coming

Messiah, Imam Al-Mahdi. Like Bernard Lewis of Princeton has said, the former president of Iran, Mahmoud Ahmadinejad, seems to believe the hand of Allah is guiding him to help set in motion a series of cataclysmic events that could bring about the return of the twelfth imam. With this radical position he holds, Iran possessing nuclear weapons brings a scary future for the entire world. His final term as president expired in the summer of 2013, but he has set in motion certain events for Islam's dominance.

Iran's president and the Islamic Republic are not afraid of restoring relations with America but must carefully calculate the benefits and damages of such a decision so independence and honor will be maintained. He said, "Access to nuclear technology is our legitimate right, and no one has the right to stop our march to progress. We *will not surrender.*"

Who Is the Twelfth Imam?

First we have to review a short history lesson on Islam. In the year AD 610 Muhammad was a forty-year-old prophet of Allah. He would retire to a cave in Mecca yearly. In the cave he received visions and revelations from Allah. He proceeded to teach and write these revelations down, and they became the Qur'an of today. He began to preach and teach these revelations to anyone who would listen. His following grew fast; these students slowly became his army, literally.

Muhammad began to conquer great areas of land in the Middle East and proceeded in the founding of the Muslim religion of Islam in about AD 622. He became the supreme authority because Allah was speaking to him. Muhammad died in AD 632 without a son as an heir. He had a daughter, who he loved deeply, and she married his cousin Ali. Before Muhammad died, he announced that he was to be succeeded by his son-in-law, Ali.

Ali became the first imam, and according to the Shiite branch of Islam, there were to be only twelve Imams and the twelfth one was to usher in one world governed by Islam, and the twelfth imam would bring an end to all sin, similar to Jesus and His second coming. So all Muslims are looking for Imam Ai-Mahdi, Islam's future messiah.

Muhammad's Death

First we must go back to Muhammad's death and the conflict that took place within Islam. After the death of their prophet, a great internal power struggle arose as to who his successor would be. This struggle divided Islam into two main branches known as the Shiite (Shias) and the Sunnis, and there has been bad blood ever since the prophet's death. Ninety percent of Muslims are Sunnis, and the remainder are Shiites. In Iran 90 percent of the population are Shiites and only 10 percent are Sunnis.

This is similar to Christianity with Catholics and Protestants. Plus the Shiite imam is similar to the Catholic pope in his authority, and the twelfth imam is more like Jesus and the coming Christian Messiah. The Shias believe that an imam was to be a direct descendant of Muhammad or his son-in-law Ali and that there would be only twelve and the twelfth imam would be the Messiah. They have Shiite clerics (mullahs) that are deputies in the absence of this twelfth imam. They believe that the twelve imams were sinless like Muhammad and that all of their revelations come directly from Allah.

The Shiites in Iran are the most radical branch of Islam. Iran was the second-largest oil producer of OPEC until the sanctions were placed on Iran. Their nuclear ambitions have dropped their ability to ship oil, and now Iraq is the second-largest producer of the OPEC nations. Iran is swimming in an ocean of crude oil. None of them are swimming in debt like Europe and the United States.

The twelfth imam was born around AD 868 at a time of great persecution of Shiites, and in order to protect him, his father, the eleventh imam, sent him into hiding. He appeared in public briefly at the age of seven, when his father died, but then went back into obscurity. Shiites believe after some twelve hundred years he continues to guide Muslims, and they expect his "messianic" return to bring order from chaos and righteousness from unbelief. When this twelfth one is to return as a messiah, it will be revealed by Allah to the inner twelve spiritual leaders of the Shiite system. Then it will be revealed to the next 331 mullahs.

President Ahmadinejad truly believes that the time is now for the twelfth imam's reappearance and that, as president of Iran, he should play a role in opening the way for his return, causing worldwide bloodshed and chaos. Ahmadinejad's term was up in 2013, but he has set in motion Iran's future place in the end times. He believes that creating world chaos will speed up the return of their Messiah.

Will Doomsday Begin in the Middle East?

The answer is *yes*. We know from the Bible that Armageddon will take place in the Middle East. There is already a plan in place, which Islam admits to, where a world war will occur to convert the world to Islam. When the twelfth Imam Al-Mahdi returns to establish global Islam, the Shiites will attempt to establish a one-world government under Sharia law with the twelfth Imam as Allah's world ruler.

Political Islam believes it will take global war for this Imam Al-Mahdi to return, and Iran is willing to cause such a disaster. Look at the unrest in the region with Egypt, Syria, Iraq, Iran, etc. The region is like sticks of dynamite with the fuse already burning. Iran with a nuclear weapon at their disposal will be a world disaster because of their radicalized thinking. Their newly elected president will try to make the world think he has changed Iran to a more peaceful nation—they only want nuclear power for domestic use.

CHAPTER 13

Bizarre Signs in the Sun and Moon

The sun shall be turned into darkness, and the moon into blood, before the great and the terrible day of the Lord come. (Joel 2:31 KJV)

And I will show wonders in Heaven above, and signs in the Earth beneath; blood, and fire, and vapor of smoke: The sun shall be turned into darkness, and the moon into blood, before that great and notable day of the Lord come. (Acts 2:19-20 KJV)

The sun and moon, as described in Acts, will be turned into darkness at the end of the final seven years. When these events take place, you will know we are approaching the Lord's return within days, not months. No one knows the day or the hour of our Lord's return. Only the Father in heaven knows, but there will be signs in the sun and moon signaling within days this final event. When you see this darkness set in, the earth will no longer be able to produce food. These events will take place during the battle of Armageddon at the end of Daniel's seventieth week, which is recorded in the book of Revelation.

We have been living in the last days since Israel became a nation in 1948. This generation that was born in 1948 will not pass away until all things will be fulfilled concerning the battle of Armageddon. A generation according to the Bible is seventy; if you have strength, eighty. On November 29, 1947, the United Nations voted thirty-three to eleven, with ten vote abstentions from the Arab nations that opposed the move, for Israel to return to her homeland and become a nation. Israel made it official in 1948. The generation born in the year of 1948 will not completely pass away until Christ's return. We know a lot of people live to see their eightieth birthday. Let's say a generation is still alive at eighty, and we add eighty to 1948—we come up with 2028.

Blood Red Moons on Passover

Since the year AD 1 we have had seven back-to-back blood-red moons that have fallen on the first day of Passover and Sukkot, with the eighth time coming in 2014 and 2015. The last two red moon cycles were on Passover in 1948 and 1967. Will this next red moon cycle be time for the second seal of Revelation 6 to open? Could this be time for the nation of Iran, more realistically Islam, to ride the red horse of the apocalypse and to take peace from the earth? Will more wars begin during these blood-red moon seasons? In all eight examples of blood-red moons, the eclipses have fallen or will fall on the first day of Passover and Sukkot, and this eighth occurrence of back-to-back blood-red moons will be in 2014–2015. Could the aggressiveness of the Islamic organization ISIL or ISIS be from these blood moons? We know Islam's ultimate goal is the destruction of Israel and America (Rev.4-18).

NASA's research data confirms these blood-red moons on the first day of Passover and the first day of Sukkot have occurred on back-to-back years seven times since AD 1. We know from history that the last two were extremely important to the nation of Israel: 1948–statehood for Israel, and 1967–the War of Independence, known as the Six-Day War. These are extremely important dates in Jewish history.

These rare red moon cycles are watched by Islam and influence their action for war. This blood-red moon is not the event spoken of in Joel and Acts but signals another sign for Islam. It is almost like Allah, the moon god, signals Islam to go to war according to past historical events.

Muhammad's father was a moon worshipper, and their flag has always been the crescent moon, even before Muhammad had formed the Muslim religion. This is an archaeological fact in the history of the Arabic nations. Ishmael left the God of his father Abraham for the idol gods in a temple in Mecca worshipped by his grandfather Terah. Islam has a black moon rock idol, or a meteor rock, housed in Mecca today. This moon rock has become an idol to the Muslim people. Millions of Muslims yearly make a pilgrimage to Mecca and they walk around the Kabah in a circle until they can touch this moon rock as an act of worship. Muhammad removed all of the idols that were in the Kabah and demanded worship be only to Allah. Muslims were to only honor the greatest of all gods, which to the Arabs was Allah.

Bizarre Signs to Evolutionists and Darwinists

NASA and the moon lander revealed bizarre, unexpected signs to the atheists, proving that the religion of evolution is nothing but a lie, myth, or fairytale. When NASA designed the moon lander, leading scientists gave their input to help keep the astronauts safe upon landing on the lunar surface. First they had big, round feet placed on the lunar lander's legs to keep it from sinking too deep in all these billions of years of the evolutionist imaginary moon dust that had accumulated since the big bang. There was a possibility of the thickness of just moon dust being over ten to twenty feet thick, even up to one hundred feet if the moon had been there twenty billion years. If evolution was a fact, then this thickness would be there and the moon lander could get stuck in the dust.

Did you notice that Armstrong had to jump from the ladder because the ladder wasn't long enough? After landing, they discovered the ladder on the Apollo Lander was eighteen inches short because it did not sink down into several feet of moon dust as expected due to the speculated blunder of billions of years of dust accumulation. Armstrong had to jump off the ladder of Darwinian speculation caused by this dumb Darwinian time machine, which randomly comes up with billions of years to support the big bang fairytale.

The moon lander ladder lacked eighteen inches reaching the lunar surface of the moon. Don't take my word for it; look at the moon landing video. This is a big deal because they only found less than half an inch of dust on the moon. This is a very bizarre sign to the atheists who had swallowed this big lie. They literally found only about six thousand years of dust on the moon. *Why* so little dust? Answer: because the universe is only about six thousand years of age, *duh*. Since the moon landing, Darwinists have been franticly trying to establish new theories to explain away this missing moon dust (*bottom line:* they were caught with their pants down). In Darwinism you never have to prove anything, just create a new theory and within a short evolution of time it evolves into hardcore *science, without even a shred of evidence whatsoever!*

The greatest proof that God's creation date of 3973 BC is real is the discovery of less than half an inch of lunar moon dust on the moon's surface. This bizarre fact about the moon dust leaves the Darwinist dumbfounded with disbelief. According to the Bible, God created this universe about six thousand years ago and there should have been less than one inch of dust on the moon. Science has proven this very *fact*. True science proves a young earth!

The following link is a great website with basic scientific proof that the big bang is a big hoax:[24]

Evolution is a lie coming from the bad angels' kingdom of darkness. This amount of dust was a bizarre sign of disbelief to the atheist and evolutionist but not to most Christians that knew God made everything in six days and the earth and moon are not billions of years old as told in the adult fairytale known as the big bang. The earth is only approximately six thousand years old, as described in the Bible. This is solid scientific proof of the age of the earth. This scientific evidence points to creation, not evolution. This small amount of moon dust leaves the evolutionists bewildered and choking in their lack of dust.

Another bizarre sign to the evolutionist is that we are scientifically losing our moon in orbit to the sum of about two inches per year. In other words, the moon has been scientifically observed slowly leaving the earth's orbit. Two inches a year is not a problem if we have only been here six thousand years, but to the evolutionist, this is a major issue. It creates a big problem for their theory; if we have been here billions of years as they claim, the earth would have been so close in only one billion years that the moon would have touched the tops of the trees and mountains.

These facts show just how ridiculous this evolution theory can be. Intelligent Design is the only answer to our origin. Evolution is a faith-based religion and is not fact-based literal science. Evolution and

---

24   http://genesisministry.org/young-earth-evidence/

creation rest upon the discoveries of exact scientific evidence. The bizarre sign is that the evidence the Darwinists want is simply not there, but the scientific evidence they don't want to be discovered is there. True science disproves this theory of evolution, and many facts can be found for a very young earth.

Another bizarre moon sign to the evolutionist is the lunar moon rocks brought back to earth. Science has proven by the moon rocks that the moon is not made of the same material as the earth. This is another black eye for the evolutionist. This destroys the big bang fairytale, and God leaves the evolutionist coughing and choking in their own imaginary moon dust. The bottom line about the moon landing discoveries is that it scientifically disproves this dangerous fairytale *religion* known as evolution.

Another sign is to look at all the moon craters on its surface, yet no one has ever observed the moon being struck. Even on earth, a huge meteor crater located in Arizona has been researched for years and millions of dollars have been spent trying to explain what happened to the asteroid that made the crater. Some come up with a theory that it vaporized and that is possible if it was ice. They have calculated the speed and size of the asteroid to be able to make such a huge crater. All of these craters and more occurred in 2317 BC when the earth's crust split open and formed fault lines. Subterranean water that was under pressure, similar to crude oil, supersonically rocketed into the atmosphere and froze into meteors and large ice asteroids.

Scientists have discovered tons of ice in the heavens, but no water is found on any of the other planets. All of this ice came from Noah's flood in 2317 BC. The Bible tells that most of the water was stored in subterranean chambers, with the crust of the earth being stretched tightly over the chambers (Ps. 24:1-2, 33:7, 136:6, Job 38:8-11).

If you want to know the truth, search YouTube for the Hovind Theory by Dr. Kent Hovind and Dr. Walt Brown's Hydroplate Theory. These Christian theories are about the global flood and the so-called Ice Age. The problem is not the truth but that some of you cannot handle the truth. Some of you do not want to know the truth so you continue to believe the *big lie!* You are afraid you will scientifically be confronted with Christian scientists and their theories will make the most common sense.

In the 1983 book *Holt Modern Earth Science*, page 51 states, "Ice meteors are common in space and are normally -300 to -400 degrees Fahrenheit." Where did all this ice come from? In *Discover Magazine* 1997 an article is titled "A Scientist—and His Theory—Vindicated." In a paper called *Science and Technology* an article's titled, "Water, Water Everywhere—in Space." Scientists make claims to ice in space, so where did all this ice originate?[25]

Bizarre Moon Evidence/a Hollow Moon

NASA started placing seismometers on the moon in 1969, and those instruments were monitoring seismic activity on the moon up until 1977, when they were switched off because it caused such a stir among the Darwinian community. Even the "moonquakes" caused reverberations through the moon that would last a remarkably long time. The moon was ringing like a tuning fork or a church bell on Sunday morning singing "to God be the glory for the things He has done." A seismometer on earth registering earthquakes would die away in less than a minute; our biggest quakes only last about two minutes.

---

[25] http://arstechnica.com/science/2014/01/water-water-everywherein-our-solar-system/

So what's going on with the moon? NASA tried to explain it away by saying that the extended length of these vibrations is most likely caused by the composition of the moon. If the Big Bang is true science, the moon should be the exact same composition as the earth. Again, the evolutionists are caught with their wooden nose getting longer like the fairytale story of Pinocchio.

Another bizarre sign this time is to the Christians. The size of the moon is almost the size of the Holy City. Revelation 21 describes New Jerusalem coming down to the new earth and tells how big New Jerusalem will be. The Holy City is described as a cube, and if you draw a circle around this cube, the Holy City is almost the same size as the moon. Now, the moon is not the Holy City but maybe the Creator of the universe wanted us to look at the moon and realize that's how big the New Jerusalem is going to be. Maybe it will come and orbit the new earth for all eternity in the same way the moon presently orbits this present earth that is *doomed* to be destroyed by *fire* in about AD 2035 and 3035, which is the real end of all time. It will only be remodeled by fire in about 2035 during the battle of Armageddon at the end of human government or as the Bible says "until the time of the Gentiles be fulfilled."

Bizarre Signs in the Sun

One bizarre sign to the evolutionist is that our sun is shrinking or burning up at a rate of about five feet per hour. This cannot be noticed with the naked eye but only scientifically, since the sun is so huge. In fact, the sun is burning up and losing mass, so that means in the past it once was larger. As creationists we believe the sun is only about six thousand years old, and that means the sun was about 6 percent larger when created. This does not create a problem for creationists, but for evolutionists this is a *scientific disaster!* However, in the evolutionary fairytale land of billions of years this is still truly no problem—they will just fabricate another weird theory and label it science. The sun losing mass is a scientific fact that has been well established. The sun is slowly getting smaller. That means it once was bigger. Before the flood there was a vapor canopy around the earth filtering out the sun rays.

The sun being larger in the past is no problem if you believe in intelligent design or creation. But if you are an evolutionist, this is an extremely bizarre sign and becomes a major problem for your burned-up worldview. The sun used to be larger, and in only one hundred thousand years the sun would have been twice its size! Duh! Hello! No life could have existed on earth under this dumb idea presented by Charles Darwin. In less than one million years, the sun would have been over ten times its size, and the earth's surface would have been toast. When you scientifically think out this Darwinian fairytale, you can easily get lost in their wonderland of unlimited imaginations. Only a person very badly deceived could be sucked into this nonscientific worldview.

The End of Government

The final bizarre signs will be at the end of human governments or the final time of the Gentiles. The smoke from everything burning on this earth will darken the skies and black out the sun. The smoke will also turn the moon blood red, and it will be out of season for a red moon. It will stay red for days from the smoke of the burning earth. When this happens, if you are still alive on this earth, then lift up your heads and start looking for the King of Kings; the Creator of all things is coming to earth at any moment to remodel the earth for the last time and set up a thousand-year kingdom. This kingdom will be a total tropical paradise on earth.

The atheists and unbelievers will hide in the rocks and "beg for the rocks and mountains to cover them and hide them from the Glory of King Jesus," for man's government has come to an end as foretold in the written Word of the Living God, and man's government will never successfully rise again. Life as you know it has ended, and a new millennium is about to be revealed. God is about to renovate this earth one more time for the King of glory and His thousand-year governmental reign. No more corrupt politicians—sounds a little like heaven on earth, doesn't it? Next we will look at fourteen reasons for doomsday AD 2028.

CHAPTER 14

Fourteen Signs for Earth's Doomsday

This chapter focuses on the evidence that points to 2028 being the beginning of the last seven years before the end of human government and Christ's coming kingdom. The following fourteen items are a list of signs and reasons supporting my theory, so I put them all in one chapter to be read showing the beginning of the apocalypse and the destruction of America in fourteen years.

The last days actually refer to the last days of human government, and the end of time will come at the end of Christ's thousand-year kingdom. Some signs are general last-day predictions and others are more specific to 2028. A theory without any evidence does not qualify as a theory but only a fairytale. For example, macro evolution has no solid scientific evidence, none, and it should be classified as a fairytale, not a theory. Evolution is not a theory but a myth. It is a smoke screen of billions of imaginary years used to blind you from the truth and baptize you into Darwinism.

This chapter offers evidence for the year 2028. Before we examine these fourteen signs, I want you to read the prophecy of Isaiah 24 concerning the end before Christ establishes His divine government.

This is coming to a city near you as the Creator of the universe brings an end to a human government that has destroyed over six billion residents of earth.

Destruction of the Earth

(This is the end of human government and God's second destruction of the face of the earth which will come by fire as foreseen by Isaiah over 2,500 years ago, concerning the Last Days.)

According to Wikipedia, a total of twenty-two copies of Isaiah were found in the Dead Sea Scrolls.[26]

> Look! The Lord is about to destroy the Earth and make it a vast wasteland. He devastates the surface of the Earth and scatters the people. Priests and lay people, servants and masters, maids and mistresses, buyers and sellers, lenders and borrowers, bankers and debtors—none will be spared. The Earth will be completely emptied and looted. The Lord has spoken! The Earth mourns and dries up, and the crops waste away and wither. Even the greatest people on Earth waste away. The Earth suffers for the sins of its people, for they have twisted God's instructions, violated his laws, and broken his everlasting covenant. Therefore, a curse consumes the earth. Its people must pay the price for their sin. *They are destroyed by fire* [the first time by Noah's flood and this second time by Fire during Armageddon], and only a few are left alive.

---

[26]   http://en.wikipedia.org/wiki/Dead_Sea_scrolls

The grapevines waste away, and there is no new wine. All the merrymakers sigh and mourn. The cheerful sound of tambourines is stilled; the happy cries of celebration are heard no more. The melodious chords of the harp are silent. Gone are the joys of wine and song; alcoholic drink turns bitter in the mouth. The city writhes in chaos; every home is locked to keep out intruders. Mobs gather in the streets, crying out for wine. Joy has turned to gloom. Gladness has been banished from the land. The city is left in ruins, its gates battered down. Throughout the Earth the story is the same—only a remnant is left, like the stray olives left on the tree or the few grapes left on the vine after harvest. But all who are left shout and sing for joy. Those in the west praise the Lord's majesty. In eastern lands, give glory to the Lord. In the lands beyond the sea, praise the name of the Lord, the God of Israel. We hear songs of praise from the ends of the Earth, songs that give glory to the Righteous One! But my heart is heavy with grief. Weep for me, for I wither away. Deceit still prevails, and treachery is everywhere. Terror and traps and snares will be your lot, you people of the Earth. Those who flee in terror will fall into a trap, and those who escape the trap will be caught in a snare. The foundations of the Earth shake. The Earth has broken up. It has utterly collapsed; it is violently shaken. The Earth staggers like a drunk. It trembles like a tent in a storm. It falls and will not rise again, for the guilt of its rebellion is very heavy. In that day the *Lord will punish the gods in the heavens* [fallen angels and demons or, to some, Ancient Aliens] *and the proud rulers of the nations on Earth. They will be rounded up and put in prison. They will be shut up in prison and will finally be punished. Then the glory of the moon will wane, and the brightness of the sun will fade,* for the Lord of Heaven's Armies will rule on Mount Zion [Christ's divine government in about AD 2035]. He will rule in great glory in Jerusalem, in the sight of all the leaders of his people. (Isa. 24:1–23 NLT)

Sign 1

The Last Generation before Armageddon

1- The coming of scoffers and mockers.

Knowing this first, that there shall come in the last days scoffers, walking after their own lusts, and saying, where is the promise of his coming? For since the fathers fell asleep, all things continue as they were from the beginning of the creation. (2 Peter 3:3–4 KJV)

2- Men in love with themselves.

For men shall be lovers of their own selves, covetous, boasters, proud, blasphemers, disobedient to parents, unthankful, unholy, Without natural affection, trucebreakers, false accusers, incontinent, fierce, despisers of those that are good, Traitors, heady, high-minded, lovers of pleasures more than lovers of God. (2 Tim. 3:2–4 KJV)

This is describing our times look at all the senseless killings.

3- Men will go to and fro upon the earth. Easy, quick global transportation is available. For thousands of years, transportation was horse and buggies, and within one hundred years we are flying globally and driving BMWs, Fords, Chevrolets, etc. It is just unreal how transportation has advanced. We are the generation that has gone to the moon and put landers on Mars.

4- Massive increase in knowledge in the last days. Look how quickly things have changed since the nineties. We are the generation of computers, microchips, and iPads. Social media consumes most of everyone's life. DNA manipulation and cloning is reality. We are the knowledge generation predicted by Daniel in the last days, and his prophecy is no longer sealed.

5- In the last days, murder and lawlessness would drastically increase. School shootings are reported almost every day and are in abundance. Do you remember the theater shooting at the Batman movie? Workplace shootings and jealousy shootings (killing girlfriend or wife and then self) are often reported on the news. The murder rates of big cities have increased. This sign alone says last days. We are the final generation that has gone mad with murder and lawlessness. It will get worse before we reach the battle of Armageddon in 2035.

6- Wars and rumors of wars: Central America, Mexican drug wars, Arab Spring, now double trouble in Egypt, and the list goes on and on. This is all just the beginning of troubles.

7- Powerless churches abandoning the Word of God and teaching feel-good messages. Denying the blood that bought them, they have a form of godliness but are denying the power thereof. Look at the Laodicean church described in the book of Revelation.

8- A doomsday spirit of fear hangs over the world population. We have doomsday preppers, doomsday movies, doomsday predictions, and doomsday books with men's hearts failing them for what is coming on the earth.

> [Jesus made this statement] I still have many things to say unto you, but ye cannot bear them now. However when He, the Spirit of truth, is come, He will guide you into all truth: for He shall not speak of Himself; but whatsoever He shall hear, that shall He speak: and *He will show you things to come.* (John 16:12–13 NKJV

Sign 2

The Parable of the Fig Tree

> Now learn a parable of the fig tree; When his branch is yet tender, and puts forth leaves, ye know that summer is nigh:. So likewise ye, when ye shall see all these things, know that it is near, even at the doors. Verily I say unto you, *this generation shall not pass,* till all these things be fulfilled. Heaven and Earth shall pass away, but my words shall not pass away. (Matt. 24:32–35 KJV)

It was prophesied that Israel would become a nation again, for they had been scattered among all the nations of the world since AD 70 and had no country or government of their own (Ezek. 37:1–17, the prophecy of the valley of dry bones). It was also prophesied that the generation of people born during the return of the Jews to their homeland will not pass away until all of these end-time prophecies be fulfilled (Luke 21:25–36). Israel is portrayed as a fig tree and the budding of the leaves is Israel becoming a nation. The generation born when Israel became a nation will be the final generation before the last seven years foretold in the book of Revelation; Israel will become a burden to all nations (Zech. 12:2–3).

> The days of our years are threescore years and ten [70];
> and if by reason of strength they be fourscore [80] years,
> yet is their strength labor and sorrow; for it is soon cut
> off, and we fly away. (Ps. 90:10 KJV)

According to this Psalm, a generation is seventy; if you have strength, eighty. The generation that witnessed Israel becoming a nation will not pass away until the end comes. This event was fulfilled in the spring of 1948. This recognition by the United Nations of the right of the Jewish people to establish their state is irrevocable.

> Therefore say, 'thus says the Lord God: "I will gather
> you from the peoples, assemble you from the countries
> where you have been scattered, and I will give you the
> land of Israel." (Ezek. 11:17 KJV)

After *nineteen hundred years*, this prophecy prediction of the Jewish people returning to their home became a reality. God is faithful concerning His promises. The United Nations voted after World War II to allow the nation of Israel to return to their homeland, and they became an independent nation. If you add the maximum generation of eighty to those who were born after 1948, you will come up with the date of AD 2028.

In the prophecy regarding the last generation, they would be like the generation in the days of Noah. The valley of dry bones in Ezekiel's prophecy was that a valley of bones would live again. This prophecy came true in 1948, and the generation that was born in that time would not pass away until all of these end-time predictions were fulfilled.

Sign 3

As It Was in the Days of Noah

There is an end-time prophecy that the end will be like the days of Noah and also like the days of Lot. During the days of Noah, it was a global destruction, but in the days of Lot it was just certain cities that were destroyed by fire from heaven. The prophecy about Lot's days will occur just prior to the rapture; probably as the church goes out, fire comes in. I believe that within that same year the tribulation period should begin with the signing of a seven-year peace agreement between the Antichrist and Israel. In the prophecy about Lot, God targets key cities of the world for heated destruction and the unleashing of His wrath against unbelievers. Destruction of the earth took place in the six hundredth year of Noah's life. Armageddon will take place after six thousand years of sinful man's life.

> And as it was in the days of Noah, so it will be also in the days of the Son of Man: They ate, they drank, they married wives, they were given in marriage, until the day that Noah entered the ark, and the flood came and destroyed them all. Likewise as it was also in the days of Lot: They ate, they drank, they bought, they sold, they planted, and they built; but on the day that

Lot went out of Sodom it rained fire and brimstone from Heaven and destroyed them all. Even so will it be in the day when the Son of Man is revealed. (Luke 17:26–30 NKJV)

And it came to pass, when men began to multiply on the face of the Earth, and daughters were born unto them, That the sons of God [always refers to angels in Hebrew, never sons of Seth] saw the daughters of men [in the original Hebrew it says "daughters of Adam," not Cain or Seth] that they were fair; and they took them wives of all which they chose. And the Lord said, my spirit shall not always strive with man, for that he also is flesh: yet his days shall be an hundred and twenty years. There were giants in the Earth in those days; and also after that, when the sons of God came in unto the daughters of men, and they bear children to them, the same became mighty men which were of old, men of renown. And God saw that the wickedness of man was great in the Earth, and that every imagination of the thoughts of his heart was only evil continually. And it repented the Lord that he had made man on the Earth, and it grieved him at his heart. And the Lord said, I will destroy man whom I have created from the face of the Earth both man, and beast, and the creeping thing, and the fowls of the air; for it repented me that I have made them. (Gen. 6:1–7 KJV)

[Man tried to keep Jude out of the Bible because he quoted from the book of 1 Enoch, and later twenty-five copies of 1 Enoch were found in the Dead Sea Scrolls, proving it to be part of the Old Testament.] And the *angels* which kept not their first estate, but left their own habitation, he hath reserved in everlasting chains under darkness unto the judgment of the great day. [the angels] *Even as* Sodom and Gomorrah, and the cities about them *in like manner, giving themselves over to fornication, and going after strange flesh,* are set forth for an example, suffering the vengeance of eternal fire. (Jude 6–7 KJV)

The wicked are too proud to seek God. They seem to think that God is dead. Yet they succeed in everything they do. They do not see your punishment awaiting them. They sneer at all their enemies. They think, "Nothing bad will ever happen to us! We will be free of trouble forever!" Arise, O Lord! Punish the wicked, O God! Do not ignore the helpless! Why do the wicked get away with despising God? They think, "God will never call us to account." But you see the trouble and grief they cause. You take note of it and punish them. (Ps. 10:4–14 NLT)

The Nephilim were on the earth during Noah's days. Will the Nephilim return in the last days? According to Daniel 2:43 and Matthew 24, they will mingle themselves with the seed of men. Read the last chapter of this book, for it covers this subject.

Sign 4

Barnabas Prophesied of Seven Thousand Years

Barnabas foretold of a virtual time clock of six thousand years for man's government and a final one thousand years for Jesus Christ's kingdom, the millennial reign of Christ. On God's time clock it was only a seven-day period—six days for Adam's race and one day for God's only begotten Son's kingdom!

When you study all seventy books of the Bible, instead of only the sixty-six books man has allowed you to have, an overview of the entire plan of God starts coming into view from beginning to end. God made all things in six twenty-four-hour days and rested on the seventh from all His labor. God didn't use a hammer. He didn't use a backhoe. He just spoke and it all happened. The English word *universe* best describes what happened: uni means single or one, and verse means spoken sentence, so we all live in a single spoken sentence. God said, "Let there be light" and it was so (universe).

We see this same six/seven pattern for the life span of all of the descendants of Adam with one exception: the days are each one thousand years long. Now to man, a thousand years is a thousand years, but to God it is only like a day. We are not referring to creation but to how long man will be able to keep time while on this earth.

In J.B. Lightfoot's translation of the epistle of Barnabas we find these three verses:

> Of the Sabbath He speaks in the beginning of the creation; And God made the works of His hands in six days, and He ended on the seventh day, and rested on it, and He hallowed it. Give heed, children, what this means; He ended in six days. He means this, that in six

thousand years the Lord shall bring all things to an end; for the day with Him signifies a thousand years; and this He himself bears me witness, saying; Behold, the day of the Lord shall be as a thousand years. Therefore, children, in six days, which is in six thousand years, everything shall come to an end. And He rested on the seventh day. This He means; when His Son shall come, and shall abolish the time of the Lawless One, and shall judge the ungodly, and shall change the sun and the moon and the stars, then shall he truly rest on the seventh day. (Barnabas 15:3-5) [In most translations of Barnabas these verses can be found in Chapter 13]

Time only exists in a window of 7,007 years. Before creation there was no time, and after the kingdom of Christ, there will be no time. To God it is seven days, and on the eighth day, in about AD 3035, He will make all things new and time will be no more.

I believe the epistle of Barnabas is the one book missing from the New Testament. It will make twenty-eight books, which can be divided by seven. The epistle of Barnabas was not allowed in the Bible because it had too many quotes from the book of Enoch. Hello, why wouldn't they quote from this most popular and oldest biblical historical book! Enoch was the third-most-popular book of the Bible during Jesus', Jude's, and Barnabas's time walking on this earth, with over twenty-five copies of 1 Enoch being found in the Dead Sea Scrolls. Jude only made it into the Bible with direct quotes from Enoch because he was one of the brothers of our Lord.[27]

Also Hippolytus, a Roman theologian, spoke about this seven thousand-year period in the third century AD. "And six thousand

---

[27]   http://en.wikipedia.org/wiki/Dead_Sea_Scrolls

holy day years must needs be accomplished, in order that the Sabbath may come, the one day which God rested from all His work. The Sabbath is a type and emblem of the future Kingdom of Christ and the resurrected saints."[28]

Lucius Caecilius Firmianus Lactantius, a Christian apologist of the fourth century, writes:

> Therefore let the philosophers, who enumerate thousands of ages from the beginning of the world, know that the six thousandth year is not yet completed, and that when this number is completed the consummation must take place, and the condition of human affairs be remodeled for the better, the proof of which must first be related, that the matter itself may be plain. Therefore, since all the works of God were completed *in six days, the world must continue in its present state through six ages, that is, six thousand years.* For the great day of God is limited by a circle of a thousand years, as the prophet shows, who says *"In Thy sight, O Lord, a thousand years are as one day."* And as God labored during those six days in creating such great works, so His religion and truth must labor during these six thousand years, while wickedness prevails and bears rule. And again, since God, having finished His works, rested the seventh day and blessed it, at the end of the six thousandth year all wickedness must be abolished from the earth, and righteousness reign for a thousand years; and there must be tranquility and rest from the labors which the world now has long endured.

---

[28] http://w0ww.ccel.org/ccel/schaff/anf05.iii.iv.i.x.ii.html

This is only a portion of the article from "The Church Fathers, Divine Institute, Book VII Chap. XIV.—Of the First and Last Times of the World."

Sign 5

In the Last Days Many Will Claim to be Christ

The Antichrist is among us. Record numbers of people claim to be Jesus Christ, the Messiah reincarnated in the flesh. We need to be watching for an additional sign of the Jewish people leaving America in large numbers. A mass exodus of Jews will leave America between 2021 and 2028, if not by the year 2015, during the blood-red moon cycles and another market crash coming within that same year, which may be worse than September 2008.

> For many shall come in my name, saying, "*I am the Christ*;" and shall lead many astray. (Matt. 24:5 KJV)

Police report record numbers of cases of lunatics claiming to be Jesus, the Messiah, and claiming the end of the world is now. Police claim that in every city they are confronted with these lunatics, and they take place almost every day. Go into any jail in America and in one or more of the cells are people who claim to be Jesus preaching the same message. Now it is the end of the world. We have always had a few lunatics but not in the mass numbers seen today with all of them proclaiming the same message: the end of time is here.[29]

---

[29] http://www.ucadia.com/me/m12/m122000.htm; http://en.wikipedia.org/wiki/Jerusalem_syndrome; http://freethoughtnation.com/dangerous-delusions-the-messiah-complex-and-jerusalem-syndrome/.

If you have a mental case, most or all of them at one time or another think that they are Jesus reincarnated and they think they need to warn the world that the end is now. Most mental cases come from past or present drug or alcohol abuse. Drugs and alcohol usually open the door to the spirit realm, which is why most liquor stores have names like Bob's Spirit Store or Your Friendly Spirit Store or Discount Spirit Store. The unseen problem is the spirit realm that's influencing their thought process. For some reason it is voodoo to say that a crazy person has deep-rooted spiritual problems and is being influenced by demon spirits. Could it be that it is just not politically correct? Doctors of mental establishments are overwhelmed, and the system has just about collapsed because of their unbelief in the Bible and the spirit world. If you do not seek a Christian psychologist, you are basically doomed before you even start. In every case in the Bible, Jesus cast out the demons before He healed the crazy persons or the lunatics.

Sign 6

The Prophecy of St. Nilus

St. Nilus was one of the many disciples of St. John Chrysostom (AD 347–407). He was an officer at the court of Constantinople, married with two sons, and later became a priest. His works, including a multitude of letters, consist of denunciations of heresy, paganism, abuses of discipline and crimes asceticism with its rules and principles. St. Nilus died around the year AD 430, and the following is what he prophesied. This amazingly accurate prophecy made in the fourth century goes as follows:

After the year 1900, toward the middle of the 20th century, the people of that time will become unrecognizable. When the time for the Advent of the Antichrist approaches, people's minds will grow cloudy from carnal passions, and dishonor and lawlessness will grow stronger. Then the world will become unrecognizable. People's appearances will change, and it will be impossible to distinguish men from women due to their shamelessness in dress and style of hair. These people will be cruel and will be like wild animals because of the temptations of the Antichrist. There will be no respect for parents and elders; love will disappear; and Christian pastors, bishops, and priests will become vain men, completely failing to distinguish the right-hand way from the left.

At that time the morals and traditions of Christians and of the Church will change. People will abandon modesty, and dissipation will reign. Falsehood and greed will attain great proportions, and woe to those who pile up treasures. Lust, adultery, homosexuality, secret deeds, and murder will rule in society. At that future time, due to the power of such great crimes and licentiousness, people will be deprived of the grace of the Holy Spirit, which they received in Holy Baptism and equally of remorse. The Churches of God will be deprived of God-fearing and pious pastors, and woe to the Christians remaining in the world at that time; they will completely lose their faith because they will lack the opportunity of seeing the light of knowledge from anyone at all. Then they will separate themselves out of the world in holy refuges in search of lightening their spiritual sufferings, but everywhere they will meet obstacles and constraints.

And all this will result from the fact that the Antichrist wants to be Lord over everything and become the ruler of the whole universe. The Antichrist will produce miracles and fantastic signs. He will also give depraved wisdom to an unhappy man so that *he will discover a way by which one man can carry on a conversation with another from one end of the earth to the other [the cell phone]. At that time men will also fly through the air like birds and descend to the bottom of the sea like fish.* And when they have achieved all this, these unhappy people will spend their lives in comfort without knowing, poor souls, that it is deceit of the Antichrist. And, the impious one! —he will so *complete science with vanity that it will go off the right path and lead people to lose faith in the existence of God* in three hypostases [the godless teaching of Darwinism].

According to Wikipedia, in ancient times the word *hypostases* had this meaning:

In its ancient usage, *hypothesis* referred to a summary of the plot of a classical drama. The English word *hypothesis* comes from the Ancient Greek ὑπόθεσις (hypothesis), meaning "to put under" or "to suppose."

Then the all-good God will see the downfall of the human race and will shorten the days for the sake of those few who are being saved, because the enemy wants to lead even the chosen into temptation, if that is possible... then the sword of chastisement will suddenly appear and kill the perverted and his servants (Second Coming of Christ).

This prophecy is almost unbelievable because it was given in the fourth century. St. Nilus in the fourth century predicted the twentieth century with chilling accuracy. These things would take place at the time when Jesus Christ will be making His return visit as King of Kings and Lord of Lords and every knee shall bow and every tongue will confess that He is Lord.[30]

Sign 7

America Prepares for Doomsday

The US government has an active doomsday plan. Within America's plan is four 747 doomsday planes. These are 747s on steroids and are ready at all times. The planes are over two hundred tons, and most everything is state of the art, but some things are old in case of digital computer failure. America is preparing for doomsday, and the battle of Armageddon is all biblical in nature. A fear of doomsday is without a doubt in the air in America, and half of the population is expecting a governmental and economic collapse at any time. America's Doomsday Center is in Colorado, and the government has created a five-acre city within a solid granite mountain fully self-contained. They actually call it the Mountain.

There are two special prophecies that are tailor-made for America. When the Bible was written, America did not exist and these prophecies were given over nineteen hundred years ago. One is found in the gospel of Luke, and the second is found in the book of Revelation. First we will look at Luke 17:28–30 and what the Bible says about the days of Lot. History says Lot pitched his tent toward Sodom because it was a well-watered plain. Finally, Lot ended up as a judge at Sodom's city gate.

---

[30] http://www.traditioninaction.org/Questions/B249_StNilus.html; http://en.wikipedia.org/wiki/Nilus_of_Sinai; http://www.fisheaters.com/nilus.htm.

Lot had several daughters while living in Sodom, and one of his daughters was burned alive at the stake for helping a poor beggar who was dying in the town square. Feeding anyone in need was a Sodom law punishable by death. Sodom's government was trying to make an example out of Lot's daughter for showing compassion to someone in need. This example was to stop anyone else from feeding the poor and hungry.

The government of Sodom was very corrupt. They approved and encouraged residents to live openly in their gay lifestyle. America's leaders also encourage gay marriage and will sell their souls for a vote on Election Day. The reason Sodom was destroyed was because the government had become so corrupt.

Likewise also as it was in the days of Lot; they did eat, they drank, they bought, they sold, they planted, they builded; but the same day that Lot went out of Sodom it rained fire and brimstone from Heaven, and destroyed them all. *Even thus shall it be in the day when the Son of man is revealed.* (Luke 17:28–30 KJV)

The day God's people were taken out of Sodom, fire came down in judgment. This Son of Man being revealed could be talking about the rapture, the taking out of God's true born-again children. On the day of the rapture, destruction will come on certain cities in America.

The second prophecy toward America is concerning a nation that did not exist nineteen hundred years ago when this prophecy was written. When John saw the vision of this mighty nation in the last days, he could only compare it to the mighty world empire of Babylon. This mystery nation has no name because it did not exist in the first century. So John named it or labeled it Mystery Babylon.[31]

Read the prophecy in Revelation 17–18. We have an unnamed nation that John called Mystery Babylon. Read it and you decide;

---

[31]   http://www.whitehorsemedia.com/articles/?d=111#.UuSGRtfnbIV

this prophecy is tailor-made for America. This prophecy was written in the first century. John had a vision of a mighty, rich nation that was likened to the Mighty Babylon of his day, so he called it Mystery Babylon. America had no name because it did not exist, but he saw it in his vision of the end times.

I challenge you to read Rev. 17-18. Compare it to the United States, and then make your decision. The characteristics that are in the prophecy are very chilling, and it has to be America; no other nation fits the bill. It talks about the economy of this new nation and mentions its purchasing power and the merchant ships that unload cargo at its seaports. John talks about how much stuff it buys and that its destruction will come in a single day. This new nation will be destroyed by fire, and John talks about the smoke of its burning. Its doomsday will come in a single day.

I think America has its own personal last seven to ten years of pretribulation woes beginning in about 2017 or no later than 2021. This final ten years in America will be a dark time of testing for the church before the rapture. This time will not be Daniel's seventieth week but will have a lot of the same characteristics. The US dollar will crash and things will become worthless, and the complete world economy will crash and experience the worst depression ever. Hyperinflation will be rampant. The middle class will almost disappear.

Banks are required to maintain only one-tenth of your deposit. There will be a run on banks, and many will lose all their savings. The government will not be able to secure the deposits, and men's hearts will fail them for what is coming on this earth.

Read this prophecy in Revelation 17–18 and judge for yourself. John was seeing America during the last days. John sees her destruction come in one day, and I am convinced this time of destruction for America will be no later than 2028. The removal of the church, in an event known as the rapture, will take place prior to America's final destruction. Then after several years of a dark time, the final seven years will begin as described in the books of Revelation and Daniel.

All great democracies have committed financial suicide somewhere around two hundred years after being founded.

The voters realize they can vote themselves money from the government treasury by electing people who promise to give them government money in exchange for their election.

The United States became a republic in 1776, which was 236 years ago. In fourteen years America, which is declining fast, will be 250 years old in 2028! We are a republic but have turned into a democracy with voters wanting more benefits. We are in a death spiral with only about fourteen years or less to live as a nation.[32]

Sign 8

Daniel's Prophecy + The Church Age = 2028

Daniel's prophecy of 490 years had a specific starting point that can be found in archaeology today. Daniel 9:25 states: "from the going forth of a commandment to restore and rebuild Jerusalem until Messiah the Prince will be 483 years." In 458 BC a decree was given to help the Jews restore Jerusalem. If you add 483 years to 458 BC, you come up with AD 26, very close to when Jesus rode in Jerusalem on a donkey as they spread palm leaves in front of Him and the people declared Him Prince and King. If we add the church age of two thousand years to that date we come up with AD 2026. This is how I estimate the

32 http://across.co.nz/democracy.html; http://answers.yahoo.com/question/
index?qid=20120623195959AACx8EF;
http://apatheticvoter.com/Article_DownfallDemocracies.htm.

following dates, and in approximately 2027 or 2028 and no later than AD 2030, the church will be removed from this earth.

This will approximately begin the final seven years predicted by John the Revelator. Children of God, lift up your heads and look up, for your redemption draws near. There is seven years of perfection in the garden before the six thousand-year period begins and seven years of pure hell on earth to end this final period of human government. It will all come to a climax with the battle of Armageddon in about AD 2035.

We truly don't know the day or the hour of Jesus' return in the clouds to remove all those that are in Christ. We truly don't know the *day* or the *hour* when He will come down to earth as conquering King, with all His angels and all of His resurrected saints following behind to help Him rule the earth. But if the calendar is correct, we will know the season and maybe the year He will redeem the Church. Only the Father in heaven knows the *day* and the *hour* of the returning King. Your purpose is to not worry but to rescue the perishing.

The key date in all history is the crucifixion of Jesus Christ and His resurrection from the dead. Take time and look very carefully; Jesus was possibly born in the seventh Jewish month (7/7/7) (Sept/Oct) or November or December of 7 BC, which is two years before Herod's death, which happened in March of 4 BC. Maybe Jesus was born in December as we celebrate and only a few days before 6 BC began (maybe 12/7/7). I know how God loves the perfect number seven, and six is just not His favorite number, but it is for man and 666 is mark of the beast. I just cannot see Jesus being born in 6 BC as I cannot agree with only sixty-six books of the Bible; there are at a minimum at least seventy books in our written Bible.

But here is a thought: maybe Jesus was born in 7/7/7 BC, in the Jewish seventh month, which is October in the Gregorian calendar, on the seventh day, and in the Roman year of 7 BC. Jesus was then crucified thirty-three and one-half years later in AD 28, which is exactly 1,993 years of the two thousand years allotted for the children of Israel. This leaves seven years for the seventh week of Daniel described in Revelation 4–18, which will close out the two thousand years of the Abrahamic Covenant found in Daniel 9 and make an end of sins, bringing in everlasting righteousness and anointing of the most holy.

Take some time and look at the seventy weeks of Daniel's prophecy as it reveals this final 490 years of the second two thousand-year covenant. It has a date to begin by a certain issuing of a document to restore and rebuild Jerusalem. In 458 BC, Persian King Artaxerxes issued this very document evidenced in archaeology. I am fully aware that two other decrees were issued, but this is the only one that adds up correctly, leading up to the Messiah being cut off. The other decrees will not end up in this AD 27 to 34 range for Jesus' death. There are many different theories and thoughts about this subject. I only wanted to make you aware of it. If you use a Jewish calendar which has 360 days, some scholars calculate Daniel's prophecy to be the exact day Christ was crucified.

If you add 490 years minus seven, you should get about the same date of AD 28. I know I have repeated myself several times. If you don't get it the first time, then maybe it will register the second or third. Children of God, be alert and don't let these events or dates catch you unaware.

The Final Judgment

"But when the Son of Man comes in his glory, and all the angels with him, then he will sit upon his glorious throne. All the nations will be gathered in his presence, and he will separate the people as a shepherd separates the sheep from the goats. He will place the sheep at his right hand and the goats at his left. Then the King will say to those on his right, 'Come, you who are blessed by my Father, inherit the Kingdom prepared for you from the creation of the world. For I was hungry, and you fed me. I was thirsty, and you gave me a drink. I was a stranger, and you invited me into your home. I was naked, and you gave me clothing. I was sick, and you cared for me. I was in prison, and you visited me. Then these righteous ones will reply, 'Lord, when did we ever see you hungry and feed you? Or thirsty and give you something to drink? Or a stranger and show you hospitality? Or naked and give you clothing? When did we ever see you sick or in prison and visit you. And the King will say, 'I tell you the truth, when you did it to one of the least of these my brothers and sisters, you were doing it to me! Then the King will turn to those on the left and say, 'Away with you, you cursed ones, into the eternal fire prepared for the devil and his demons. For I was hungry, and you didn't feed me. I was thirsty, and you didn't give me a drink. I was a stranger, and you didn't invite me into your home. I was naked, and you didn't give me clothing. I was sick and in prison, and you didn't visit me. Then they will reply, 'Lord, when did we ever see you hungry or thirsty or a stranger or naked or sick or in prison, and not help you? And he will answer, 'I tell you the truth, when you refused to help the least of these my brothers and sisters, you were refusing to help me. And they will go away into eternal punishment, but the righteous will go into eternal life.'" (Matthew 25:31–26:13 NLT)

Jesus Heals Two Demon-Possessed Men

When Jesus arrived on the other side of the lake, in the region of the Gadarenes, two men who were possessed by demons met him. They lived in a cemetery and were so violent that no one could go through that area. They began screaming at him, "Why are you interfering with us, Son of God? Have you come here to torture us *before God's appointed time?*" (Matt. 8:28–29 NLT)

There is an appointed day of doom and judgment set for the unbelievers and the entire world. Nothing will change this appointed date. Only you can change your destiny with this date. Give your heart and life to Christ, who was crucified for your sins. It is a free gift wrapped just for you.

Sign 9

Doomsday Calendars

So we ask the question why 2027? This is the year when the Aztec Calendar Round restarts. Unlike the Mayan Calendar, which ended in 2012, the Aztecs had no tradition of the Long Count; they only had the Calendar Round. The Five Suns prophecy states that the sun has been remade four times prior to this and we are now waiting the fifth and final sun. What we have is an Aztec prophecy and an Aztec calendar that restarts in 2027.

2027 the End of the Zapotec Calendar in Mexico

The Mayan Calendar ended in December 2012. They had no actual doomsday prophecy. However, the Aztecs and the Zapotec had a doomsday prophecy at the end of their calendar in 2027.

Jewish Calendar/Bumping Six Thousand Since Creation

The start of the coming kingdom should be AD 2035 if 2028 is correct in the Gregorian calendar, considering the final seven years.

> The people of Israel had lived in Egypt for 430 years. In fact, it was on the last day of the 430th year that all the Lord's forces left the land. On this night the Lord kept his promise to bring his people out of the land of Egypt. (Ex. 12:40–42 NLT)

The Sanhedrin in Judea ceased to function or to maintain calendar experts. While Hillel II is credited with the present fixed calendar, it is the result of centuries of development and the aim to perfect a system of fixing the calendar. It was not until Christianity became dominant and Christian rulers forbade the Jewish religious leadership to proclaim leap years or to communicate with the Diaspora that it was decided to abandon the method of official proclamation of the months and years and to fix the calendar in a permanent form.

In AD 2028 we find the year 5808 since creation in the Jewish calendar. The calendar only allowed 210 years for the Egyptian bondage, so we are going to add an adjustment of 190 years for their stay of 400 years in Egypt, and seven years still awaiting the tribulation period. With all adjustments, it gives you a Jewish calendar with 6,005 years since God created all things. Subtract Adam's time in the garden before he sinned, seven years and one month and seventeen days, and you have 5,998 years, very close to six thousand for man's rule since the fall of man or, to God, six days. Now we are ready for the seventh day of rest, the coming one thousand years of Christ's kingdom. Historically, the Jewish calendar is the result of a long series of revisions and adjustments. We just made one more adjustment. The Egyptian bondage is found in Genesis 15:13–14 and also in Acts 7:6, and after all their work on the calendar they only could find 210 years for slavery in Egypt. I put no trust in the Jewish calendar except for the first three thousand years. But this shows just how close we are to six thousand years since Adam first sinned.

Sign 10

2027: Target Completion Date—New World Order

A source that wants to remain anonymous says the talk among the top elite of the New World Order is that no later than 2027 the NWO will take over global governments. If you want to know how this global government is going to operate, then go back and watch films and read articles on the Nazis and the Third Reich. The New World Order will be like Hitler on ultra-steroids after it has complete control, with death camps and gas ovens. The difference is Hitler only eliminated or killed about fifty million total. The NWO has to destroy seven billion, with a B, to get things down to a manageable population. Satan and the fallen angels have big plans for mankind in these last days, as prophesied in the book of Revelation. The earth again will be physically invaded by thousands of very bad angels masquerading as ancient aliens. They literally will take over the earth, as they did in the days of Noah.

Sign 11

Science Community Has a Doomsday Clock

This doomsday clock is about to strike midnight, midnight being doomsday. The hands of the infamous "Doomsday Clock" will remain in their place at five minutes until midnight, which symbolizes earth's destruction, as announced in 2013 by the science community. Google "Doomsday Clock holds at five until midnight" or "pictures of doomsday clocks," and you can see a picture of an assortment of scientific doomsday clocks.[33]

Scientists keep their outlook for the future of humanity very dim. This group of scientists also wrote an open letter to President Barack Obama that urges him to partner with other global leaders to act on climate change.

Their doomsday clock is a symbol of the threat to all humanity from nuclear or biological weapons, climate change, and other human-caused disasters. In making their deliberations about how to update the clock's time this year, the Bulletin of the Atomic Scientists considered the current state of nuclear arsenals around the globe and the slow and costly recovery from events like Japan's nuclear meltdown. A nuclear war is becoming more likely as Iran develops a nuclear weapon. North Korea may have perfected a miniature atomic weapon that can be concealed within a normal suitcase. Wake up! The end is here! It is a question of how much time do we truly have?

> The sun shall be turned into darkness, and the moon into blood, before the great and the terrible day of the Lord come. (Joel 2:31 KJV)

---

[33]   http://www.slate.com/articles/technology/future_tense/2013/01/doomsday_clock_from_the_bulletin_of_the_atomic_scientists_for_2013.html

Shall not the day of the Lord be darkness, and not light? Even very dark, and no brightness in it? (Amos 5:20 KJV)

The sun shall be turned into darkness, and the moon into blood, before that great and notable day of the Lord come. (Acts 2:20 KJV)

Sign 12

Major Earthquakes/Different Places

According to the Bible, earthquakes will be a major sign of the last days. The massive increase in the number of earthquakes will bring doomsday by fire over the entire earth. Google the number of major earthquakes since 1900 and look at a few government charts to prove we are quickly approaching the last days with this drastic increase in seismic events. After you examine the government charts, you will see how major earthquakes have greatly increased since 1990. You could bury your head in the sand and ignore the signs that are all around us. However, Jesus said there would be signs to warn us that the end is here.

Earthquakes will increase. There is a massive increase in earthquakes and national disasters.

The Lord's wrath will be executed upon the earth around 2028 till 2035 during the last part of the final seven years of man's time.

And great earthquakes shall be in diverse places, and famines, and pestilences; and fearful sights and great signs shall there be from Heaven. (Luke 21:11 KJV)

And I will bring distress upon men that they shall walk like blind men, because they have sinned against the Lord: and their blood shall be poured out as dust, and their flesh as the dung. Neither their silver nor their gold shall be able to deliver them in the day of the Lord's wrath; but the whole land shall be devoured by the fire of his jealousy: for he shall make even a speedy riddance of all them that dwell in the land. (Zeph. 1:17–18 KJV)

Sign 13

The Papal Prophecy of the Final Pope

There were two different men giving us two prophecies of the final Roman Catholic popes before the end of time; the sixteenth-century Nostradamus and St. Malachy, an archbishop from the twelfth century. Both prophesied the last pope, which is in office now, would be in power when Christ returns.

We have two prophecies seemingly coming together from two men who have been very accurate at predicting things over the years. On November 2, 1148, St. Malachy prophesied an end to the Roman Catholic Church and predicted the fates of the popes up until Judgment Day. Pope John Paul II has died. Are the Catholic prophecies warning humanity of a great apocalypse at hand? The last pope was to be the 112th and was just elected on March 14, 2013. But the prophecy said he would be called Peter the Roman. Even though the new pope is from Argentina, his parents were Italian immigrants. Italy was a part of the old Roman Empire. The new pope picked the name Francisco, which has the name Peter within it. So now the final prophecy has come to fulfillment. St. Malachy was very exact in his predictions of the other 111 popes. Now the final pope is in office, making him number 112.

St. Malachy, an archbishop of Argentina, was known as a great prophet. While in Rome in 1139 he received a vision showing him all the popes from his day to the end of time.[34]

St. Malachy was reported to have possessed the powers of levitation, healing, and clairvoyance. While on his way to the Vatican to assume the post of papal legate for Ireland, he fell into a trance and saw a line of papal reigns stretching from the successor to Innocent II and extending through centuries to the last of the line, identified as Peter of Rome. Malachy assigned short descriptions in Latin to each pope when he committed his vision to paper.

From the twelfth century to the twenty-first, his prophecies have turned out to be amazingly accurate, even prophesying the date of his death. In all, 112 popes and their characteristics are listed from 1143 to the alleged doomsday end of the world, or perhaps religion as we know it. The archbishop's final words in the prophecy were: "Rome, the seat of the Vatican, will be destroyed and the dreadful Judge will judge the people."[35]

Nostradamus had a prophecy of the last pope. "Century 5 Quatrain 49" of Nostradamus's prophetic masterpiece "Les Propheties" would cool the odds makers who bet that the next pope will be a Latin American. Nostradamus' inference to Spain includes candidates arising from her former colonial territories. This is only a part of the prophecy.[36]

---

[34] http://www.bibleprobe.com/last10popes.htm

[35] http://digitaljournal.com/article/345949; http://www.livescience.com/27827-papal-conclave-triggers-doomsday-theories.html.

[36] http://worldnews.nbcnews.com/_news/2013/03/10/17238040-are-cardinals-electing-the-last-pope-if-you-believe-nostradamus?lite

Sign 14

NASA has discovered an asteroid that will encounter earth's atmosphere on August 7, 2027.

On Friday, April 13, 2029, the asteroid Apophis will have a near collision with the earth. It will also come close to the earth in 2036.[37]

This following fairytale circulates among the evolutionists: an asteroid struck the earth 65 million years ago that killed off all the dinosaurs. They have no proof of this event, and all evidence points to the fact that man and dinosaurs shared this planet together less than six thousand years ago. Evidence in the fossil record points to a global flood; this is exactly what took place during Noah's days, about 2317 BC, when the earth's surface was destroyed for the first time.

Information concerning a possible future asteroid impact comes from the NASA scientific community, a governmental organization with which everyone is well-acquainted. This asteroid 1999 AN 10 was discovered by the Linear telescope on January 13, 1999. More sources say that a large asteroid *could* miss the earth by only 38,000 kilometers in 2027, according to new astronomical observations.

The near-miss trajectory of a newly discovered asteroid, called 1999 AN10, was announced. Now the observational data of Australian astronomer F. Zoltowski allows calculations of just how *close* this asteroid may come to earth.

Other astronomers at the Minor Planet Center at the US Smithsonian Astrophysical Observatory also used Zoltowski's work to calculate an estimated approach distance for AN10 of 56,500

---

[37]   http://www.space.com/19226-asteroid-apophis-gives-earth-a-close-shave-in-2029-infographic.html;   http://www.worldend.org/2029/asteroid-impact/apophis_p1.html.

214 | *Fourteen Signs for Earth's Doomsday*

kilometers from earth. The fly-by will occur on *August 7, 2027.* Notice they all come up with different calculations, some 56,600 and someone else 38,000 kilometers, which is about 19,000 miles, but all have the same date of arrival. What this says is that they don't truly know just how close it will come to earth.

They predict it could be much closer than our moon's orbit, in fact, only one-tenth the distance of the moon's orbit. They know it is headed on course to impact or come extremely close to our planet. They are a government agency and will not frighten you because they don't need a panic on their hands; plus, someone could lose their job.

Calculations suggest the asteroid will not impact. But the new calculations confirm the initial speculation that the asteroid might approach within the earth's sphere of gravitational influence. It could therefore be disrupted in such a way that it might impact earth a few years later, approximately 2036–2039, on one of its return orbits. This date is about the time of the second coming and the battle of Armageddon. This return date is well within the range of the final seven years—a time such has never been and never again will be.

Others Scientists Say It Is Impossible to Predict Orbit

Dr. Benny Peiser of John Moore's University in England makes the following statement: "The chaotic behavior of this asteroid makes it practically impossible to predict all possible approaches for more than a few decades after any close encounter." He also says, "The orbit will remain dangerously close to the orbit of the earth for several years."

On the official NASA website, the following article was posted concerning this coming asteroid:

Notes about this article posted by NASA: They say the miss distance is still uncertain and tell you it could pass outside the moon's orbit. What they don't tell you is that it could be much closer but they don't know how much closer. Already they predict it could pass within a distance 1/10 the orbit of the moon. They just don't know until it get much closer and they track it for a while. This is a sign of coming doom and the end of time.[38]

Posted by kdawson on Tuesday April 15 2008, @11:22PM from the little-child-shall-lead-them dept.

Spiracle writes "A German schoolboy, Nico Marquardt, has revised NASA's figures for the chances that the Apophis asteroid will hit earth. Apparently if the asteroid hits a satellite in 2029, its path could be diverted enough to cause it to collide with earth on the next orbit, in 2036. NASA had calculated the chances as 1 in 45,000 but the 13-year-old, in his science project, made it 1 in 450. NASA agreed." Giant meteorite hits central Russia, caught on film, more than 500 people hurt February 13th 2013. Go to YouTube. You must see this for yourself.[39]

---

[38] http://neo.jpl.nasa.gov/news/news017.html
[39] http://science.slashdot.org/story/08/04/16/001241/schoolboy-corrects-nasas-math-on-killer-asteroid

CHAPTER 15

Giant Humans, UFOs, Angels, and Aliens

Ancient Civilizations Discovered

Archaeologists around the world are constantly finding ancient civilizations. Since the 1930s, the *Golden Graves* in the city of Vani unveils the ancient kingdom of Colchis in what is today the Republic of Georgia.

Other unknown civilizations have been discovered: the Solomon Islands, ancient cities in Central America, Tell Mardikh, Hamouar, Tiahuanaco, Han China, the Mayans, the Incas, and the Aztecs, only to name a few. All around the Black Sea and throughout the Middle East (i.e., Lebanon, Cambodia, India, Iraq, Egypt, and Peru), researchers are finding proof of ancient advanced civilizations that mainline science ignores in total defiance to the present artifacts. Ancient Mayan cities still await to be discovered in the jungles of the Yucatan peninsula. Most of the information about Mayan sites have been mistranslated and misdated. These cities were not abandoned by the Mayans as many confusedly claim. Instead, these megalithic structures were built by Nephilim civilizations that were wiped out by the flood.

The Nephilim, a hybrid race, were wiped out on purpose by Noah's Flood in 2317 BC. According to the Dead Sea Scrolls, the Nephilim were cannibal hunters of the original human race. At the time the flood waters began to descend upon the earth, Noah and his three sons were the only surviving humans left whose DNA had not altered by the bad angels. Millions of Nephilim were destroyed by the flood.

The Nephilim fossil record totally exposes the *big lie* of Darwinism. In fact, every time an archaeological shovel digs in the dirt, another stainless finishing nail is placed into the coffin and a silver spike is driven deeper into the dark heart of Darwinism. Only a darkened or deceived individual could believe such lies that ignore all true scientific evidence. The problem is you don't want to believe in God. You don't want anyone telling you what to do and not to do. Disbelieve if you like but it does not make God disappear. You will face eternal judgment all alone without Jesus at the Great White Throne. Jesus loves you and died for your sins. Give your life to Him today and be rebirthed in your human spirit.

An international archaeological expedition to Lake Issyk-Kul, high in the Kyrgyz Mountains, discovered an ancient advanced civilization at the bottom of Lake Issyk-Kul. Many advanced civilizations are discovered in the Andes Mountains, such as Machu Picchu, under Lake Titicaca. How did these underwater anomalies occur at such high elevations if it was not for Noah's global flood? Most of these unknown civilizations were destroyed by the Great Flood in 2317 BC. Science still will not acknowledge this flood because it was a God-orchestrated global judgment, and God does not fit into their distorted way of thinking. Due to evolving technology the old main line science of Darwinism is becoming a *big joke* among people possessing an open mind and common sense. Constant scientific discoveries are exposing the big lies of Darwinism.

Is Mainstream Science an Illusion?

Mainstream science and archaeology are so deceptive with their tunnel vision approach to artifacts. They are determined, until hell freezes over, to indoctrinate everybody in their imaginary caveman myth of origins. But the Nephilim fossil record and basically all of the archaeological record definitely *do not* support what they erroneously declare in mainline science. Darwinism is a state-run religion supported only by your tax dollar donations. If tax donations were taken away, Darwinism would die like a fish out of water.

Giant skeletons with elongated skulls, with strange DNA, and having one-third larger brain capacity than normal humans have been discovered all around the world. However, this is *forbidden history here in America*. Read the book *The Ancient Giants Who Ruled the Americas* by Dewhurst. The book is filled with over three hundred pages of newspaper articles and clippings from the late 1800s and early 1900s. This was a time before the evolutionists developed such a stranglehold on the media and the science community. There is free information on strange artifacts of giants found in all of these earthen mounds here in America. However much of the fossil record revealing the Nephilim has been hidden, destroyed, or ignored in our country by the science community headed up by the Smithsonian.

A Hidden Goal

Why is this taking place within our nation? The answer is that these fossil remains do not fit their godless fairytale called Darwinism. So the bottom line is this *big lie* must be taught to our children as historical scientific fact, even though it is false. The future New World Order cannot govern people who believe they have inalienable rights given to them by a Creator. So their hidden goal is to destroy the Judeo-Christian belief system and its foundation, which is creation.

However, a new theory has emerged lately with literally tons of archaeological evidence and is supported widely by the fossil record. This theory is given time on the History Channel and H2, and they call it the ancient alien theory. Evidence in abundance supports their theory. This extraterrestrial idea is one interpretation of these artifacts, and it is very interesting to watch and listen to their theory. They have a very good argument for what they believe and have solid historical artifacts supporting their beliefs.

This ancient alien theory reveals something very different than what is taught by mainline science, causing a very sickly pall to further hang over the big lie of Darwinism. The evidence found for the ancient alien theory adds another plank to the wooden coffin of this monkey-to-man myth.

Misunderstood Theory of Ancient Aliens

This theory of aliens—who they were, how and when they arrived on earth, plus the history of the dinosaurs—can more accurately be explained within the context of the Bible and the Dead Sea Scrolls. We all have witnessed very large stone structures and strange skeletons, but the alien idea is only a guess as to how and when they fit into our ancient history. The evidence is true, and their interpretation appears to be correct until you examine the Word of God. The Bible reveals that ancient aliens are far from being an accurate interpretation of these artifacts.

The biblical writings can better explain the evidence presented for the ancient alien theory and their arrival on earth with a very accurate biblical date and timeline. You first have to ignore the Darwinian time machine myth filled with confusing millions and billions of imaginary years. Darwinian dating is as bogus as a six-dollar bill. Darwinian dating has affected the dates claimed in the ancient alien theory and has deceived many Bible scholars into believing this earth to be very old. Atheists are slowly brainwashing the entire world.

Ancient Writings

The ancient writings claim that several gods, known as the Anunnuki, descended to earth to live with man. Many believe that these so-called gods were nothing but ancient aliens and were misinterpreted by the people of that era to be gods as they witnessed their descent from heaven. The Bible has a better answer with the Nephilim in Genesis 6, the human giants found in the Dead Sea Scrolls, and the earthly arrival of some very bad renegade angels in 3114 BC.

In fact, two hundred watcher angels descended down to Mt. Hermon at the start of the Mayan calendar. These bad angels, according to the Bible and the Dead Sea Scrolls, came to cohabit with the beautiful young daughters of Adam. Angels have the ability to take on different forms, so they took different human forms—some took part-human, part-animal forms. But they gave up their eternal state to procreate with women and produce hybrid children. These children were the giants that were on the earth during Bible times before the flood and descendants from the line of Ham during the time of King David as he fought Goliath (1 Sam. 17). "There were giants in the earth in those days; because when the sons of God came in unto the daughters of men, and they bore children to them. Those men became mighty men who were of old, men of renown" (Gen. 6:4).

These sons of God who procreated with the daughters of Adam were the watcher angels that were assigned to watch mankind. They gave up their eternal state or domain to live an earthly life and die like humans. They were tempted with live pornography, by secretly watching men enjoying sex with beautiful women.

They were angel watchers given a special assignment as described in the Dead Sea Scrolls. This temptation was more than they could resist, so they took human form and cohabited with these beautiful daughters of Adam. The hybrid children they produced were called the Nephilim. To mankind, these bad angels were misinterpreted as gods because of their great powers and abilities. Some manifested as half-human and half-animal beings, as recorded on the Egyptian petroglyphs, and had wings and supernatural abilities.

> And angels who did not keep their own domain, but abandoned their proper abode, He has kept in eternal bonds under darkness for the judgment of the great day, *just as* Sodom and Gomorrah and the cities around them, since they *in the same way* as these *indulged* in gross *immorality* and went after *strange flesh*, are exhibited as an example in undergoing the punishment of eternal fire. (Jude 1:6–7 NASB)

This particular group of bad angels are interpreted in the ancient alien theory as extraterrestrials or ancient aliens. I can see how they reach this conclusion. But did these two hundred angels who abandoned their eternal domain to be like mankind die and leave a fossil record? If Psalm 82 is referring to these bad angels then it is possible. We know their hybrid children, some with elongated skulls and others with enormous skulls, are recorded in the fossil record. But did these watcher angels leave fossils? Man's body once was eternal but now is destined for death. Could the same be true for these two hundred bad angels?

Do Angels Have Bodies?

Angels have eternal bodies, but could this particular group of two hundred that abandoned their domain and left their own habitation (Jude 6–7) have been judged and faced death like Adam? They came to earth, taking physical form, and masqueraded themselves as gods that created mankind. They fooled mankind and were worshipped as gods. Adam had an eternal body before he sinned, and death was part of his sentence. According to Psalm 82, this group of bad angels that lived like men and procreated with the daughters of Adam received the same sentence of death as Adam, who himself was once eternal. If you want to live like mankind and have sex with the daughters of Adam, you will die like mankind.

> I said, you are gods, and all of you [200 angels] are sons of the Most High. [In the Old Testament, angels were referred to as sons of God.] Nevertheless you shall die like men, and fall like one of the princes. Arise, O God, judge the earth; for thou shalt inherit all the nations. [And God did judge the earth with a global flood in 2317 BC.] (Ps. 82:6–8)

God Judged Two Hundred Angels

God severely judged these two hundred angels before the flood and then sent the global flood to destroy their hybrid offspring. These angels rebelled against their proper place or abode as recorded by Jude. God sent the Archangel Uriel, and he cut the earth open and created Tartarus, a special prison for these watchers. He had these two hundred renegade watcher angels chained by this archangel, and

Uriel is assigned as a prison guard until the end of time, which is approaching at light speeds. They were not given any freedom as God gave the original fallen angels who sinned at the beginning. They must have died like mortal men. The purpose of the flood was definitely to destroy their evil genetic hybrid offspring, which we can see in the fossil record today.

Another thing these fallen angels left was thirty-six magnificent stone cities they built for their hybrid children. They started a major building program with the construction of these thirty-six cities we find around the earth today. The building of these thirty-six cities is recorded in the Dead Sea Scrolls. These cities were the mighty pyramids of old that we find under the sea and on dry land today.

They cut temples into solid stone mountains and made perfect statues from solid stone, as in Egypt. A few examples: Angkor Wat in India, the Grand Canyon caves in the United States, Mayan and Aztec ruins in Central America, and the Egyptian ancient ruins. The accuracy in these extremely large stone structures cannot be duplicated to this very day. These structures and statues were not made by Stone Age people, as mainline scientists would have you believe. Some solid stone petroglyphs, statues, and obelisks are created with perfect accuracy from solid stone and cannot be duplicated even with modern technology.

Did Aliens Create Mankind?

The ancient alien theorists believe that we are a human race genetically created from Neanderthal with altered DNA by ancient aliens. And this is exactly what the kingdom of darkness would have you to believe, especially if they are not able to convince you of Darwinism. Now, I may have some ancestors who hung by their necks, but they never hung by their tails.

The kingdom of darkness wants to keep you believing anything that is godless since you won't believe in evolution. There is far more evidence for ancient alien intelligence in the past with the giant skeletons and pyramid structures than there is evidence for this dumb theory of tadpole to monkey to man myth, which is riddled with deception. Are you not sick of this Darwinian deceptive mess being crammed down your children's throats? Then you should homeschool your children or invest into private schooling rather than new cars, new clothing, and new houses as you keep up with your neighbors. *Where are your priorities?* These fools are stealing the minds and hearts of your children.

UFOs/Abductions/Space Aliens/*Really?*

Do you truly believe in flying saucers and humans being abducted by space aliens? What in this world is going on? Are we truly being taken over by aliens from another solar system? Is there truly life out there in this vast universe? Remember uni means single and verse means a spoken sentence. Could everything literally be wrapped up into one single word, *uni-verse*? When atheists speak of the universe—in this one word they are unknowingly declaring the glory of God.

God said it, and all life came into being. Then He had it all recorded over time in the greatest book ever written, the Bible! The Bible is also the most accurate history book, recording 7,007 years from the creation to the future end of this earth. God recorded that the total surface of this earth has and will be destroyed two times—2317 BC by the flood and coming soon the battle of Armageddon in AD 2035.

I am going to try and make this as simple as possible. I want to help you understand what Jesus meant when He said (Matt. 24:37): "As it was in the days of Noah so shall it be when Christ returns." We have reached the end, and you need to know what to expect so your heart will not fail you because of the strange things that are coming on the earth. Google "the demonic alien deception" and watch the first hour of this YouTube video.[40]

We Live in an Interdimensional Realm

We humans are restricted to a dimensional realm while living in an interdimensional realm with angels, demons and strangely enough UFOs. In these last days bad angels are masquerading as UFOs and aliens from another universe, deceiving mankind as they did in the days of Noah. This realm is divided into the unseen spiritual realm and the actual physical realm you can see and feel. If you don't know how it was in the days of Noah, as recorded in Genesis 6, you are going to be easily fooled and deceived as bad angels repeat a physical invasion of earth as before the flood. In about 3114 BC two hundred angels physically took over the earth. In these last days thousands will manifest to mankind as UFOs, space aliens and other creatures in an effort to scare or deceive you.

God created these realms with certain laws. The physical realm is a four or more dimensional realm—with width, height, depth, time, and maybe more. The spirit realm—for better words—is an interdimensional realm, and we cannot fully comprehend it. The spiritual realm is divided into two kingdoms, competing for the souls—minds, wills, emotions—of mankind. You have God and His holy angels on one hand and Satan, the fallen angels, and the demonic spirits on the other.

If you want to see how Satan and his realm are openly operating then you have to go no deeper than the manifestation of alien encounters. Satan represents a realm of deception. God represents the

---

[40] https://www.youtube.com/watch?v=BPF2hK77ifg

realm of truth. The kingdom of darkness works relentlessly to keep you from believing and trusting in God, the Creator of the uni-verse. They try to affect your worldview with doctrines of demons, Darwinism, works-based religions, atheism, and the ancient alien theory. This is the foundation of their doctrinal deception and worldview. The alien theory makes the most sense—with all physical evidence presented—if it were not for the Bible and the Dead Sea Scrolls.

The darkened kingdom must remove you from the Genesis foundational account of God the Creator and six days of creation. If they can change your worldview with these foundational truths— moving you off the rock of creation and onto the shifting sand of millions of years—they successfully have you into their camp or kingdom. They will destroy your faith. One of their secret formulas is to make you believe in their worldview of millions of years instead of a six-day creation that which occurred roughly six thousand years ago. This is the big lie of the religion of Darwinism.

The fallen angels will do anything to keep you from believing in the divine Creator. As they prepare for the events recorded in the book of Revelation, they want you to believe that ancient aliens created man for their purposes and have been frequently checking on man to see how their creation has progressed. Thousands of UFO sightings have been recorded. A poll taken lately reveals that 75 percent of the population believes in UFOs. Then what is taking place in our skies? The Bible says that in the last days there will be a great falling away in Christian beliefs. Many will abandon the Judeo-Christian faith.

The Bible says in the Judeo-Christian worldview, "All things were made by the God most high and without Him nothing was made that was made."

The origin of all things has to be accepted by faith alone, so where do you place your faith? My suggestion is always stick to the Bible and run from all of those theories that try to eliminate God from the equation. If you are one of those doubters affected by the Darwinian smokescreen of millions of years or if you always look for an alternative other than God the most high—you have a foundational problem. You cannot build a solid Christian worldview with a rotten foundation filled with doubt. Immediately pray to God for wisdom, eyes to see and ears to hear so that you may be given understanding. The truth will literally set you *FREE!*

Vanishing UFOs in Our Physical World?

Why do UFOs appear and then vanish? If they were true physical nuts and bolts spacecraft, they should be subject to our physical laws. UFOs that are able to vanish and defy the laws of physics are not from another solar system but the fallen angelic dimension. After Jesus was resurrected, He moved from our physical world into this invisible world, what I want to simply call the angelic or spiritual dimension. He had the ability to pass through solid walls and vanish at will. There are definitely two different dimensional realms in this present world.

> Now it came to pass, as Jesus sat at the table with them, that He took bread, blessed and broke it, and gave it to them. Then their eyes were opened and they knew Him; and He vanished from their sight. (Luke 24:30–31 NKJV)

Are we dealing with angels and demons instead of aliens from another planet? They are interdimensional beings from our planet in the unseen spiritual dimension of angels and demons. When you study the characteristics of angels, they are identical to alien and UFO activity. Angels and demons are successfully creating the great end time deception with UFOs and supposed extraterrestrials from another star system. In Chuck Missler and Mark Eastman's book *Alien Encounters*, you will find research on most UFO encounters. The following is a remarkable quote from this well-written book:

> Among the thousands of cases of UFOs reported in the last 50 years, more than 700 cases have been reported by *experienced airline and military pilots*. The reliability of such witnesses and the physical evidence left at landing sites are powerful indicators to many investigators that the phenomena are real.[41]

The kingdom of darkness does not want to play by the rules set down as part of their punishment. We see these rules in the story of Job. In any prison, those who are sentenced still have certain rules to abide by or get additional punishment with solitary confinement. Could this be what happened in Genesis 6 with two hundred angels cohabiting with the daughters of Adam? Or could these two hundred angels be more good angels gone bad, as recorded in Psalm 82? Whatever happened, they received an extreme punishment, and these two hundred angels are still chained in a dark abyss named Tartarus. Their sin was so bad that they were made an example to deter other angels both fallen and good from sexually defiling their bodies with the daughters of Adam. Read Jude 6 and 7.

---

[41]   Chuck Missler and Mark Eastman, *Alien Encounters* (CITY, STATE: PUBLISHER, YEAR), 66.

As It Was in the Days of Noah

The fallen angels are breeding hybrid offspring today by artificial insemination. Search for hybrid fetus discoveries on YouTube. They are impregnating abductees and then taking the fetuses after about two months and placing them into some kind of incubators. Could they be reconnecting the demon spirits to hybrid bodies? Just a thought! These UFO abductions are not aliens from another solar system but angels and demons in another dimension of our unseen spirit world. Their hybrid breeding program is somewhere on this earth or under the earth or waters. Their hybrid offspring should be subject to the same laws of earth as mankind. But could they be injecting the old Nephilim demon spirits into these new hybrids and giving them life instead of God giving life at birth?

In the last days it will be like the days of Noah—the earth was filled with the hybrid Nephilim. If you don't understand Genesis 6, you will be fooled. The fallen sons of God are abducting women today all over the earth for hybrid breeding purposes. These bad angels are not defiling their bodies with women by sexually impregnating them as in Genesis 6—for fear of the judgment of God. But Satan soon will be cast into Tartarus—the abyss or bottomless pit—for possibly impregnating some girl with his son, the Antichrist. When Christ returns, Satan and the whole kingdom of darkness will be imprisoned because of this end time hybrid breeding program. The bad angels and demons will all be imprisoned for one thousand years during Christ's kingdom reign.

We wrestle not with flesh and blood but against spiritual wickedness in high places. UFO sightings today are real and are part of this alien deception. These sightings are a manifestation of fallen angels trying to deceive mankind into believing they are ancient aliens that seeded mankind on this earth. They are not from another planet but from a fallen angelic dimension of spirit beings. They are interdimensional beings that have the ability to vanish and reappear at will. Wake up, America—you are being sucked into the great deception!

Thousands of people have seen the UFOs streaking across the sky on many different occasions. *National Geographic* lists the top ten mass sightings of these UFOs in America, not counting the many NASA sightings recorded on camera.[42]

The Bible says *if it were possible these fallen angels would deceive the very elect,* born-again believers that are indwelled by the Spirit of the Living God. This book is designed to help you see the truth and help you to not be deceived by the kingdom of darkness.

In these last days, not only do we have all these sightings, but there have been thousands of abductions with surgical procedures being done to the abductees. Read Missler's well-documented book *Alien Encounters.* There have been too many reputable people, and they have the surgical scars to prove their encounter. All abductions cannot be dismissed in unbelief. If true abductions are taking place, then what do you think these angels and demons are up to?

The Nephilim governed the earth during Noah's days, but will they return to govern the earth in these last days, found in the book of Revelation? Are they getting ready to destroy seven billion humans leading up to the battle of Armageddon? Will the Antichrist be a Nephilim hybrid? Will the ten kings of the New World Order be Nephilim kings?

---

[42] http://channel.nationalgeographic.com/channel/chasing-ufos/articles/top-10-mass-sightings-of-ufos/

Ancient Historical Manifestations

If you don't understand Genesis 6, you will be among the ones who are deceived. An open manifestation on earth of two hundred bad angels occurred in 3114 BC at the beginning of the Mayan civilization. These fallen angels made their descent to Mt. Hermon in the Middle East on the thirty-third parallel (Google facts about the thirty-third parallel). This manifestation of these two hundred renegade angels and their efforts to physically take over the earth happened during the biblical time of Jared. God ended their altering of DNA with their imprisonment and later with the flood during the days of Noah in 2317 BC. Jared was the father of Enoch, and Jared was born about 460 years after the creation. Jared, born in about 3514 BC, lived to a ripe old age of 962 years, almost as long as Enoch's son Methuselah; talk about genetics!

Historically these bad angels abandoned their proper domain and actually manifested, with intentions to physically live on earth among men, at the beginning of the Mayan calendar. This calendar was *not back dated as many have claimed* but was created by these bad angels during the days of Jared. The Mayan civilization actually began in 3114 BC, and they lived before the great deluge in Noah's days.

Half-Animal and Half-Human Genetics

These renegade angels came down to earth, and we have their pictures historically carved on rock walls called petroglyphs. Most of them are shown with wings and usually appeared as half-human and half-animal creatures as seen in the Egyptian stone art carvings. Watch the *Ancient Alien* series on the History Channel or H2 and realize that all this stone work was done by renegade angels before Noah's flood.

The Easter Island statues were created by these bad angels called star beings some time before Noah's global flood. Most of the statues were partly covered up with flood sediment like the Sphinx in Egypt, duh!

The Greek god Pan was half-human and half-goat; centaurs were half-human and half-horse. There was the monster Minotaur with the head of a bull, etc. They were worshipped as gods, and history has recorded them on stone petroglyphs in Egypt before the flood.

Some of these so-called gods appeared with a bird's head and others with the head of a jackal and even an alligator. Don't listen to the evolutionists who write all of this off as myths and legends. The only true myth today is Darwinism. The human race worshipped these weird-looking creatures, and their magical powers and their ability to fly like Superman or Thor convinced humans that they were gods. People worshipped them and were deceived into believing them to be truly gods. But they were not gods or extraterrestrials—only bad renegade angels from the spirit realm.

These are not to be confused with stone carvings showing weird half-animal hybrid creatures. Fallen angels genetically engineered half-animal hybrids through genetic modification. Fallen angels in past history have been involved in a program of evil genetic breeding with animals and humans, truly making a mess of God's original creation. You have to discern between petroglyphs of bad angels pretending to be gods and their half-animal offspring, some being shown like pets with chains around their necks in some cases. Go to YouTube and look up the eight weirdest fossils ever discovered. These are some fossils of half human creatures with horns, an actual mermaid skeleton and also a Cyclops's skull. Evolutionists try to hide and distort these forbidden fossils but bones don't lie.

These lesser gods or star beings were only rebellious angels from the angelic dimension deceiving mankind. Young, beautiful women even began to interbreed with these strange beings, and they produced a royal offspring that the common man also worshipped. This ungodly union produced the Nephilim, which dominated the earth during Noah's days. If you misinterpret Genesis 6 then you will not understand these last days. Biblical prophecy tells us that the Nephilim will again populate the earth during the last days. In this twenty-first century, fallen angels are masquerading as aliens and UFOs from another planet. They are involved in a hybrid breeding program producing again the Nephilim. This is what UFO abductions are all about. They need women to produce the modern hybrid Nephilim for the end time.

The Nephilim Are Here Now

This breeding program began with UFO abductions at about the time Israel became a nation. Abductions by the fallen angels are presently taking place on earth. Only one generation will exist after 1948. This will bring a conclusion to man's rule on earth at the battle of Armageddon.

The kingdom of darkness wants you to believe that the ancient aliens have returned to the earth to help mankind, whom they created! It could be that Bigfoot is a Nephilim hybrid as they again genetically breed with the animals like in Noah's days, or they could be fallen angels masquerading as Bigfoot creatures. Brandon Watson, a missionary friend relentlessly working in the mountains of Mexico, woke up from his sleep to discover this big tall hairy Sasquatch creature standing at the end of his bed. It miraculously vanished like it materialized after Brandon determined in his heart that it could not hurt him, so he covered his head and went back to sleep. This was an effort of the fallen angels trying to scare Brandon away from preaching the gospel of Jesus Christ to the indigenous people of that region. None have ever been killed, and the few that have been shot have disappeared before the shooters' very eyes. Beware lest you entertain angels unaware; fallen angels also have that ability. However, hybrids do die and can be killed like any animal or human.

Mermaids are leftover Nephilim from Noah's days because they lived in water and were not destroyed by the flood. They travel with schools of whales to avoid predators. Go to Google and search for "mermaids found" or "evidence for mermaids." Research the Discovery Channel's documentary on the subject. You decide if they exist. [43]

Some theorist put forth the idea that extraterrestrials grew tired of the man they had genetically made, so they are the ones who sent the flood to get rid of humans. The Bible says God sent the flood to rid the earth of the Nephilim or alien genetic experiments as recorded in the Dead Sea Scrolls. In these last days, bad angels will be manifesting themselves to be ancient aliens that created the first man. But I know God created the human race in about 3973 BC and about 3114 BC two hundred bad angels came to earth. Their purpose was to corrupt man's bloodlines so the Messiah could not be born. God judged them and their hybrid children. God washed the earth of their mutations of human and animal DNA.

In these last days, the fallen angels are prepping the population of the earth to disbelieve in the Creator God and the frame of time of 7,007 years. They are using the History Channel series called *Ancient Aliens* and all the UFO sightings to help accomplish this. Watch the new series on H2 called *Hanger 1: the UFO Files*.

We have several UFO crashes or landings, like Rendlesham forest, Phoenix lights (in 1997), in America's Area 51 in Roswell, New Mexico, and many UFO sightings in Russia. These are only a few examples, but

---

[43]   http://www.youtube.com/watch?v=zn4psImr25w; http://www.youtube.com/watch?v=fz1NOgrpipE

there are thousands. The fallen angels need human women to produce the Nephilim. This is what happened before the flood, and it is quietly taking place now. I think the fallen angels are genetically trying to keep the Nephilim from growing so tall like the giants did during Noah's days.

The Present Deception

In our lifetime angels and demons have masqueraded themselves to be alien creators of man. They have come to protect mother earth and to mine gold. The deception is that these aliens interbred with the so-called Neanderthal race to produce better and more intelligent slave laborers. The DNA mutation caused by this interbreeding produced the Homo sapiens race, or this is what they want you to believe. Go to YouTube and watch anything produced by Chuck Missler. He is very scientifically intelligent about this subject. You can also watch *Ancient Aliens* on YouTube or just watch the History Channel or H2.

Theorists say these ancient aliens have been overseeing earth for the last ten thousand years, and they are the missing link between monkeys and man. They mean no harm and only want to guide man in the right way. This is all a bad angel deception, and this book is written to true believers so you will know the truth and the truth will set you free. This is the reason the book of 1 Enoch is so hated by the kingdom of darkness throughout the ages and even today, because it reveals the past history of bad angel activity and their hybrid children, the Nephilim.

According to the complete seventy biblical-book record, we now have evidence unveiling man's true history. The Bible unveils a great deception that is hanging over and deceiving mankind. This bad angel deception began in the Garden of Eden. Then, about nine hundred years later, we had two hundred bad renegade angels descending to earth and mingling sexually among the daughters of Adam and animals for about one thousand years before Noah's flood. Evidence is presented in the fossil record showing these bad angels corrupting things with a second creation of man and animals though genetic engineering. Look at the fossil record; bones don't lie.

Finally, in these very last days it will be as it was in the days of Noah. Fallen angels manifest themselves as UFOs streaking across the skies, for they manifest as angels of light. These alien spaceship sightings are prepping a population for what is about to come on this earth. The Bible says men's hearts will fail them in shocking unbelief for what is taking place on this earth; they had misinterpreted Genesis 6. I do not want God's children to be in shock, so I write to help you understand what is happening.

The better part of the population has always believed that God created mankind despite what deceiving atheists and evolutionists teach. However, the constant teaching of evolution to the end-time generation is taking its toll on the way they think. Unbelief has become rampant among youth. The kingdom of darkness is working twenty-four/seven in preparation for the great end time deception.

A Spiritually Ignorant World

The fallen angels are deceiving a world that is spiritually ignorant of their ability to manifest. This is the reason they tried to destroy the book of 1 Enoch and any writings that revealed their ancient manifestations. The bad angel manifestation and the origin of giant humans in past history are widely revealed by some biblical books found in the Dead Sea Scrolls. These books were removed from our Bible by the very influence of these fallen angels through the Pharisees, Emperor Constantine, and the Laodicean early church. Fallen angels can be the most active members in your church. They are very active in religious affairs and manipulate religious leaders around the world.

Our complete seventy-book Bible, unveiled in the Dead Sea Scrolls, reveals this fallen angel deception. The Bible has seventy books instead of the sixty-six that our religious leaders have put in the biblical canon. The complete historical Bible reveals how bad angels have had influence in the recording of history. The truth will set you free, so these bad angels want to keep mankind ignorant about their true past history. We wrestle not against flesh and blood but spiritual wickedness in high places.

The Battle for the Bible

Could the fallen angels have censored the number of books in our Bible today? This, as a Christian, is just unthinkable, but I have found that fallen angels and demons have infiltrated religious affairs. It was the religious crowd that crucified the Son of God. Religious men, controlled by demons and bad angels, have tried to restrict access to these four missing historical books of the Bible for thousands of years.

Even the sixty-six books of the Bible we have today have been kept from the common man for hundreds of years. Only through much shedding of blood, prayers, and modern technology has it been widely made available in these last days. Uncovering the truth is a constant battle. The Devil is a liar and the father of lies. Atheists and evolutionists are only following in their father's footsteps.

The kingdom of darkness restricts the Word of God in communist countries to this very day. Demons work overtime in free countries to keep us from reading and studying the Word of God. You cannot see them, so they cause distractions for you with other people and your stuff in any way possible. The kingdom of darkness hates the Word of the Living God; it exposes their evil agenda for mankind. Yet, despite their efforts, the Bible is still the most powerful and influential book in the whole world. When you discover all seventy books instead of sixty-six, you will become complete in your understanding of the truth in past history.

Is Our Religious Freedom Being Threatened?

Religious freedom is the very subject America was founded upon, and in the spirit realm there is a great war going on to change America's religious freedoms. The Bible says in Ephesians 6:12, "For we do not wrestle against flesh and blood, but against principalities, against powers, against the rulers of the darkness of this age, against spiritual hosts of wickedness in the heavenly places" (NKJV).

Only within the last five hundred years has God's written Word been made available to the common man, and only within the last sixty or so years have the complete seventy books been made available. You must not be deceived by these religious demons in these last days! We have seventy books in our great historical Bible.

I do not have the time and the pages to argue this subject anymore. You must search your own heart and let the Spirit of God reveal this truth, if you are a true believer. First John 2:27 says, "The anointing which ye received of Him abides in you, and ye need not that anyone teach you; but as His anointing teaches you; concerning all things, and is true, and is no lie" (KJV). You have the anointing of Jesus if you are a born-again believer. Now make use of this great gift.

Making the Argument Again

The two following historical books were uncovered in the Dead Sea Scrolls. First was the book of 1 Enoch, and a second book was authored by Moses, the book of Jubilees. According to Wikipedia, who has no religious axe to grind, the first book of Enoch was the third-most-popular book of the Bible in Jesus' days, and Jubilees was number seven out of the forty-two books. Only forty different OT books were in the Dead Sea Scrolls; the book of Esther and the ancient book of Jasher were not found, but the scrolls have not all been researched and assigned.

The ancient book of Jasher is quoted in two verses of the Bible. It needs to be examined but appears to be authentic. This is the only book of the missing three OT books that I am not sure of; you will have to decide. In the New Testament, the epistle of Barnabas is missing. Barnabas was also not in the Dead Sea Scrolls, as were none of the Greek NT manuscripts. This epistle was removed from the Bible NT because Barnabas quoted from the hated book of Enoch. Also, Barnabas is the only book of the Bible that reveals man's 6,000-year destiny as an exact fixed time allotted for mankind. How the book of Jude made it in the Bible, I don't know, because he quoted from the hated book of Enoch also, but Jude was the half-brother of Jesus and, this is probably the reason he made it in the Bible.

> Now Enoch, who lived seven generations after Adam, prophesied about these people. He said, "Look, the Lord is coming with thousands of his holy ones. He will bring the people of the world to judgment. He will convict the ungodly of all the evil things they have done in rebellion and of all the insults that godless have

spoken against him." These people are grumblers and complainers, doing whatever evil they feel like. They are loudmouthed braggarts, and they flatter others to get favors in return. (Jude 14–16 NLT)

We now have forty-two Old Testament books and twenty-eight New Testament books, totaling seventy. These books are our complete Bible in these last days. Through religious man the kingdom of darkness has tried to keep God's Word from us. But we have it in our possession, for heaven and earth will pass away but God's Word will endure for all time, as witnessed in the Dead Sea Scrolls!

My Responsibility to You

I have a responsibility from God to tell you the truth. I am a seeker of truth and not man's approval. I do not have to make you believe these truths but only unveil them to you. What you do with the truth is up to you. One thing I do know for sure is that the truth will set you *free*. On the judgment day you will be responsible for what you did with the truth given to you.

If you are a true born-again believer and are being led by the Spirit of God, you will know that what I am writing to you is true. Search your heart and be not deceived. You see, I believe the Bible, all seventy books. It is a very accurate historical record of time and events. I have discovered that nothing, except God, existed before 3973 BC. I believe that God created everything in six literal days. God created the angels on the first day, and all of them were good. In fact, everything God created was good, but we were given free will and a creative ability.

Yet You have made him but a little lower than God, and
You crown him with glory and majesty. (Ps. 8:5 NASB)

Man was not made a little lower than the angels according to this passage. Angels, both fallen and good, are lower than born-again believers.

Later, after the creation, one-third of the angels followed Lucifer in a rebellion against the Creator—at the least one thousand angels but I think many more. Some of the angels became jealous of God's special attention being given to the creation of Adam and him being made higher than the angels. They did not like the fact that they were to be servants to this inferior creature called man.

Angels Created Lower than Man

Man was made a little bit lower than God, which is documented in the original Hebrew text. This verse was mistranslated in the Septuagint (lower than angels), from which verses were quoted in the book of Hebrews. The angels, with all their supernatural power, were made to be servants to man and God. Jealousy became a problem for Lucifer, the leading angel. He wanted to be like the Most High and exalt his throne above God's. He was jealous of the fact that he was much more powerful than man, yet God had made him to serve this less-powerful being.

God created both angels and mankind with a free will. God wanted His creation to love and worship Him of their own free will, so He gave them this powerful gift, known as the freedom of choice. And after almost six thousand years of history, we are still given that same choice today. You are reading this book because of that choice given to all. The free will is power. Free-will decisions can enslave you or set you free.

A Free Will to Chose

The Creator created free will in your original ancestors, and it was passed on to all descendants. You are exercising this free will today. I love and serve God because I want to, not because someone forces me. I am now asking you to choose *life in Jesus Christ,* or you can choose death and deception with the dark angels. There are no other options. This is a six thousand–year-old question. We all have to make choices with our free will every day of our lives.

You do not have to truly choose eternal death. You are automatically on the eternal dark death road because it was chosen for you by your ancestor Adam. But you do have to make a choice to get off of this road headed down to dead man's curve. Choose life in Jesus Christ. Jesus came to restore to you what Adam lost in the Garden of Eden. Jesus came to offer you the gift of eternal Zoë life, which is the DNA of God, and to give it to you abundantly.

Jesus came to restore the DNA of our heavenly Father that was originally given to mankind. Don't be foolish and be deceived by the kingdom of darkness, for that is their craft. Deception is what they are skilled at, and they have had thousands of years to fine tune their craft. If you have been born again, you have authority given to you over these fallen angels and demons.

The Great Ancient Alien Deception

According to ancient alien theorists, a phrase dominantly used by the History Channel, they contend that the manifestation of these gods or bad angels is actually ancient aliens. Like Moses and the burning bush, Elijah and the fiery chariots, Ezekiel and the spacecraft with wheels, they contend it is just ancient aliens returning to check on their creation.

Angels Are in a Different Dimension than Man

There is a spiritual world not of the same dimension as the one we are in. These aliens and UFOs are fallen angels deceiving the world and operating in that spiritual dimension. Many have seen UFOs streak across the skies at thousands of miles per hour and changing direction in a split second. If they were truly physical aliens, then they would be subject to our laws, as Chuck Missler explains. Angels are not subject to our laws, like the law of gravity, because God created them to live and operate in another dimension, but their hybrid offspring are subject, as we are, to this world.

The Nephilim Are a Hybrid Race

Was mankind put here by aliens millions of years ago, or is mankind a human race created by God less than six thousand years ago? The original creation has been mutated by fallen angels and heavily influenced by demon spirits. These demon spirits originally came out of the dead bodies of the Nephilim. Demon spirits are the spirits of the dead Nephilim, according to the Dead Sea Scrolls. The takeover of the earth by two hundred renegade angels and their activities was the cause of the great flood of Noah's day. *They'll be back* for the final seven years and Armageddon.

A Repeat of the Problem

Many do not want to believe about this second creation of genetic manipulation by bad angels, but the skeletons are in the fossil record. They are a witness to this fact. Don't be a fool and be sucked in by the religious theory known as the sons of Seth and the daughters of Cain. This is a false doctrine from the kingdom of darkness. Good Christians have been deceived with this Sethite theory.

The giant skeletons and strange skulls are part of the fossil record. My fellow believers in Christ, take a look at the fossil record; *bones don't lie*. This is forbidden archaeology among evolutionists and even some religious leaders in America. The Nephilim skeletons and skulls are all over the earth.

Produce a Witness or Be Silent

If you did not live thousands of years ago and if you do not have any eyewitness to this period, then *who are you* to discredit the Bible? Enoch was an eyewitness of this time. These so-called gods to some and ancient aliens to others came to live with men and are referred to in ancient writings as the Anunnuki. Enoch was an eyewitness to this period and recorded it in history. In fact, Enoch was a scribe who was recorded as being greatly loved by God, so loved that God took him off the earth and he never died. I have a live eyewitness with an exact time and the correct narrative of their visit on earth. Enoch is God's recorded eyewitness, and I have a copy of his deposition in the Bible and the Dead Sea Scrolls. So the Judge says, "Produce your witness or you have no credible case."

The Nephilim are Coming

In these very last days these Nephilim will again populate the earth. In the last days, these fallen angels will claim to be aliens from another planet that created the Homo sapiens race sometime in the past. These bad angels fight against the truth of their origin and constantly try to alter and hinder the written Word of God from being proclaimed. Deception is their job description among mankind.

Bad angels have in the past mingled sexually with the human race. I know some of you have a problem with that, but the truth will truly set you free. You have to distort and stretch the Scriptures to come up with your Sethite theory.

> And it came to pass, when men began to multiply on the face of the Earth, and daughters were born unto them, That the sons of God saw the daughters of men that they were fair; and they took them wives of all which they chose. And the Lord said, My spirit shall not always strive with man, for that he also is flesh: yet his days shall be an hundred and twenty years. There were giants in the Earth in those days; and also after that, when the sons of God came in unto the daughters of men, and they bear children to them, the same became mighty men which were of old, men of renown. And God saw that the wickedness of man was great in the Earth, and that every imagination of the thoughts of his heart was only evil continually. And it repented the Lord that he had made man on the Earth, and it grieved him at his heart. And the Lord said, I will destroy man whom I have created from the face of the

Earth; both man, and beast, and the creeping thing, and the fowls of the air; for it repented me that I have made them. But Noah found grace in the eyes of the Lord. (Gen. 6:1–8 KJV)

Also read Jude 6, 1 Peter 3:18–20, and 2 Peter 2:1–5.

The Bible labels them as Nephilim, and according to the prophecy of Daniel, the Nephilim will populate the earth in these last days, maybe at the end of the Mayan calendar. Could more of these fallen angels have come in 2012 and mingled again with the daughters of men? I am sure these UFO abductions have something to do with a modern-day genetic breeding program to produce Nephilim that look more like modern man and not the giants of past history.

The new Nephilim may be in the wombs of the daughters of men, this being 2014 as I write. As it was in the days of Noah so shall it be in the coming of the Son of Man. The Nephilim, a hybrid half-breed race, covered the earth in an effort to corrupt the human bloodline so Jesus Christ could not be born. Well, we know they failed, and they will fail at the battle of Armageddon. I know this because I have read the last chapter, and they will fail at deceiving God's born-again children.

Hybrid Offspring Produced

The Nephilim population grew to millions, maybe even billions during their stay on the earth, while corrupting the pure bloodlines of mankind for over one thousand years before the flood. Possibly Noah was the only family bloodline that had not been corrupted by the fallen angels' DNA. One or two of Noah's daughters-in-law must have had Nephilim DNA in them, causing the giants to reappear in the Promised Land after the flood. In our lifetime they will come with a different agenda and a purpose to prepare for wars that will be created to destroy mankind instead of protecting them. Read the book of Revelation if you have any doubts.[44]

According to the Dead Sea Scrolls and certain verses in the Bible, bad angels produced a hybrid kingly line of half-breeds appearing in human history beginning about 3114 BC; these bad angels were called by some as the Anunnuki and their children were the Nephilim. They materialized as men and had sexual relations with the daughters of descendants of Adam up until the great flood in 2317 BC. Bottom line, angels had sex with humans.

Giant Hybrid Cannibals

Anunnuki means "the kingly blood line"; theorists say it means "from heaven they came to earth." Either one, they were adored and worshipped by the human race. Their children, the Nephilim, ruled the earth in violence and cannibalism for the latter part of their reign, which lasted over one thousand years. They basically ate or cannibalized the human bloodlines before the flood. This all started sometime after the creation of the Mayan calendar in 3114 BC. This reign of terror lasted until God judged the Nephilim during the flood about 1,656 years after the creation. Those two hundred watcher angels were judged and imprisoned for their treason by the only true and living God, as told in Jude 6–7, 2 Peter 2:1–6, 1 Peter 3:18–20, and the Dead Sea Scrolls. Did these two hundred angels sin separately from the original fall at the beginning?

---

[44] http://beginningandend.com/bloodlines-of-the-nephilim-a-biblical-study/; http://lastdayscalendar.tripod.com/genesis_5___6.htm.

> For if God spared not the angels that sinned, but cast
> them down to hell [tartarus], and delivered them into
> chains of darkness, to be reserved unto judgment;
> And spared not the old world, but saved Noah the
> eighth person, a preacher of righteousness, bringing
> in the flood upon the world of the ungodly. (2 Peter
> 2:4–5 KJV)

Notice that Peter uses a different Greek word for hell that is not used anywhere else in the Bible, but it is found only in Greek mythology. Tartarus is the pit within the earth where God banished these two hundred treasonous, rebellious, and renegade watcher angels in judgment. Their judgment was so severe that other fallen angels would think twice before defiling their bodies with humans. God imprisoned in chains these two hundred angels as an example to other angels to keep them from doing the same thing. Could Greek mythology actually be recorded history instead? Could this latest movie, *Thor: the Dark World*, be a glimpse of the abilities of these two hundred gods (renegade angels) during a time before Noah's flood?

Impossible Architecture

Have you ever wondered about these underwater architectural ruins that are on ocean floors and lakes? There have been over 130 ancient structures and complete cities discovered, not counting the above-ground pyramids, mounds, and cities. Fallen angels and Noah's flood are the only answers for them. Some of these ancient structures would be impossible to reconstruct, even with modern technology. Most of these mysterious pyramids of ancient civilizations, such as the Mayan, Egyptian, and Aztec civilizations, have puzzled scientists for years. The

Great Pyramid of Giza was actually an ancient power plant, not a tomb. There are probably ancient power plants underwater in the Bermuda Triangle and the Devil's Triangle still producing power causing strange interferences with electrical instruments.

These structures were constructed during a time period before Noah's flood, about 2317 BC. This flood is a known fact, for it is historically recorded by every civilization, plus many ancient flood records, including the Bible, tell of a race of giants that ruled the earth prior to the flood. They all have flood stories, and they are not myths as labeled by mainstream scientists. The ancient historical records and the fossil record of Noah's flood are true. If you don't believe in God the Creator and the flood, you are a fool. Atheists deny and hate this flood because it demonstrates God's ability to bring judgment on His own creation.

Dead Sea Scrolls

The Dead Sea Scrolls openly reveal the activity of these two hundred bad angels pretending to be gods. The scrolls reveal them as architects of all these mysterious ancient pyramids and mounds. The scrolls claim these angels built these remarkable cities that cannot be reconstructed to this day. So we must be aware of fallen angels masquerading as aliens and UFOs in the twenty-first century. This is what it means when the Bible says, "As it was in the days of Noah so shall it be when Christ returns." (Matt. 24:37)

The Nephilim Fossil Record

Giant human skeletal remains can be found today in the fossil record. The flood left fossil remains, fossil evidence, and proof of their time on earth, which helps to unveil their existence. The human giants can be found in the Bible, the Dead Sea Scrolls, and the fossil record. Will the Nephilim return in these last days?

You are just one or two clicks away from having the truth revealed. But a lot of *you can't handle the truth!* That is the reason you adopt the religious Sethite theory. Type in your search window "strange skulls" or "giant skeletons" and prepare yourself for the results, or go bury your head in the sand and deny until you die. Read a very scholarly book titled *The Rise, Fall, and Return of the Nephilim* by Rob Skiba for the truth about Genesis 6.

These fallen angels and the spirits of their children have tried to control the lives of mankind and events on earth since the creation. They have plotted and tried to censor the Bible, hoping to keep Christians ignorant of the historical truth by keeping out certain books that reveal the Nephilim. I am trying to correct this; if my heavenly Father is willing, my next books will be available at zoebooks. org. *Forbidden History of the Ancient World as it was in the Days of Noah* and *The Book of Life (Zoe life) Tracing God's DNA* (see page 266).

The Return of the Nephilim

Could the Mayans have tried to synchronize their calendar 5,125 years ago with God's six thousand-year countdown calendar? If so they only missed it by about twenty years—unless the end of the calendar was the year more Anunnuki silently returned to the earth to genetically change the DNA of the human race in preparation for the destruction of seven billion people in the last seven years and the battle of Armageddon. This new alteration of human DNA will produce new Nephilim hybrids in human women as in the days of Noah. Satan is getting ready for the wars that are coming on this earth. The Nephilim almost destroyed the human race before the flood, and they will attempt it again between 2028 and 2035. Read the book of Revelation for a glimpse of the future for humans.

> And whereas thou did see iron mixed with miry clay, they shall *mingle* themselves with *the seed of men.* (Dan. 2:43 KJV)

In Daniel's prophecy of the final one-world power, he predicts the return of the Nephilim in the last days. They had begun mingling with the human race (1 Enoch 7:3) about 3114 BC and were destroyed by the flood about 2317 BC. The Nephilim genomic DNA was in Ham and Japheth's wives, as we see in the Old Testament. The giants that were in the Promised Land ancestry can be traced back to some of Ham's children. The Nephilim were on the earth twelve hundred years before the flood and twelve hundred years after the flood, up to the time of King David—all from one incursion of two hundred bad angels in 3114 BC.

These bad angels also contaminated the animal bloodlines. They were taking on animal form, messing with animal DNA (1 Enoch 7:5) in an effort to create monsters. This was an effort to mess with God's creation, and these creatures also produced a fossil record that is with us today. On YouTube, look up the eight weirdest fossils ever discovered.[45]

Google and check out the fossil found of a mermaid and the fossil of a person with wings. Bad angels set out on a mission to destroy God's creation. No wonder God was disgusted with man and wished He never made him, destroying all but eight persons and the animals God sent to Noah to put on the ark. God sent the great deluge, known as Noah's flood. God washed the earth of bad angel DNA experiments that had filled the earth with corruption.

---

[45] https://www.youtube.com/watch?v=UHyCdTOZ70E

Again, I challenge you, these truths are just a click or two away on your computer; type in your search engine "strange skulls" or "giant skeletons" and brace yourself for what you will find. Archaeology is speaking to you today, if the real truth is not censored. Evolutionists are very busy attacking and trying to deceive the public by distorting these findings as Photoshop frauds, but they are present in the fossil record. Don't be a fool; their bones are there.

The Last Days Have Arrived

The last days are here, and the demons and fallen angels all have a date with destiny when God's clock quits ticking, and they know it. They know their time is short and their judgment is sure. The demon spirits of the giants begged Jesus to let them go into the pigs, but first they asked Jesus, *"Have you come to torment us before our time?"* The kingdom of darkness knows they have a date with destiny. They also recognized Jesus as the Son of the Most High God (Yahweh) and not Allah, because Allah has no son.

> And when he was come to the other side into the country of the Gergesenes, there met him two possessed with devils, coming out of the tombs, exceeding fierce, so that no man might pass by that way. And, behold, they cried out, saying, What have we to do with thee, *Jesus, thou Son of God?* art thou come hither to *torment us before the time?* And there was a good way off from them an herd of many swine feeding. So the devils besought him, saying, If thou cast us out, suffer us to go away into the herd of swine. (Matt. 5:28–31 KJV)

OVERALL BOOK SUMMARY

If you have completed the journey and reached this portion of the book, I want you to remember the following things.

We all live forever beyond these physical earth suits. The question is where do you want to spend eternity? It is truly your choice. Jesus Christ, the last Adam, came to restore to you a godly dimension of life know as Zoë life or the DNA of God within your human spirit. This Zoë life is what the first Adam lost in the Garden of Eden, and you can recover a portion of God's glory instantly. You can live for eternity with Jesus or you can live for eternity in the second death separated from God by rejecting God's Son as your sin offering, which is truly your choice. But know that Jesus is the only way to God and to have eternal Zoë life.

> For as the Father has Zoe Life in Himself, so He has granted the Son to have Zoe Life in Himself, and has given Him authority to execute judgment also, because He is the Son of Man. Do not marvel at this; for the hour is coming in which all who are in the graves will hear His voice and come forth—those who have done good, to the resurrection of Zoe Life, and those who have done evil, to the resurrection of condemnation. (John 5:26–29, translated from original text)

We have examined the unbeliever's worldview and have come to a conclusion that they too have to believe their worldview by faith, which is the Darwinian theory or the ancient alien theory. They have to exercise their faith in these unseen and unknown theories. I have never seen God, yet I believe in the God of creation, and His only intercessor is Jesus Christ. We all have different things that make us believe in each worldview. It is not an issue of science versus religion—no, no, no—but religion versus religion. It is on all sides totally believed by faith. They have no eyewitness of the origins but only circumstantial evidence. We have noticed that the Darwinian believers tend to scoff at our beliefs in a higher Intelligent Designer. We have discovered that this was predicted to take place around the end of man's time as recorded in the Bible. This would be a sign to believers that the end has arrived.

We took a quick history lesson of the world's three leading religions and discovered that they all originated from the Middle East and had some ties to a man named Abraham. We looked at Abraham's childhood, trying to find what caused a man of such statue to have such faith in only one God, named Yahweh and His coming Son, Jesus Christ. We discovered that one of Abraham's sons abandoned Abraham's God and followed the most popular deity of the Middle Eastern people of that time, which was known as Allah, and we discovered Allah was a god that had no son. Abraham's son worshipped a different god than the one Abraham served, even though Ishmael was the DNA child of Abraham. Ishmael never chose his dad's religious beliefs, as many offspring do today.

A six thousand-year time clock was discovered ticking down to Armageddon, which is a fixed and appointed time on God's calendar. We also discovered what caused this clock to start ticking: the first sin of Adam and Eve. Plus, the clock cannot be stopped or disarmed and will end man's government as we know it.

We examined the time clock and the time factor involved. God sees it as six days, and to man it is six thousand years because one day in heaven to God is as a thousand years on earth to man. God only gave mankind six days to rule from start to finish. We discovered it was broken down into three two-day or two thousand–year periods, and the final two thousand years was for the church-age, AD 28 to 2028.

Chapter 7 revealed that the complete seventy-book Bible contained a 7,007-year window of time from the creation of all things until the total destruction of this earth as it leaves its orbit. Then a new heaven and earth will be created for God's children to live on forever. In this book we believe the Bible to be the true, accurate history of the world and the only history book ever written that can be trusted in this crazy world, a world that is controlled by the mythological Darwinian time machine that is a big part of the atheist fairytale world they label as science.

In chapter 8, a key factor was given in understanding the exact or approximate dating of all world events—the crucifixion of Jesus Christ, which was in AD 28. The flood during Noah's days destroyed the ancient world, and 2317 BC is a date that separated the ancient world and their artifacts from Noah's descendants of today. We looked at the writings of Daniel and his end-time prophecies plus the world planners of a New World Order, coming soon to a city near you. We looked at the United States and Iran on the world stage. We found some wonderful signs in the moon confirming the creation event over the Darwin fairytale.

Then we examined fourteen signs and prophecies pointing to the final days of America and the end of all things as we know it and the picking of 2028 as our possible final year before the rapture of all believers from this earth, which ends the church age! The final chapter brought the word count of this book above seventy thousand words. The final thoughts presented pertain to amazing structures found on earth and under the oceans and the giant skeletons found in the fossil record all over this earth, known as the Nephilim. We discussed the ancient alien theory and how their accumulation of evidence destroys the Darwinian Theory. We established that the Bible had a better explanation for the alien and UFO events. We also offered evidence for the present alien activity going on around the world, and it was fallen angels and demons masquerading as aliens and UFOs that live in a different, unseen angelic dimension. They only let you see what they want you to see. This is the great end-of-time deception, and this is the meaning of the phrase "as it was in the days of Noah" as we compare events to Genesis 6.

I hope you are awakened by this book concerning the times in which we live. Christians, be careful about going into debt, and be submissive to all government authorities. Maybe store some freeze-dried foods, which have a twenty-five-year shelf life. Troublesome times are coming within the next fourteen years. Be careful about banks; our national debt will soon destroy us as a country. No democracy has ever lasted much over two hundred years, and we are at age 236 and counting. When America financially falls, it will happen overnight and will be sudden. Do not rebel against the new coming government for it will be ordained from God. When the United States is later destroyed, it will also be sudden, in one day, according to the Bible in the book of Revelation.

Pray about everything you do, and seek God's guidance before doing all things. Jesus said He could do nothing unless His heavenly Father showed Him (John 5:19, 30, 8:28, 15:5). Maybe we need to be more like our Lord in these end times in which we live. Don't let this book scare you. Cling to your Bible and the words of Jesus for comfort. Only faith pleases our heavenly Father, so believe in the words of Christ.

I am nothing, nobody in this world today, just a voice crying from within a doomed nation. "Make straight your paths, give your heart to Jesus, and always be led by the Holy Spirit in all you do." May God bless you and keep you. I am working on a website, zoebooks.org. Check this site for future books and more information about this book, as our next step is to have it translated into Spanish.

May God richly bless you and keep you, and may He expand your learning curve for His glory. God is all about truth. He looks for those who worship Him in spirit and in truth. May the words I have written, under the direction of the Holy Spirit, enrich your lives. The truth will set you *free*! It will help to deliver you from the King of Darkness and goofy religious beliefs. There is only one God. His name is Yahweh, and He has a Son named Jesus. He is the God of Abraham, and His name *is not Allah*, who has no son! Jesus is the only path to Yahweh, the only true God and the giver of eternal Zoë life, *period*. Don't be fooled by other religions, because as death finds you so shall the *judgment*!

> Be on guard, so that your hearts will not be weighted down with dissipation [the act of using all or a lot of money, time, etc., in a foolish way] and drunkenness and the worries of life, and that day will not come on you suddenly like a trap; for it will come upon all those who dwell on the face of all the earth. But keep on the alert at all times, praying that you may have strength to escape all these things that are about to take place, and to stand before the Son of Man. (Luke 21:34–36)

TIME CHARTS OF ALL HISTORY

(CHART# 5) INTRODUCTION TO CHARTS

Time is described within a 7,000-year window.
6,000 years for Man's government
1,000 years for Christ government.
On God's time table it is 7 days,
6 days for man & 1 day for His Son.

The 6,000 years or 6 days are divided
into 3 - 2,000-year or 2-day segments.
CHART #1 Adam to Abraham is the first 2,000 years
      (Days 1 & 2)
CHART #2 Abraham up to the Crucifixion is
      the second 2,000 years (Days 3 & 4):
      1,993 years are history. The final 7 years
      will begin after the Rapture. Rev.4-18
CHART #3 Church age until the Rapture covers
      the third 2,000 years (Days 5 & 6)
CHART #4 Covers the final 1,000 Years for
      Jesus Christ's Kingdom (Day 7)
CHART #6 Covering Hosea's 3 Days compared
      to God's 7 Day Master Plan
CHART #7 Covering the 7,007-Year Theory of David.

This chart covers all time from the Creation until the end of all TIME!
Time consists of seven days in God's eyes but to all of mankind it is
7,000 years. With man 1,000 years is 1,000 years on man's time table.

2 Peter 3:7-9 But by His word the present heavens and earth are
being reserved for fire, kept for the day of judgment and
destruction of ungodly men. But do not let this one fact escape
your notice, beloved, that with the Lord one day is like a thousand
years, and a thousand years like one day. NASB

259

CHART # 1: The First 2,000 Years for Man's History or 2 Days on God's Time after Adam sinned.

3973 BC

7 On the day Adam sinned, God begins mankind's 6,000-Year Clock counting down toward Armageddon.

1966 BC

The Birth of Abraham

God's first two days or 2,000 years for Man

1,656 Years after Creation / GLOBAL FLOOD in Noah's Days

The Reign of the Nephilim (Giants)

God removes Enoch to Heaven without death at age 365...

6,000-YEAR TIME LINE

Adam sinned on the 7th year, 2nd month, & 17th day

Enoch's Birth in 3343 BC

2317 BC
God cleansed the Earth of Giants with a Global Deluge!

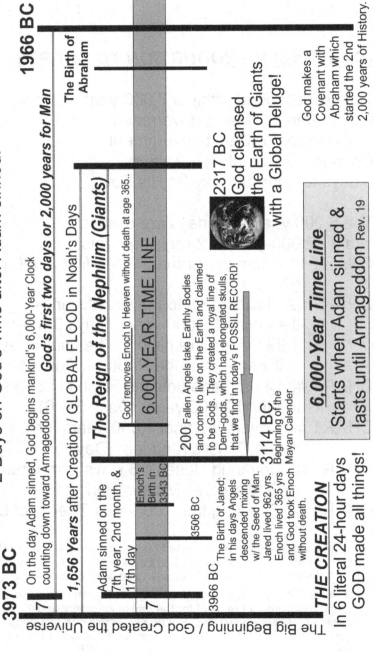

God makes a Covenant with Abraham which started the 2nd 2,000 years of History.

3506 BC

200 Fallen Angels take Earthly Bodies and come to live on the Earth and claimed to be Gods. They created a royal line of Demi-gods, which had elongated skulls, that we find in today's FOSSIL RECORD!

3114 BC
Beginning of the Enoch Mayan Calender

6,000-Year Time Line
Starts when Adam sinned & lasts until Armageddon Rev. 19

3966 BC The Birth of Jared; in his days Angels descended mixing w/ the Seed of Man. Jared lived 962 yrs. Enoch lived 365 yrs and God took Enoch without death.

7

THE CREATION
In 6 literal 24-hour days GOD made all things!

The Big Beginning / God Created the Universe

260

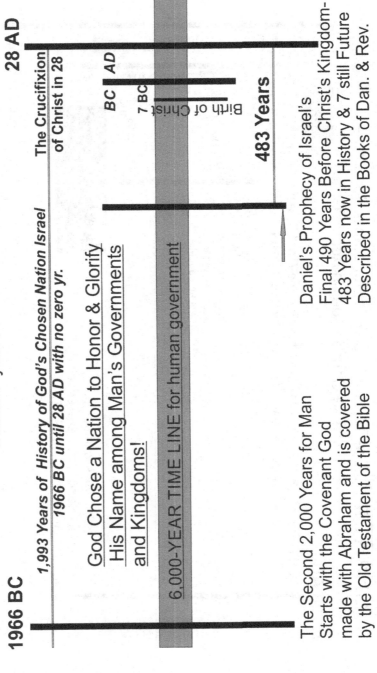

CHART # 2: The Second 2,000 Years for Man's Government minus 7 years / Daniel's 70th week

1966 BC

28 AD

The Crucifixion of Christ in 28

1,993 Years of *History of God's Chosen Nation Israel* 1966 BC until 28 AD with no zero yr.

God Chose a Nation to Honor & Glorify His Name among Man's Governments and Kingdoms!

6,000-YEAR TIME LINE for human government

BC   AD

7 BC

Birth of Christ

483 Years

The Second 2,000 Years for Man Starts with the Covenant God made with Abraham and is covered by the Old Testament of the Bible

Daniel's Prophecy of Israel's Final 490 Years Before Christ's Kingdom- 483 Years now in History & 7 still Future Described in the Books of Dan. & Rev.

261

CHART # 3: The Third 2,000 Years for Man's Government
The Church Age an Age of Grace

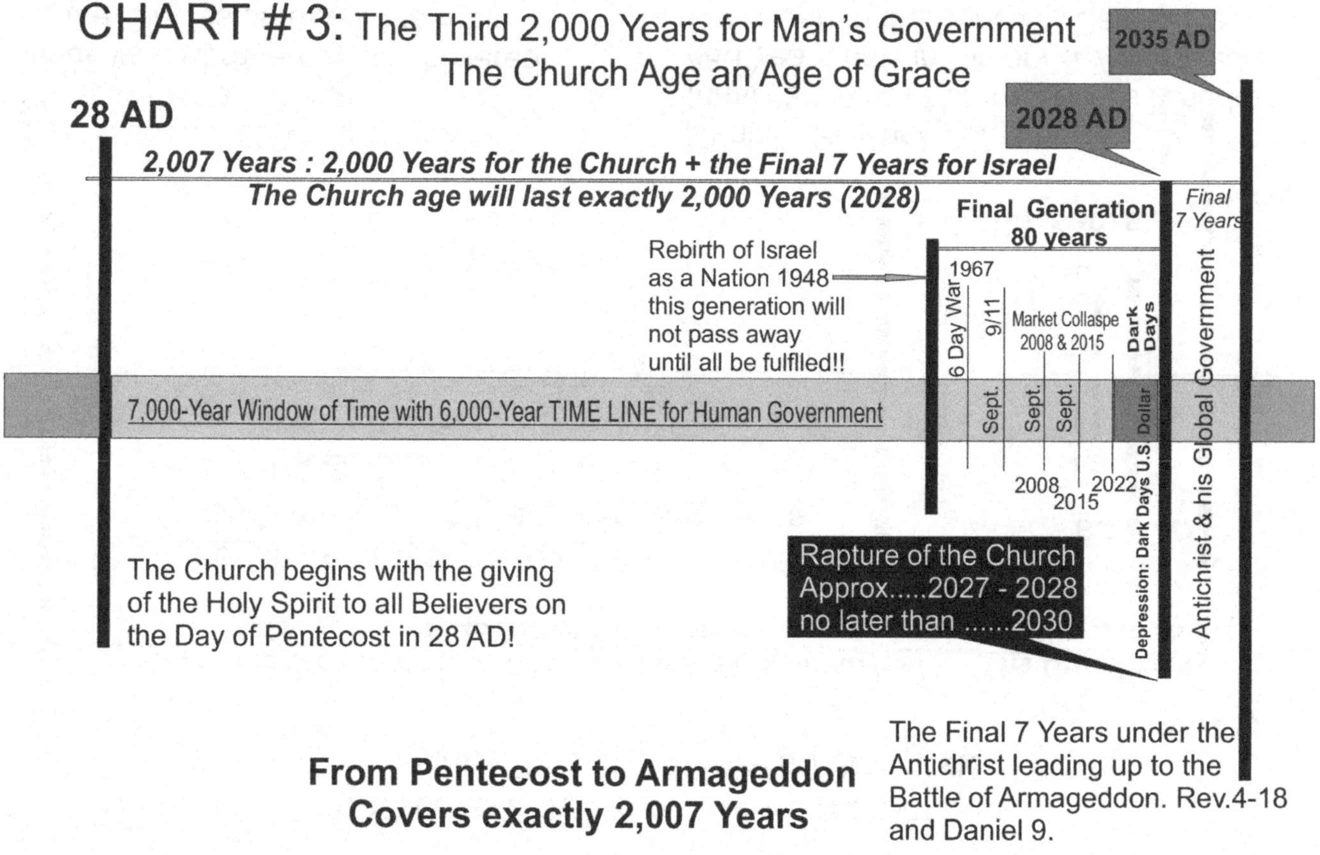

28 AD

2035 AD

2028 AD

2,007 Years : 2,000 Years for the Church + the Final 7 Years for Israel
The Church age will last exactly 2,000 Years (2028)

Final Generation
80 years

Final
7 Years

Antichrist & his Global Government

Dark
Days

Depression: Dark Days U.S. Dollar

Market Collaspe
2008 & 2015

2022
2015
2008

Sept.
Sept.
Sept.

6 Day War

9/11

1967

Rebirth of Israel
as a Nation 1948
this generation will
not pass away
until all be fulfilled!!

7,000-Year Window of Time with 6,000-Year TIME LINE for Human Government

Rapture of the Church
Approx.....2027 – 2028
no later than 2030

The Church begins with the giving
of the Holy Spirit to all Believers on
the Day of Pentecost in 28 AD!

The Final 7 Years under the
Antichrist leading up to the
Battle of Armageddon. Rev.4-18
and Daniel 9.

From Pentecost to Armageddon
Covers exactly 9,007 Years

CHART # 4: The Final 1,000 Years of Divine Government the Kingdom of Jesus Christ

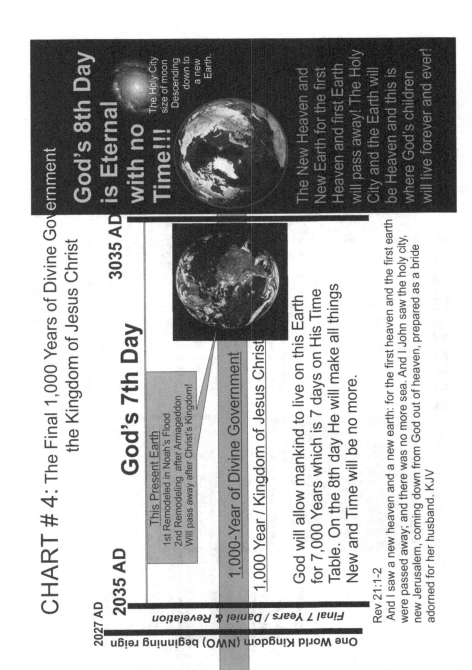

God's 8th Day is Eternal with no Time!!!

The Holy City size of moon Descending down to a new Earth.

The New Heaven and New Earth for the first Heaven and first Earth will pass away! The Holy City and the Earth will be Heaven and this is where God's children will live forever and ever!

3035 AD

God's 7th Day

2027 AD
2035 AD

This Present Earth
1st Remodeled in Noah's Flood
2nd Remodeling after Armageddon
Will pass away after Christ's Kingdom!

1,000-Year of Divine Government

1,000 Year / Kingdom of Jesus Christ

God will allow mankind to live on this Earth for 7,000 Years which is 7 days on His Time Table. On the 8th day He will make all things New and Time will be no more.

Rev 21:1-2
And I saw a new heaven and a new earth: for the first heaven and the first earth were passed away; and there was no more sea. And I John saw the holy city, new Jerusalem, coming down from God out of heaven, prepared as a bride adorned for her husband. KJV

Final 7 Years / Daniel & Revelation

One World Kingdom (NWO) beginning reign

Chart # 6 HOSEA's 3-Day
Compared to God's 7-Day Master Plan

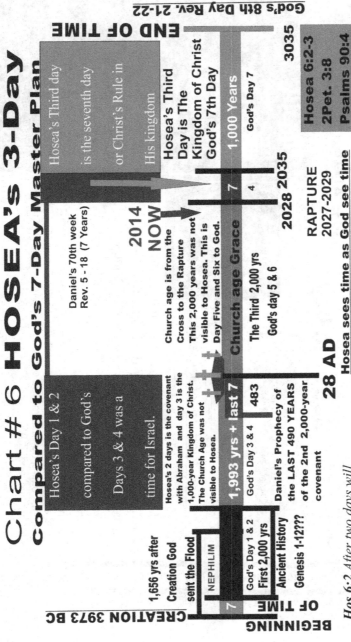

END OF TIME

God's 8th Day Rev. 21-22

Hosea's Third day

is the seventh day

or Christ's Rule in

His kingdom

Hosea's Third Day is The Kingdom of Christ God's 7th Day

1,000 Years

God's Day 7

3035

Hosea 6:2-3
2Pet. 3:8
Psalms 90:4
Barnabas 15

Daniel's 70th week
Rev. 5 - 18 (7 Years)

2014 NOW

Church age is from the Cross to the Rapture This 2,000 years was not visible to Hosea. This is Day Five and Six to God.

Church age Grace

The Third 2,000 yrs
God's day 5 & 6

7

4

2028 2035

RAPTURE
2027-2029

28 AD

Hosea sees time as God see time three days equaling 3,000 years

Hosea's Day 1 & 2

compared to God's

Days 3 & 4 was a

time for Israel.

Hosea's 2 days is the covenant with Abraham and day 3 is the 1,000-year Kingdom of Christ. The Church Age was not visible to Hosea.

1,993 yrs + last 7

God's Day 3 & 4

483

Daniel's Prophecy of the LAST 490 YEARS of the 2nd 2,000-year covenant

1,656 yrs after Creation God sent the Flood

NEPHILIM

God's Day 1 & 2
First 2,000 yrs

Ancient History Genesis 1-12???

7

CREATION 3973 BC

BEGINNING OF TIME

Hos 6:2 After two days will he revive us: in the third day he will raise us up, and we shall live in his sight. KJV

2Peter 3:8 But do not let this one fact escape your notice, beloved, that with the Lord one day is like a thousand years, and a thousand years like one day. NASB

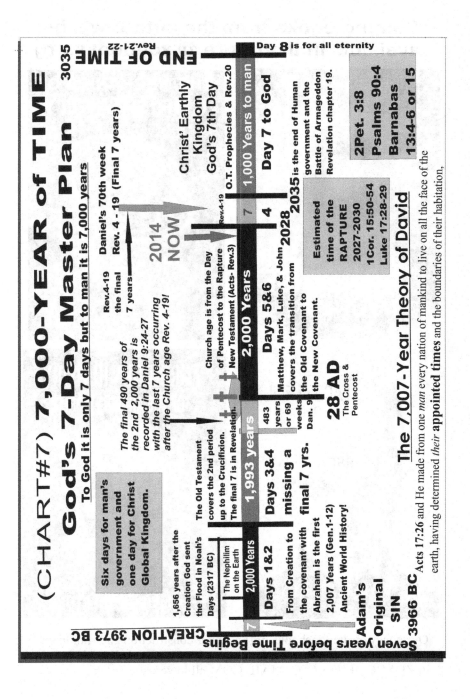

(CHART#7) 7,000-YEAR of TIME
God's 7-Day Master Plan
To God it is only 7 days but to man it is 7,000 years

3035

END OF TIME
Rev.21-22

Day **8** is for all eternity

Six days for man's government and one day for Christ Global Kingdom.

Christ' Earthly Kingdom God's 7th Day

O.T. Prophecies & Rev.20

7 **1,000 Years to man**

Day 7 to God

Rev.4-19 the final 7 years

Daniel's 70th week Rev. 4 - 19 (Final 7 years)

The final 490 years of the 2nd 2,000 years is recorded in Daniel 9:24-27 with the last 7 years occurring after the Church age Rev. 4-19!

2014 NOW

Rev.4-19

4

2028

2035 is the end of Human government and the Battle of Armageddon Revelation chapter 19.

Church age is from the Day of Pentecost to the Rapture New Testament (Acts- Rev.3)

The Old Testament covers the 2nd period up to the Crucifixion. The final 7 is in Revelation.

2,000 Years

Days 5&6

Matthew, Mark, Luke, & John covers the transition from the Old Covenant to the New Covenant.

Estimated time of the RAPTURE 2027-2030 1Cor. 15:50-54 Luke 17:28-29

2Pet. 3:8
Psalms 90:4
Barnabas 13:4-6 or 15

1,993 years

483 years or 69 weeks Dan. 9

28 AD
The Cross & Pentecost

1,656 years after the Creation God sent the Flood in Noah's Days (2317 BC)

The Nephilim on the Earth

Days 3&4 missing a final 7 yrs.

From Creation to the covenant with Abraham is the first 2,007 Years (Gen.1-12) Ancient World History!

2,000 Years

Days 1&2

7

Adam's Original SIN

3966 BC

CREATION 3973 BC

Time Begins

Seven years before Time Begins

The 7,007-Year Theory of David

Acts 17:26 and He made from one *man* every nation of mankind to live on all the face of the earth, having determined *their* appointed times and the boundaries of their habitation,

265

Coming books from the author will be available in the future @ zoebooks.org

DAVID NETHERTON

THE BOOK OF LIFE

(ZOE LIFE) The TRACING of GOD'S DNA

THE MECHANICS OF
CHRISTIANITY

DAVID NETHERTON

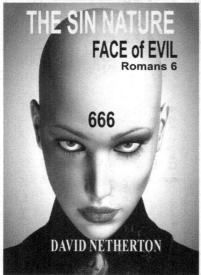

THE SIN NATURE
FACE of EVIL
Romans 6

666

DAVID NETHERTON

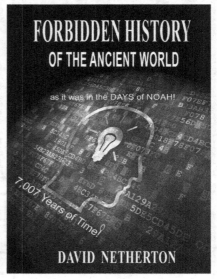

FORBIDDEN HISTORY
OF THE ANCIENT WORLD

as it was in the DAYS of NOAH!

7,007 Years of Time!

DAVID NETHERTON

Our new website (zoebooks.org) is under construction and should be available some time in 2015. We can be contacted through email at ZOEBOOKSLLC@GMAIL.COM all lower case letters.